THE VANGUARD
LEADER

THE
VANGUARD
LEADER

Becoming A Strategic Leader

FRANK DAMAZIO

CITYBIBLE
PUBLISHING

www.citybiblepublishing.com

Published by City Bible Publishing
9200 NE Fremont
Portland, Oregon 97220

Printed in U.S.A.

THE VANGUARD LEADER

ISBN 0-914936-53-0

Cover By Jon Walusiak *www.designpointinc.com*

Contents

Foreword ix

Introduction xi

The Challenge: Confronting the Twenty-First Century ... 1

The Conquest: Penetrating a Babylonian Culture 33

The Mission: Fulfilling God's Eternal Purpose 53

The Commission: Advancing God's Army 83

The Strategy: Taking the City 105

The Mandate: Building Unshakable People 125

The Character: Marks of Authenticity 143

The Witness: Discerning False Ministry 161

The Standard: Moral Purity 181

The Authority: Holy Spirit Anointing 203

The Motivation: Divine Blessiong 233

The Commitment: Covenant Relationships 263

The Legacy: Passing the Baton 281

Appendix: Things I Have Learned 313

Bibliography 317

Foreword

The Vanguard Leader is not only a primer for those aspiring to be leaders, but it is also a checklist for those who find themselves in a leadership role. As one would expect from Frank Damazio, this work is clear, biblical, and well illustrated! Frank has mastered the skill of taking biblical principles and linking them together in a powerful manner. The results of this effort will not leave you disappointed! One thing that I've always appreciated about Frank is that he lives what he teaches.

Having had the privilege of reading the initial manuscript for this book, I found myself challenged in the practical aspects of my role as a leader in the Body of Christ, and as a believer I was spiritually blessed.

If you are interested in growing in your own leadership abilities or in communicating the principles of leadership to others, this book is for you.

I whole-heartedly commend this book to you. It could change your life and ministry.

Dr. Joe C. Aldrich
President Emeritus
Multnomah Bible College
Portland, Oregon

Introduction

Times are strange and challenging for everyone, including Christian leaders who desire to make the traditional church relevant to modern culture. Morality, religious beliefs, and traditional values have been shifting. Leaders must encounter and assimilate change without sacrificing values, without losing the non-changeables of God's Word and kingdom.

A vanguard stands at the forefront of a movement and at the head of an army. Advancing in the twenty-first century, church leaders march in the vanguard, moving in front of the body of Christ. Leaders in the vanguard move ahead, understanding that God already lives in the future. Nothing surprises or confuses Him. He is very comfortable with change, simple or complex. God's vanguard leaders have His equipping Word, Spirit, and wisdom for these times.

I'm believing that simple, old-fashioned, biblical values will again become immensely popular. I'm believing that the church will make needed adjustments because Christ, the head of the church, is in tune with the times. The Word of God already points the right way to face today, tomorrow, and a million more tomorrows. Jesus is the same yesterday, today and forever (Heb. 13:8). God's truth is relevant for the twenty-first century and every century thereafter until Christ returns.

The vanguard leader has a basic attitude, mindset and ministry, which are examined in the following chapters.

John the Baptist set a standard for all vanguard leaders. He stood between two eras, two time periods, and two covenants. He was a forerunner. Something new followed his ministry, yet he faced the future with confidence given by God. Consider the characteristics and distinctives of vanguard leaders such as relational integrity, the difference between hype and anointing, and the kind of success God can bless.

Vanguard leaders are innovative, unafraid to introduce new ideas, methods, structures, or programs. They are motivated, courageous, goal-oriented, knowledgeable, honest, optimistic, enthusiastic, risk-takers, energetic, persuasive, principled, wise and balanced. What follows is a painting—with broad brush strokes and some detailed pencil sketches—of church leaders of the future.

The Challenge: Confronting the Twenty-First Century

John the Baptist bridged the gap between two time periods—the end of one era and the beginning of another. He lived in a time of momentous change, confusion and expectation. He stepped out of obscurity to become a vanguard announcing Christ's coming. His voice cried in the wilderness to prepare the way of the Lord (Mal. 4:1-6; Matt. 3:1-12; Mark 1:1-8; 6:14-18; John 1:19-28).

Vanguards point the way for others. They run forward to scout the future. They advance ahead of others to see what awaits the main body. As forerunners, they have the ability to live in the present and look into the future. They stand in the gap between two generations.

During periods of change, people look for leaders to follow. They cry for a new kind of leadership to take them into a new kind of world. The approaching twenty-first century presents a host of challenges. Extraordinary changes occurs at lightning speed. This age rapidly disappears. The dawn of another arises. Navigating the church through this period requires vanguards to march in the forefront, leading others in the move of the Holy Spirit and leading the church in revival and restoration. A leader's ability to change and to help others change will determine his success in this era.

The vanguard's voice cries today in a wilderness of humanism, syncretism, immorality and failing religious systems. Many church leaders have become stagnant and impotent, more comfortable in managerial than vanguard duties. What a challenge they face today: to be leaders like John the Baptist.

In his book, *In Search of Excellence,* Tom Peters praised 43 companies for the enlightened way they did business. Now 14 of the companies he wrote about are bankrupt. Why? They failed to respond to change, a major business magazine reports. Alvin Toffler calls the span from the mid-1950s to 2025 the hinge of history. Lance Morrow, who wrote *The Coming Millennium,* calls this period a cosmic divide.

To prepare the way for a new time, the church today needs a new breed of leaders like John the Baptist, vanguards willing to make changes in the church world. One of history's most influential preachers, he called for action and produced it. He did not deal in theological subtleties but in the reality of life. The emergence of John the Baptist was one of the hinges on which history turned. Today God is raising vanguards to minister in the close of this age as He opens something new.

Awesome responsibility of vanguards

Five scriptural realities face men and women who would lead others into the future.

1. Through their influence, leaders have the potential to ruin the future of God's people. When

Israel came out of Egypt and prepared to enter the Promised Land, Moses sent vanguards ahead to spy out the land (Num. 13:1-16). Twelve men went ahead. When they returned, ten of them expressed doubts about Israel's ability to conquer the land. Their unbelief struck fear into the hearts of the people. They brought back an evil report that frightened the people from entering the land God had given to them. Vanguards have the unique responsibility to see into the future with prophetic insight yet to be able to take the people pastorally, without discouragement, from the present into the future.

2. *Vanguards go into God-given vision ahead of the people.* Joshua, the leader who succeeded Moses, was told to "go over before this people" (Deut 3:28). A vanguard goes ahead before the rest of the people get there (Josh. 1:12-14). Joshua was a true vanguard who brought people into their inheritance. He went ahead of the people with the ark of the covenant and led the people into the vision.

3. *In faith, leaders take action in times of crisis.* God uses His leaders to turn crises into miracles. Gideon and his remarkable band of three hundred warriors turned a crisis into a miracle. Acting on a word from God and a confirming sign, he moved out when others sat still. He went ahead of his men who defeated the enemy (Judges, chapters 6 and 7). A vanguard moves out in faith when there is no natural way to solve a problem.

4. *A leader endures when others quit from exhaustion.* David and his men returned home from a military excursion once to find their homes burned, their families missing and all their belongings stolen (1 Sam. 30:6-20). David's military leaders were disheartened but David received a word from the Lord to pursue the enemy. David's six hundred men

had fought for several weeks and they were already tired, but they followed David. Along the way, two hundred men were too exhausted to cross a ravine to engage the enemy. Four hundred men received strength from God and the renewal of the Holy Spirit to keep going. They went ahead as a vanguard.

Vanguards have endurance and perseverance that enable them to go further than others. When others give up, they keep going. When others get tired, they draw strength from a supernatural source. When others let discouragement rob them of the coming victory, vanguards rise up and push ahead.

5. *Unconquered carnality causes leaders to forfeit privileges.* Carnality has robbed many great leaders of the destiny and vision God had for them. Moses spent forty years with the church in the wilderness, leading them into the promise (Acts 7:38). He asked God to let him enter the Promised Land. But Moses was not allowed to go in because he had disobeyed the Lord in frustration and in full view of the people (Deut. 3:23-29; Num. 20:7-12).

Vanguard responsibility carries significant consequences. You may see the vision and not possess it. You may allow an unconquered area of carnality to rob you of the privilege of marching in with the people of God.

John the Baptist's life shows seven characteristics/distinctives of vanguard leadership.

Distinctive #1: Prophetic pastors

A vanguard sees something emerging prophetically and prepares others pastorally to move into it.

> This man came for a witness, to bear
> witness of the Light, that all through

him might believe... John bore witness of Him and cried out, saying, "This was He of whom I said, 'He who comes after me is preferred before me, for He was before me.'" And of His fullness we have all received, and grace for grace. For the law was given through Moses, but grace and truth came through Jesus Christ (John 1:7,15-17).

For all the prophets and the law prophesied until John (Matt. 11:13).

We need to understand the historical context of John the Baptist's ministry

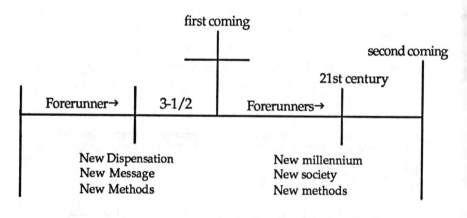

The diagram above illustrates the significance of John the Baptist's ministry for the twenty-first century. John was a prophetic messenger. As a forerunner, he prepared the way for the Messiah. He had a new, unorthodox message. He preached repentance to change people's minds and hearts to receive Christ.

Today, we prepare to enter the twenty-first century as forerunners and vanguards like John. A new era dawns bringing a new society with a new kind of culture, more diverse, secular, increasingly urban and a world of single parents, working women and multiple choices. The new cultural morality is undefinable but is punctuated by low commitment to God, Bible and family. We have shifted from being family-centered to being job-centered. Most of our time is spent on the job. Close friends are at work and we will move for the job. We live and die for our companies. We live busy lives, overextended, and losing the true value of life itself. It has caused fractured relationships, lonely people and a culture without roots.

Meanwhile, society wallows in distractions. The seductive power of the media continually tempts people to spend more money than they have and to be dissatisfied with the material possessions they own. Rock and roll, and country music shape the minds of people in the United States as they have for the past fifty years.

The world for which many leaders prepared no longer exists.

The spiritual significance of leadership during times of transition cannot be down-played. Every nation of the world desires to hold its family units together and to know some true God, even as values decay around them. People age and get fatigued, systems become rigid and purposes get lost. The world for which many leaders prepared no longer exists. It has changed. Culture has changed and, certainly, the church has changed.

To minister effectively in this new century, the church must adopt methods and attitudes to prepare people for Christ's second coming. Vanguards in transitional eras need to read the times and apply the Word of God to them without compromise. Leaders need to be in touch with culture but not in tune with it. They must understand it but not become like it. Transitional leadership must perceive the future and the past clearly to maintain continuity. They must save the best of the past yet change with the times.

Leighton Ford, in his book *Transforming Leadership*, said, "History is filled with instances when powerful leaders have failed to meet the challenge of the future." Lazy churches do long-range planning as if the future will be simply an extension of the present. Coming changes will catch them by surprise as always. Christian organizations and leadership are very slow to adapt to change.

While changing the form, we must keep biblical principles intact. The Amish people froze at a historical point in time. They decided to no longer be in tune with or understand the culture around them. They decided to be a subculture. They decided not to live their moment in history. They take no cues from United States culture, and their culture is frozen in the 1830s. They talk it; they live it; they dress it. The Amish are wonderful people, nevertheless, the church is not to copy their example. We are to know our time in history and live it out according to the Word of the Lord.

Transitional leadership balances prophetic insight with pastoral zeal. Maturing leaders keep youthful zeal without youthful disorder. They grow to maturity without hardening into aged rigidity. While dealing with things that are wrong, they take care not to upset things that are right. All changes may not represent progress, but without change there would be no progress at all. When faced with change, the Duke of Edinburgh said, "Any change at any time for any reason is to be deplored." A leader in Christ's church cannot afford the luxury of nurturing an attitude like the Duke's.

A transitional leader's most difficult responsibility is to help churches decide to change. Organizations tend to stagnate and deteriorate. Decision-making toward change begins with leaders who understand that the church must move into the future.

Wing walkers who entertain crowds at air shows by walking on the wings of old-fashioned airplanes in mid-air always obey the first rule of wing walking: Always get a hold of something else before you let go of what you've got. Reaching for the future means spending some precarious time in mid-air.

Leaders who have prophetic eyes and a pastor's heart must understand emerging spiritual trends of the twenty-first century. Trends come and go. Here are some that are currently emerging:

•The trend of *cell groups having church* instead of churches having cell groups. This trend offers new definitions of group purpose and church growth.

•The trend of *lay ministry becoming the dominant force* in the church. Some call this the "new reformation" returning the ministry to the people. This trend holds positive and negative ramifications. The people need to be the force of ministry in the church, but taken to extremes, this trend can harm church government and authority.

•The trend toward *more aggressive and more creative strategic church planting*. Hundreds of organizations plan to cooperate to plant thousands of churches. This is a positive New Testament model for evangelizing the world.

•The trend toward *seeker services,* as founded by Willowcreek Church's Bill Hybels, and other variations of reaching the unchurched Harry and Mary.

•The trend toward church program and church *schedule consolidation* to fit with the busy lifestyle of the modern family. The United States is in a giant rat-race, running itself ragged. Being overextended is epidemic. Pressures of this age push people to the edge of their time and their energy. Churches need to ask, "How much time and energy can the church and its leaders reasonably expect from people?"

•The trend toward *multiple services on different days* and times. Churches have begun to offer Friday night and Saturday night services as well as several services on Sunday.

•The trend toward *partnership in mission projects* by local churches and mission agencies. Networking consolidates funds and places people into needed ministries around the world.

•The trend toward *multicultural, multiracial congregations.* More ethnic groups in the cities forces the church to ask, "Should we start Spanish churches, Indonesian churches, etc., and separate African-Americans from other Americans?" Some groups do not want to mix with Caucasians. The greatest challenge for leadership in the twenty-first century will be to build multicultural, multiracial congregations where all flow together.

•The trend toward *belief in the supernatural,* angels, spirits and in miracles. These beliefs will come from a twisted synchronizing of different religions and philosophies, not from the Bible.

•The trend toward *anti-Christian bigotry.* The bias against the historic Christian world view will escalate. It is evident already in academic circles and in the major media. Christian-bashing will be one of the few acceptable discriminations remaining.

Distinctive #2: Spiritual roots

The second characteristic of a leader in the vanguard is his ability to understand his spiritual roots, discern his God-given destiny and pursue it with single-minded passion (Luke 1:5-15,76; John 5:35).

> But the angel said to him, "Do not be afraid, Zacharias, for your prayer is heard; and your wife Elizabeth will bear you a son, and you shall call his name John" (Luke 1:13).

John the Baptist came from a long line of priestly families reaching back to Aaron. His parents, Zacharias and Elizabeth, served as priests in a multi-religious culture that did not entirely embrace the ways of Jehovah. They were godly prayer warriors who prepared for the coming of the Messiah.

More than 20,000 priests in 24 divisions received annual assignments to work in the temple. Zacharias was in the eighth division called Abijah. He worked two weeks each year performing his priestly duties. With so many priests on the roster, some were never able to go in and burn incense before the Lord. However, this lot fell to Zacharias on the Day of Atonement. As he went in to offer up the prayers of the people, an angel of the Lord appeared. The angel spoke about a son that Zacharias' wife would bear. He was to be named John and would be a prophet of the Most High (Luke 1:76).

John understood his spiritual roots. He knew his parents were priests. He knew they were intercessors with vision for the future. John also knew he had a prophetic destiny by the stories he heard his father tell about the angel who announced his birth (Luke 1:15; Matt. 11:10).

Because of his destiny, John knew he was to have serious dedication. He was not to touch wine or strong drink to derive strength or inspiration. His strength was to come from the Holy Spirit. According to Numbers, chapter six, this was the law of the Nazarite. Like a Nazarite, John was to live his entire life in total consecration to service for the Lord. John would be a prophet with spiritual depth. He was filled with the Spirit from his mother's womb, a fact that honors his godly lineage.

Empty chambers in the soul of a leader must be filled with God's Holy Spirit...

A vanguard leader needs spiritual depth. Empty chambers in the soul of a leader must be filled with God's Holy Spirit so he can minister with spiritual depth. This kind of depth comes only through serious dedication. John's dedication to his call led him to live a strange and poor life in the wilderness. He lived in obscurity except for the brief time his and Christ's ministries overlapped. History records many great people who were obscure during their lives—like John, Zacharias and Elizabeth—but remembered for thousands of years.

John the Baptist was great in the sight of the Lord.

> For he will be great in the sight of the Lord, and shall drink neither wine nor strong drink. He will also be filled with

the Holy Spirit, even from his mother's womb (Luke 1:15).

He lived his life to please God, not to please men. He knew God's evaluation of all things is true. He was not moved by the wicked king or by the people in his government. Living to be great in God's sight shortened John's life because he was beheaded by the king, Herod the Great, who was great in his own sight but not in the sight of the Lord. A great man shows greatness by the way he treats obscure men.

John discerned his God-ordained destiny and pursued it with single-minded passion. Because of the word of the Lord and preparation by godly parents, John was able to dedicate himself and receive the Holy Spirit in power. He was a messenger who prepared the way for the greatest change in history. He was a prophet with a consuming passion. He was like a burning torch. His life caused a spiritual earthquake.

Distinctive #3: Wilderness training

The third characteristic of a leader in the vanguard is being spiritually prepared by frequent journeys into God-ordained spiritual deserts and wildernesses (Luke 1:80; 3:1-2; Exod. 3:1; Deut. 32:10; Matt. 14:13-15; Isa. 48:21).

The voice of one crying in the wilderness: "Prepare the way of the Lord, Make His paths straight." John came baptizing in the wilderness and preaching a baptism of repentance for the remission of sins (Mark 1:3-4).

Leaders in the making will spend time in the desert school of God. God calls them out of the world's noise to commune with Him. Spiritual deserts become fertile soil for God's work in the human spirit. Here He shapes the soul's purpose and forms the character of the human spirit. These are days of destiny that truly change anyone who enters the school.

The desert school of God is a place of solitude, suffering and self-denial, yet it makes men and women grow mighty in spirit. It is the pain required before true healing takes place.

Deep agape love can be developed only in the school of suffering.

When Michelangelo meditated on a great design, he would shut himself away from the world. People would ask, "Why do you lead such a solitary life?" He would reply with just one word, "Art. Art. It is a jealous god. It requires the whole and entire man." The calling of the Lord also requires the whole and entire man. You may not be a Michelangelo. You may not be a Billy Graham or a D.L. Moody, but you are a servant of God. The confirmation that you have been chosen for vanguard duties with Christ in His kingdom comes in your desert experiences and wilderness times. In that school you will grow strong in the Spirit until the day for you to appear (Gen. 32:24; Job 31:17; Luke 9:18).

The desert school is a place of suffering. Henry Ward Beecher, the great preacher of the last century said, "Do not be afraid to suffer. Do not be afraid to be overthrown. It is by being cast down and not destroyed, by being shaken to pieces and the pieces torn to shreds that men become men of might and that one a host."

Tribulation is necessary to dethrone self. Deep agape love can be developed only in the school of suffering. Suffering on the cross came before the resurrection. Without suffering there is no glory. As we are driven into the desert schools of God we will experience our own forms of suffering body, soul and spirit (1 Pet. 4:12-15).

> But may the God of all grace, who called us to His eternal glory by Christ Jesus, after you have suffered a while, perfect, establish, strengthen, and settle you (1 Pet. 5:10).

The wilderness strips a leader of his outer confidence and gives him something much greater: a knowledge of the Most High.

In the desert school, God strips men of their self-confidence. Before Moses was driven into the wilderness, he commanded Egyptian armies and was a statesman, philosopher, and educator. As he returned from the wilderness he was afraid to speak. He stuttered. He had no strength left in himself and he realized that he was merely a man. In the wilderness we learn what we cannot do on our own. The wilderness strips a leader of his outer confidence and gives him something much greater: a knowledge of the Most High. Moses had encountered God and was able to return to Egypt in the power of the Spirit, not the power of the flesh.

The desert school of God is nothing to be ashamed of. It is of the Lord's making and produces a fresh anointing that is alive and authentic. It prepares leaders to march in the vanguard. It strips them of humanistic thinking and modern theology that has gone amiss. It strips them of their own ways to take on God's ways.

Embrace the wilderness as a banqueting table, as a chamber where the Lord wants to speak with you. Embrace it with great faith and vigor.

Distinctive #4: Convictions like iron

The fourth characteristic of a leader in the vanguard is courage to stand with iron-like convictions in times of uncertainty and change in culture, philosophy, theology, and immorality (Luke 3:1-2).

John ministered in a context of spiritual and moral bankruptcy similar to conditions today. However, events today move at a much faster speed. Contemporary civilization is like a giant spaceship rocketing into orbit, powered by the engines of confidence in intelligent order, faith, and divine providence. Yet the blast from takeoff destroyed the guidance system. As a result the spaceship hurdles at supersonic speeds into the future but lacks instruments to track its course and tell its passengers where they have been, where they are and where they are going.

Building a conviction starts with the Word of God, not with human thoughts, culture or experiences.

The church has a responsibility to minister to this fast-moving civilization of multiplied uncertainties.

Society today needs the iron-like convictions of leaders like John the Baptist.

Building a conviction starts with the Word of God, not with human thoughts, culture or experiences. Using proper hermeneutics and meditation, we study the Word of God to draw out the truth that lies there. We construct principles that reflect the truth of the Bible. These principles need to be articulated as convictions that people can apply in life's circumstances. Convictions in harmony with the message of the Bible usually oppose our lower nature's basic desire.

A conviction is a scriptural principle we purpose to obey whatever the cost. A conviction never changes. It allows absolutely no turning or compromise. Leaders need to articulate the absolutes of the Bible to a society that has lost its way. Society has no convictions for family, values, morality, honesty, or integrity. Sadly, many church leaders have compromised their values and morality but stayed in leadership. This has brought great reproach on the church.

The church needs leaders who will stand in the gap and hold the principles and convictions God has given them. A leader in the vanguard needs convictions covering the word of God, holiness, and the church. If we are going to minister like John the Baptist to a culture that has lost its morality and theology, we cannot surrender to modern philosophy or to new so-called Christian philosophies that rob the church of the truth of the Bible.

Distinctive #5: Few mentors

The fifth characteristic of a leader in the vanguard is to emerge at a time when mentoring fathers are scarce and a search for models holds certain dangers.

> While Annas and Caiaphas were high
> priests, the word of God came to John
> the son of Zacharias in the wilderness
> (Luke 3:2).

John the Baptist emerged when no other prophets could act as mentors for him. He was raised in the wilderness away from the corrupt, perverted religious system and he was alone. He had no mentor, no elder prophet to look to. He had old manuscripts he could read and learn about Isaiah, Jeremiah, Ezekiel, Daniel and probably his favorite prophet, Elijah, but no one discipled him.

Today young leaders search desperately for models they can imitate and look up to. Today's leaders live when heroes have flaws and fail and when dreams have died. When religious systems are corrupt and modern ministry does not offer a mentoring model, young leaders may end up following wrong models.

From the 1950s to the 1990s God raised up leaders in the wilderness as He did with John the Baptist. Because God shaped them sovereignly, they may feel that all leaders should be shaped sovereignly and alone. Many of those leaders never were mentored and have not become mentors to others, but older leaders need to have a mentoring, father's heart that will reach out to younger leaders and raise them up. Every one does not need to go through the same school of hard knocks to learn. A vanguard must pass on his wisdom. He must pass on everything he has learned to upcoming leaders so they don't make the same mistakes he made. It's time for men and women to take responsibility to disciple others.

Even leaders who were raised in the wilderness by God can begin mentoring others. Mentoring is biblical. Moses mentored Joshua. Elijah mentored

Elisha. Paul discipled and mentored Timothy, his son in the faith. Naomi discipled and mentored her daughter in the faith, Ruth. (See 1 Kings 19:15-21; Num. 27:16-23.)

A pastor's leadership energies are often caught in the leadership of programs rather than people.

God wants leaders to mentor other leaders. God will still supply wilderness experiences and sovereign dealings, but that does not remove the responsibility from older leaders to be mentors. Mentoring is a pastoral leadership necessity. Mentors commit time and emotional energy to relationships with understudies. Often this commitment is intense. A pastor's leadership energies are often caught in the leadership of programs rather than people. Preoccupation with administrative duties can absorb much of the pastor's time causing him to miss the important discipleship ministry God has given him. Mentoring is one of the wisest investments a leader can make.

Great teachers are known for the students who have surpassed them.

Mentoring may be the greatest multiplying ministry strategy you will ever employ. "A mentor," according to Fred Smith, "is not a person who can do the work better than his followers; he is a person who can get his followers to do the work better than he can." Great teachers are known for the students who have surpassed them. Select leaders with potential, ones who seem to show low risk and high return. Be very careful whom you choose. Choose wisely. Be honest but gentle with those you have to turn down. Nevertheless, you can mentor only a certain number of people. If you devote your time to a wrong person, life can be discouraging. Remember, Jesus chose the twelve after he had prayed the whole night. Paul did not choose Timothy until later in his ministry.

Mentoring is transferring life. Bob Schank says, "Mentoring is a deliberate transfer of wisdom from one person to another with an emphasis on credibility, experience, time and relationship in the transfer process." We need to transfer integrity, humility, authenticity, ability, experiences. Mentoring does not require perfection, but it does demand commitment. You don't have to be at the top but just ahead of the person who follows you.

Distinctive #6: Prophetic preaching

The sixth characteristic of a leader in the vanguard is the courage to preach prophetically to a syncretistic religious society and passive religious community (Luke 3:1-3,18; Mark 1:2; Matt. 11:12; Mark 1:14-15; Acts 10:37; 13:5,24,28).

> For this is he of whom it is written:
> "Behold, I send My messenger before
> Your face, who will prepare Your way
> before You" (Matt. 11:10).

Preaching without the anointing is only unproductive entertainment, a kind of showmanship, small talk, rhetoric.

John the Baptist came preaching under a specific anointing to penetrate the hearts of people. Preaching is the power to persuade and birth new life through inspiration. It is God Himself breaking into the affairs of men and confronting them with a demand for decision.

Preaching is not a style; it is an anointing on the person speaking. Preaching is more than form. Form must not become more important than substance. Oratory or eloquence are not the essence of preaching. Preaching without the anointing is only unproductive entertainment, a kind of showmanship, small talk, rhetoric.

We need to balance preaching and teaching. Teaching is the ability to establish, deepen, define, channel and protect the truth that has been birthed. In the last generation many became fine teachers and expositors of the Word because we had such a lack. We have missed thundering preachers who bring forth the Word of God under a preaching anointing. People of this generation need to be birthed into greater things of God and this society needs to be penetrated by the anointing of God. Today the hearts of people are so hard and confused they need the anointing of God to break in upon them. We need preachers who can preach with teaching, to bring forth the Word of God with substance and with anointing (John 3:2; 2 Tim. 1:11; Acts 13:1; 1 Cor. 12:28-29; Acts 13:35; Col. 1:28; 3:16).

> Then one came and told them, saying, "Look, the men whom you put in prison are standing in the temple and teaching the people!"(Acts 5:25).

for which I was appointed a preacher
and an apostle—I am speaking the truth
in Christ and not lying—a teacher of the
Gentiles in faith and truth (1 Tim. 2:7).

Leaders must preach the Word of God with
authentic anointing and prophetic voices in the
twenty-first century (Titus 1:1,3; Amos 2:11-12; Mal.
4:4; Isa. 58:1; Ezek. 3:17; 33:7; Hag. 1:13; Matt. 2:7; 3:1).
Faithful messengers will discharge their duties in
spite of all risks and deliver messages entrusted to
them by God. They speak without ambition to
promote themselves.

The ministry of preaching is spoken about in
Scripture in hundreds of places. Here are a few (Isa.
61:1; Luke 16:16; Acts 20:7):

Preach the word! Be ready in season and
out of season. Convince, rebuke, exhort,
with all longsuffering and teaching (2
Tim. 4:2).

and did not spare the ancient world, but
saved Noah, one of eight people, a
preacher of righteousness, bringing in
the flood on the world of the ungodly (2
Pet. 2:5).

The Hebrew definition of preaching means an
annunciation of a specific message with specific
recipients, with an intent to elicit a specific response,
a planned encounter, a confrontation. The Greek idea
of preaching is to publicly proclaim or announce
news of something to come. It speaks of a forerunner
who delivers a message with authority (Matt. 3:1;
4:17; 10:7,27; 24:14; Mark 1:4; 16:15).

The New Bible Dictionary says preaching is not the relaxed recital of interesting but morally neutral truths. Martin Lloyd Jones, in his book *Preaching and Preachers*, says, "My true definition of preaching must say that man is then to deliver the message of God, a message from God to those people he is ambassador."

Preachers need to forcefully penetrate this society.

Shallow preaching is a disease that threatens to carry into the twenty-first century. It is without biblical purpose. It meets only a temporary need or a surface problem.

> Some fell on stony ground, where it did
> not have much earth; and immediately
> it sprang up because it had no depth of
> earth (Mark 4:5).

Shallow preaching places emphasis on experience, stories and illustrations more than the Word of God. Shallow preaching is charm, giftedness, fake friendliness, hypnotic voice. It is dominated by the preacher's personality rather than by the presence of God.

Preachers need to *forcefully* penetrate this society. They bring forth the Word of God with substance and anointing. They stand before God to receive His message and deliver that message accurately. A preacher is a mouthpiece, a spokesman, a speaker, an agent of another, one who has special communication to deliver (Gen. 50:16; 1 Sam. 4:17; 23:27; Prov. 25:13; 1 Sam. 42:19).

And from the days of John the Baptist
until now the kingdom of heaven
suffers violence, and the violent take it
by force (Matt. 11:12).

Common hindrances come to all who desire to
preach better. Unexpected long, dry periods make
preachers concerned that they have done something
to quench the anointing or that God has withdrawn a
measure of anointing without explanation. Times of
great dryness do not mean that God has withdrawn
Himself. You will have dry times.

Rejection of the preacher's personal ministry by
those he is ministering to brings discouragement. It
can distract him from study and prayer and dampen
his fire and power in preaching. Even though
rejection is temporary, it causes a loss of confidence.
A man or woman turns this around by stirring
themselves, reminding themselves of the calling to
preach the Word of God, which restores their
confidence.

When inspiration evaporates, the preacher may
be lingering too long outside his spiritual gift
and calling.

A preacher hurt or wounded in his ministerial
responsibilities may become harsh toward others,
cynical or apologetic. It is not the intensity of the
trouble that causes him to criticize others. You have
to be little to belittle other people. Do not take out
your discouragement on the people of God. Do not
become harsh in the pulpit. Be gentle and speak
comfortably to the church.

When inspiration evaporates, the preacher may be lingering too long outside his spiritual gift and calling. Maybe administrative duties, program management and people problems take up too much time. Dryness and apathy set into his ministry. Speaking becomes more work and less anointing. This is a sign to return to your knees and open the Book. Study for yourself and spend less time outside of your gifting.

Severe satanic attack can cause fear, guilt or a loss of confidence. Accusations may make a preacher feel he lost his anointing. Sometimes he has to preach in this atmosphere. It's amazing, but sometimes more people respond and get ministered to than when he feels he has the greatest anointing in the world. It is a paradox. When we are weak, He is strong. When we are empty, He is full. When we are dry, He seems to have a well full of water. God's ways are different than our ways. I have included a chart I constructed some years back after a study on the history of preaching. Please notice that the most productive years in church history were when expository preaching was at its zenith.

History of Preaching

Apostolic	4 - 69	Preaching of Jesus and the Apostles Proclamation of the Word with power, followed by signs and wonders The supernatural
Patristic	70 - 430	From about 70-300 the laymen preached. Nonprofessional and untrained, they had a great impact on the world. From 300-430 there was a remarkable rise in the power of preaching. Within the church, more form in sermons, a finished canon, more biblical preaching, more orderly worship service, stability in doctrine and the culture. The training of preachers added power to the pulpit. People loved oratory and education. Basil the Great, Gregory of Nyssa, Chrysostom, Ambrose, Augustine, Polycarp -Bishop of Smyrna (68-160), Ignatious-Bishop of Antioch (30-110), Clement-Bishop of Rome (50-100)
Early Medieval	430 - 1095	Preaching based in the Word declined. Preaching with power was all but destroyed. Preachers became corrupt; liturgy strangled the power of the pulpit. Preacher became priest; doctrines were corrupted. Allegorizing was rampant. 476 Fall of Rome: period of decay, decline and hopelessness. Preaching was affected by this event; Augustine's "City of God". During this period the Papacy was finally established. Gregory the Great (590-604) established Catholic ceremony, chanting, Latin used, purgatory, rise in monasticism, no real preaching to the people from the Bible. 7th-11th centuries considered the Dark Ages of preaching.

Central Medieval	1095 - 1361	Age of scholasticism ushered in new concern for learning. Mysticism was strong. Preaching became popular again. Period of great cathedrals, clergy ranked top of the social order. Intellectualism was on the rise with the founding of many universities. Great crowds gathered to hear preaching which was given with dramatic presentations. Expository methods used. Francis of Assisi, Dominic.
Reform-ation	1361 - 1572	Two distinct periods: Renaissance 1361 - 1499 and Reformation 1500-1572 The renaissance was a time of new thinking, new art, new attitudes. Classical scholarship, intellectual interest, philosophy, independent of theology. Translation of Bible into English in 1382 by John Wycliffe. Martin Luther (1517) 93 theses against the Catholic Church Luther in Germany; Calvin in France; Zwingli in Zurich; Knox in Scotland The development of printing brought the most influence in this age. 1446 John Gutenberg invented movable type for the printing press. Preaching was revived. Biblical preaching was at its height.
Early Modern	1572 - 1789	John & Charles Wesley and George Whitfield formed a team of preachers resulting in The Great Awakening. Evangelistic movement known as pietism. Known as the golden age of preaching. Age of literary giants: John Bunyan, Shakespeare. Preaching was once again mainly verse by verse exposition. Church services continued for hours with heavy context. Greek/Latin flowed profoundly. Homiletics became the form of preaching. Many books written on preaching. The beginnings of the natural style of preaching, less artificial style.

Later Modern	1789 - 1900	Influence of international, national and religious pressures. Unemployment, riots, telephone, socialism, Karl Marx, industrialization, urbanization. Time of great pressure, but also time of great preaching. Revivals of Finney, Moody, gave way to Bible conferences, YMCA, Salvation Army birthed. Church membership declined. Rise in biblical criticism, liberalism. Science became predominant replacing religion, stressing self sufficiency. Preaching method was topical rather than expository. Nearly 2/3 of all preachers were students of Hebrew, Greek, Latin. Great missionary age.
Contem-porary	1900 - 1950	World War I/World War II and the Great Depression. Darwin's evolution became prominent. Existentialism became world view of philosophy. Henry Drummond, Henry Ward Beecher challenged the decay. The new technology came in, influence of scientific thought, higher criticism, materialism, psychology that ignored the fall of man, spirit of liberalism, questioning inspiration of Bible, virgin birth, deity. Age of Bible translations: RV/NAS, Moffat, Goodspeed. 1905-1930 time of much church construction in suburbs. Preaching declined in content, new popular approaches to preaching, poor quality, little word.

Modern Preaching	1950 - present	Intense studies in psychology. Personality mixed with humanism, higher criticism and the influence of television and/or modern art has greatly damaged preaching today. Sermons begin with life problems rather than scripture passage. They are much shorter (15-25 minutes average). American Sermon—"Need oriented" relevance plays the important role in today's preaching. (Problem preaching, life situation).

Distinctive #7: Elijah's spirit and power

The seventh characteristic of a leader in the vanguard is ministry in the spirit and power of Elijah. Elijah-style ministry confronts an ungodly culture to restore hope for the future and prepare a people for the second coming of Christ (Luke 1:17; 3:3).

> He will also go before Him in the spirit and power of Elijah, "to turn the hearts of the fathers to the children," and the disobedient to the wisdom of the just, to make ready a people prepared for the Lord (Luke 1:17).

John the Baptist had the same spirit as Elijah. Both men confronted their cultures without fear or compromise. Both stood before wicked kings and spoke the Word of God boldly. Both spoke with absolute faith that God would back them up. Neither hoped for man's favor or feared his dislike.

The Elijah ministry restores families and turns the hearts of fathers to their children. In the past forty years, the institution of the family has deteriorated but it can be restored. An Elijah ministry takes restoration of the family seriously. The Elijah message is repentance, not modern psychology.

Leaders in the vanguard need to carefully discern modern psychology...

In Luke 3:7 John the Baptist cries out, "O generation of vipers." These words were not kind nor condemning. They were factual. John had seen many vipers in the wilderness where he grew up. He knew their treacherous ways and their nature. He knew what it was like to lift a rock and find a viper. The ungodly religious culture reminded John of poisonous snakes hiding under the rocks in a wasteland.

> He who has ears to hear, let him hear! But to what shall I liken this generation? It is like children sitting in the marketplaces and calling to their companions, and saying: "We played the flute for you, and you did not dance; we mourned to you, and you did not lament" (Matt. 11:15-17).

Conversion describes a radical change of mind and of heart—a complete turnaround. It requires repentance, genuine sorrow for sin, and earnest resolve to break with evil. Conversion produces evidence or fruit of repentance. Leaders in the vanguard need to carefully discern modern psychology promoted in seminaries and Bible colleges offering substitute ways to change people's lives. We need to understand principles of biblical counseling. The Bible is the source of all principles for proper counseling. Dealing with the knowledge of psychology and the complexity of the human soul becomes so confusing we lose the simplicity of the message of the Bible.

John the Baptist preached to a sin-ridden, hopeless generation of perverted people in many religions. Many had broken homes. Many businessmen had mistresses. Many worshiped at the temple of Diana that housed male and female prostitutes. Many emperors were homosexual and had harems of young men. John the Baptist's day was no different than our perverted day. He did not preach, "Psychology, for the kingdom of God is at hand." He preached, "Repent, for the kingdom of God is at hand."

Modern psychology is a lie that confuses instead of changes people. Modern psychology has caused unrest in many churches. People have left Bible-preaching and Bible-counseling churches on the advice of counselors whose counsel does not line up with the Word of God. Healing of memories, inner healing and other trends of psychology have surfaced in this day. We can draw resources and information from studies done on human nature and the habits of people, but we must submit these resources to the Word of God. We must not reverse the process. The Word of God is the last court of appeal. It is the only truth that will actually improve a person, changing him into a new creation.

If people under your pastoral care counsel with advisors outside the church, at least find out if they are being counseled with the Bible and biblical principles. Ask to attend a session with them. Write to the counselor and ask for his understanding of sin, God, adultery, fornication, homosexuality and abortion. Ask the counselor what he believes about inner healing, healing of the memories, how a person breaks a habit, and who holds responsibility for it. Find out what he thinks about Freud.

John the Baptist came preaching repentance. Repentance was enough to deliver people from their sins and prepare them to walk in the ways of the Lord. John the Baptist saw the coming of the Lord as real and prepared for it himself. He prepared for Christ's first coming as leaders in today's vanguard need to prepare for Christ's second coming. It may be ten or one hundred years from now, but people need to be equipped, fit and ready for the coming of Christ.

Vanguard leaders stand in the gap between two eras and take seriously the challenges of the coming age. The church needs authentic vanguards to raise up a whole generation of people who know the Lord, who move in the power of His might.

2

The Conquest: Penetrating a Babylonian Culture

In the midst of a culture given to evil, Daniel served as a messenger for God. With impeccable character and deep prophetic insight, he confronted the culture as a mouthpiece or spokesman for God. Babylon, where Daniel served, represents evil throughout Scripture. Moral impurity, blasphemy, and hatred of God and His people filled Babylonian society.

God's vanguard leaders will fill roles similar to Daniel's in the last days. They will rise to confront a culture very much like Babylon. As messengers prepared and empowered by the Holy Spirit, they will stand before God to receive a message to speak clearly, without compromise, and with Christlike compassion. This new breed of prophetic, vanguard leaders will interpret history, predict the future and articulate God's plan and purpose for their generation (Ezek. 3:17; 33:7; 1 Kings 17:1; Mic. 3:8; Amos 3:7-8; 2:11-12; Isa. 58:1).

Daniel and his three friends, Hananiah, Mishael, and Azariah, were taken captive in Jerusalem in about 606 B.C. when Jehoiakim was king of Judah.

Babylonian King Nebuchadnezzar had conquered Judah and had taken Hebrew aristocrats with leadership gifts and abilities as captives. (This was the first of three defeats for Judah at the hands of Babylon. Ezekiel and others were brought to Babylon about 598 B.C. Zedekiah and the rest of the tribe of Judah was taken to Babylon about 587 B.C. when the city of Jerusalem was destroyed.)

Daniel was thrust into a foreign culture and lifestyle to face new challenges. The Babylonians made every effort to break his faith and convictions, however, he lived sixty years in Babylon without becoming Babylonian.

Howard F. Vos, historian and archaeologist, describes the magnificence of Babylon in his book, *Archaeology In Bible Lands,* as follows:

> Adjacent to Nebuchadnezzar's main palace and just to the east of it was the great Ishtar gate through which passed Procession Street, the main street of the city. In honor of the god Marduk, this roadway was paved with imported limestone and sometimes reached a width of 65 feet. It was bordered with sidewalks of red brick. Walls on either side of the road were faced with blue enameled brick and decorated with life size yellow and white lions and dragons. The city's major structures opened on this roadway. The Ishtar gate was a double gate flanked with towers of blue enameled brick decorated with alternating rows of yellow and white bulls and dragons. Nebuchadnezzar's palace was a huge complex of buildings protected by a double wall. Rooms in the palace surrounded five courtyards. The white plastered throne room, which was 56' x

170' had a great central entrance flanked by smaller side doors.

The city itself, roughly rectangular, sat aside the Euphrates. The wall, eleven miles long and 85' thick was protected by a moat filled with water from the Euphrates. Actually, the wall was double. The outer wall was 25' thick and the inner one 23' thick with an intervening space filled with rubble. Watchtowers stood 65' apart on the walls. There were eight or nine gates in the wall with the Ishtar gate entering from the north. As mentioned, the palace of Nebuchadnezzar, the ziggurat and the great temple of Marduk all opened on Procession Street. Altogether there were 43 temples in the city of Nebuchadnezzar's day. The population of greater Babylon in the sixth century B.C. has been estimated at about one-half million.

To the church today and in the last days, Babylon refers to the network of evil spiritual powers that seeks to control men's minds, values, beliefs and destiny. The influence of demonic spirits can be seen in educational institutions, economic and political systems, and in unbiblical religious organizations. The Babylonian system opposes God's true church and seeks to destroy it.

The Bible records the beginning of Babylon's history in Genesis 11:1-9, and the major prophets repeatedly use Babylon as a stereotype for evil. Revelation 17:1 to 21:9 give at least thirteen major descriptions of the evil powers of Babylon. Ultimately, Babylonian evil is judged (Rev. 16:17-21; 17:1-18).

Vanguard leaders will encounter the spiritual powers of Babylon in the last days. The Bible calls

Babylon "the great harlot...with whom the kings of the earth committed fornication and the inhabitants of the earth were made drunk with the wine of her fornication" (Rev. 17:1-2). Not only is Babylon a place of gross immorality, but it also is filled with the spirit of blasphemy (Rev. 17:3).

Blasphemy, humanism, deception, false powers, false prophets, persecution, demon spirits, and the Antichrist are all part of the Babylonian system. Babylon is filled with abominations. All that is perverse, abominable and unacceptable to God is found in Babylon (Rev. 17:4).

Babylon represents people and institutions that hate the church and who will persecute and murder the saints of God. Babylon is a culture, a value system. It is a spirit, an attitude. It is prevalent today. Hatred of righteousness and of the church of Jesus Christ is rising (Rev. 17:6).

Babylon is evident in every generation. Kings and kingdoms, symbolized by mountains, will rise and fall. The last king and kingdom to arise in power in these last days will be the Antichrist (Rev. 17:9).

The Babylonian spirit rules over entire nations. It seduces and manipulates the minds of leaders to bring multitudes of people under its influence. It denounces the Word of God and positions itself against the church of Jesus Christ. It is well organized evil. Like a great city, Babylon has its own government and rulers (Rev. 17:14-18).

Babylon is a prison house of demonic powers. It houses every foul spirit and every unclean, hated bird. In Matthew, chapter 13, Jesus points out that birds represent demonic spirits trying to snatch away the Word of God and harm the disciples of Christ (Rev. 18:1-2).

The Babylonian spirit encompasses all the evil in the pit of hell that is injected into this culture. Everyone runs the risk of being influenced by the spirit of Babylon and needs to guard his own mind and heart. The cry of the Holy Spirit through the apostle John was for the people of God to come out of Babylon and be set free from this hideous spirit (Rev. 18:4).

Babylon is a system of ungodly beliefs and philosophies that bind the hearts and minds of men to ungodly lifestyles. Christians should not share in Babylonian sins, beliefs and philosophies. They should walk a separate path because they are a separated people. They compose the church of the Lord Jesus Christ. Church leaders in this generation need to have the kind of spirit Daniel had. Daniel resisted the Babylonian culture and philosophy and stood strong for sixty years as a prophetic voice in the midst of perversity.

The book of Revelation pronounces judgment on the whole Babylonian system and all the evil represented in it. The system and culture will be judged by the wrath of God and will be destroyed quickly (Rev. 18:5, 19, 21).

Like Daniel, Christians today have been taken from Jerusalem to Babylon. Western civilization has declined. Believers find themselves in the midst of dragons, temples, and the god, Marduk, as they walk down Procession Street. But believers should not be seduced by the wonders of Babylon. They should not be deceived by all the sights and sounds of this culture. Nothing they see or lay their hands on in this world is eternal. All they see will decay and pass away in the twinkling of an eye. It will melt in the heat of God's judgment on this world at the second coming of the Lord Jesus Christ.

Vanguard leaders must continually remind the people of God that they live in a temporary world, eat temporary food, wear temporary clothes, drive temporary cars, and live in temporary homes. The world is not their home. They are only sojourners on the earth. The Babylonian system and everything in it will be judged by God. All those who partake of its sins and fornication will be judged. Vanguard leaders must sound the trumpet, "Come out, come out."

The word *Babylon* means disintegrate, fragment, disunite and confuse. It describes the type of work Babylon does.

Daniel was trained in the Babylonian court to serve the Babylonian king. Yet Daniel's heart would not relinquish loyalty to Jehovah, the true king. He would allow only godly values and convictions to shape his life. Daniel lived in Babylon but Babylon did not live in Daniel. Daniel was in Jehovah, or as we say today, Daniel was in Christ. Even though he was living in this culture, he lived in Christ.

> Then the king instructed Ashpenaz, the master of his eunuchs, to bring some of the children of Israel and some of the king's descendants and some of the nobles, young men in whom there was no blemish, but good-looking, gifted in all wisdom, possessing knowledge and quick to understand, who had ability to serve in the king's palace, and whom they might teach the language and literature of the Chaldeans. And the king appointed for them a daily provision of the king's delicacies and of the wine which he drank, and three years of training for them, so that at the

end of that time they might serve before the king. Now from among those of the sons of Judah were Daniel, Hananiah, Mishael, and Azariah (Dan. 1:3-6)

Qualities in Daniel and his young leaders

Seven features of Daniel and his three friends characterize today's vanguard leaders as well.

Royal lineage. They were from noble families. The New Testament priesthood derives its royalty from Christ's kingly line, according to 1 Peter 2:9.

Free of defects. They had no physical or mental handicaps. "Therefore there are now no disabilities or handicaps in Christ" (Rom. 8:1; paraphrased). Vanguard leaders have all they need in Christ, the Bible, and the Holy Spirit. They do not accept the world's evaluation of their abilities.

Good-looking. Like all believers, vanguard leaders are God's workmanship, created in Christ Jesus, accepted in Christ, and made beautiful in Christ (Eph. 2:8).

Intelligent. They possessed wisdom. Today's leaders have the ability to apply knowledge wisely to any task or decision. They have understanding the world is looking for because they have the wisdom of God.

Understanding. They were "quick to understand." Leaders today have God-given perception to distinguish between what is false and what is true, what is evil and what is good. They have discernment to separate what appears to be real from what is real. They can see through deception because of discernment God has put into them.

Knowledge. They knew revealed truth. The Living God gives vanguard leaders the proper adaptation of His laws and enables them to live well-ordered, purposeful lives. He imparts meaning and value to all he has fashioned.

Ability to serve. They were competent, capable young men. Vanguard leaders have been equipped to be competent to serve the true king, the Lord Jesus Christ.

Daniel and his three friends were placed in an academy called the Chaldean school. This school trained a class of influential Babylonian priests noted for their study in astrology, divination, magical arts and soothsaying. The Chaldean language was a sacred tongue which required years to master and was used in intricate, mysterious religious rituals performed by the priests.

Under the influence of these Chaldean priests, students came under pressure to conform. They were squeezed into the Babylonian mold. Today universities, colleges, and higher-education institutions take choice young people and try to neutralize and re-educate them into the school's philosophy. Bending their minds to fit an accepted ideology, the schools decree what students must think and dictate what they must believe. Millions of young people today enter into the Babylonian squeeze.

Shifts in science, philosophy and morality

The worldly Babylonian influence in western culture has caused major shifts in how society views science, philosophy, and morality.

Science is the knowledge of general principles or truths relating to any subject. It is comprehending truth or facts in the mind. Early scientists believed a reasonable God created the world. Faith in the God of the universe was the foundation for faith in modern science. Science and the Bible do not conflict under this foundational, philosophical approach. Christians view the world as an object of genuine, objective, and serious study. English mathematician and physicist Sir Isaac Newton (1642-1727) was loyal to the Bible's teaching. He began his scientific experiments with the assumption of the existence of a personal God who created the universe. He studied the Bible intensely. French mathematician and philosopher Blaise Pascal was a dedicated Christian scientist who did not view people as meaningless specks of dust in the universe. He knew people were precious because Christ died for them.

However, modern science has shifted from the concept of the uniformity of natural causes in an open system to the concept of uniformity of natural causes in a closed system. Everything that exists is part of a total cosmic machine. Nothing exists outside this cosmic machine. This new view is called the modern, modern scientific view. It has pushed God from the center, to the edge, and finally out completely. The cosmic machine has been made the creator and judge.

Philosophy is an attempt to explain values, beliefs, and underlying reality. As long as society adhered to a philosophy based on the biblical teaching of an absolute God who ruled with absolute principles, it fostered optimistic attitudes. A seeker could find reality because God's absolutes were not hidden.

Modern, modern science concocted a cosmic God with no absolutes, which led to the development of existential philosophy. Existentialism teaches that nothing is real except what the individual can experience for himself. It was the foundational philosophy of the 1960s that produced the hippie movement, rebellion against authority, and the search for truth through drugs. It has led society from optimism to pessimism. Man gave up hope of finding real answers for his individual and collective problems. He searched for meaning in a vacuum. All things, including man, are merely the result of chance. Truth is in one's own mind. The only reality in existentialism seems to be autonomous freedom. The shift to this new philosophy has caused confusion, loss of moral standards, and a shift away from the Christian world view.

Drugs were touted as vehicles to find the truth in an individual's own mind. Peace is in personal experience, therefore the peace movement and the drug movement were supposed to usher in the ideal life. Instead, a whole generation of people who did not find truth have turned to look for meaning in a materialistic society running rampant with narcissism and humanistic, existential philosophy.

When experience becomes a god, occultism is the result. The shift to existential philosophy opened new opportunities for eastern religions, which dot the nation's landscape today. It gave the occult fertile soil to grow in western minds. Religions like Hinduism and Buddhism that exalt experience as their main thrust have found great hope in America. Both drugs and eastern religions seek truth within one's own mind. Both negate reason. Both negate absolutes. Both negate the God of the Bible.

The Babylonian shift in philosophy was demonstrated in the Humanist Manifestos of 1933 and 1973. The lie had taken root in United States society. The Humanist Manifestos reveal the purpose behind humanism. Their first three tenets reveal their evil, Babylonian mindset. The tenets state:

1. Religious humanists regard the universe as self-existing and not created.

2. Humanism believes that man is a part of nature and that he has emerged as a result of continuous process.

3. Holding an organic view of life, humanists find the traditional dualism of mind and body must be rejected.

Sadly, secular humanism is now the established religion in public schools. Neutral education is impossible. Teaching knowledge without God is the religion of secular humanism. The United States Supreme Court's 1973 decision to legalize abortion was based on humanistic reasoning.

The shift from the Word of God to secular humanism has removed western civilization from its Judeo-Christian foundation. Humanism teaches that man's religious culture and civilization are the products of gradual development and interaction of environmental and social factors. Humanism asserts that the nature of the universe makes any supernatural or cosmic guarantees of human values unacceptable. Humanism says, "We are convinced that the time has passed for theism, deism, modernism and the several varieties of new thought."

It is clear that western civilization has experienced a shift in philosophy. All traces of Christianity are being removed from public schools and institutions because of the misapplication of the idea of separation of church and state. Marriages and families are being destroyed by the liberalization of divorce laws. The family is being attacked by children's rights laws. Christian parents are being sued for giving their children a godly education. If leaders do not return culture to the Word of God, life as we have known it will be destroyed.

New York's highest court ruled on July 8, 1982, that a 32-year-old homosexual man could adopt a 43-year-old homosexual as his son.[1] Humanistic permissiveness has made suicide the leading cause of teenage deaths. Immorality has produced an epidemic of venereal diseases such as herpes 1, herpes 2 and AIDS. A church council in Minnesota published a booklet urging churches to accept homosexuals and lesbians and to help them celebrate their lifestyle.[2] These are clear signs that society has shifted from the Word of God to a vain, evil Babylonian philosophy. Out of this Babylonian system, the Antichrist will arise and find human hearts that he can rule over. His main weapon always has been deceit, and deception is prevalent in the shifts in science and philosophy.

Even in Christianity, existentialism and humanism have produced a shift in theology. The sure foundation of God's Word has been challenged by a higher criticism that negates supernatural truth and teaches the Bible has mistakes. The new theology includes no resurrection and no eternity. In this so-called church, liberal theology prevails. Humanists calling themselves modernists or liberals have infiltrated Christianity and, in many places, are in firm control. A social gospel rules.

The liberal minister denies at least five basic truths. He denies (1) the inspiration of the Holy

---

[1]Adult Anonymous II, SUNY Supreme Court, July 8, 1982, 452 NY52d 198.

[2]Minnesota Council of Churches, Statement on Ministry to and with Gay and Lesbian Persons, October 1982.

Scriptures and only sees the Bible as a book of history, (2) the virgin birth of the Lord Jesus Christ, (3) His atoning death, (4) His literal bodily resurrection, and (5) the literal coming of the Lord Jesus Christ.

When ministers discard the Bible as the absolute moral standard for living, another philosophy must prevail. The church has declined and entered into an apostate spirit when so many ministers have adopted these liberal viewpoints. The ordination of homosexuals, advocation of easy abortion, easily breaking the marriage vows, all are signs of a shift in theology.

In addition to shifts in science and philosophy, a shift in *morality* has occurred. The new morality follows no definite rules or principles. Its only basis is individual experience. It is also known as situation ethics.

In 1987, the graduating class of the Harvard School of Public Health tossed hundreds of condoms into the air encased in envelopes bearing the latin message, "Ad veneren securiom," translated: "For safe sex." In June of that same year, ABC *Nightline* moderator Ted Koppel spoke to the graduating class at Duke University in Durham, North Carolina. He warned the student body of the threat to the nation's future from the shifts occurring in society

> We have actually convinced ourselves that slogans will save us. Shoot up if you must, but use a clean needle. Enjoy safe sex whenever and with whomever you wish, but wear a condom. No. The answer is no, not because it isn't cool or smart or because you might end up in jail or dying in an AIDS ward, no because it is wrong. Because we have spent 5,000 years as a race of rational human beings trying to

drag ourselves out of the primeval slime by searching for truth and moral absolutes. In its purest form, truth is not a polite tap on the shoulder. It is a howling reproach. What Moses brought down from Mount Sinai were not the Ten Suggestions.

Babylonian culture seeks to indoctrinate people—to change their minds and convictions. King Nebuchadnezzar wanted to make Daniel and his friends into Babylonians. He wanted them to think and dress like Babylonians and to become accustomed to Babylonian ways. He wanted them to eat like Babylonians, and in eastern tradition, sharing a meal with another person implied a commitment to friendship and loyalty. Sharing the king's food meant compromise and moral defilement for Daniel. Therefore Daniel decided not to eat it but to stand for godly absolutes.

> But Daniel purposed in his heart that he would not defile himself with the portion of the king's delicacies, nor with the wine which he drank; therefore he requested of the chief of the eunuchs that he might not defile himself (Dan. 1:8).

Daniel's convictions were based on principles from the Word of God. He had built his convictions over time. Scriptural convictions stand in harmony with the whole message of the Bible and usually oppose the desires of man's lower nature. If a man obeys scriptural convictions, he will develop godly character, and if he does not obey them, he will pay the consequences.

Morals and values rest on absolutes. Absolutes are unchanging standards that can be applied in any situation. If a man's ideas and opinions are his ultimate authority, he has no appeal to an impartial standard when his ideas conflict with the moral judgments of others. Conflicting opinions have no resolution. Absolutes give meaning to man's existence. They define reality for him. Only if he has absolute science, philosophy, theology, and morality can he rest assured that reality corresponds to what he thinks he knows.

Daniel and his friends had to adjust to live in an environment at odds with their religious convictions. They had to think through the principles involved in their actions and abide by those principles. Every Christian must live in a Babylonian system without letting Babylon live in him. It is a tremendous challenge.

Daniel's life principles

Daniel lived by the following five basic principles:

1. He took a stand. Daniel risked being different. He stood his moral ground. His motto was not: "When in Rome, do as the Romans do." He risked his life for convictions and standards.

2. He stood by his final decision. Once Daniel made up his mind, his priorities were firm. He resolved to do what God wanted regardless of the consequences.

3. He respected authority. Daniel had good rapport with the country's leaders. Even though the king was ungodly, Daniel never treated the king or his officials with contempt. He showed sincere goodwill and faithfulness to those over him. He worked through the proper chain of command.

4. He relied upon God. Daniel prayed three times a day, faithfully. His refusal to deny the Lord and stop praying got him thrown into the lion's den. Daniel remained totally dependent upon God. He and his three friends received special ability from the Lord because of their faith and willingness to take a stand.

5. *He adjusted and applied his expertise.* Daniel adjusted to a new culture without adopting it. Without becoming involved in magical arts, he acquired wisdom and understanding in Babylon. He never resorted to pagan practices to predict the future or to interpret history. His only resources were prayer and the Word. He surpassed the professional heathen diviners and magicians. He interpreted the dream about the statue with feet of iron and clay smashed by the stone. No one except Daniel could interpret the dream of the tree falling. Only Daniel was able to interpret the handwriting on the wall.

Daniel inspires the confidence of every vanguard leader who looks to him as a model. He predicted the future and led people into it leaning only upon the Word of God, prayer, fasting, and meditation. The Holy Spirit gave him wisdom to see simplicity in a complex culture and society. Ministers of the Gospel must believe that God will give them divine words to fit their culture and that they can accurately predict where society is headed. Daniel's life shows that pressures to compromise cannot overcome strong convictions.

Trusting God does not always keep true believers free from pressure, struggles or suffering. However, vanguard leaders will trust in God to the point of death and will not apostatize.

> But now, thus says the Lord, who created you, O Jacob, and He who formed you, O Israel: "Fear not, for I have redeemed you; I have called you by

your name; you are Mine. When you
pass through the waters, I will be with
you; and through the rivers, they shall
not overflow you. When you walk
through the fire, you shall not be
burned, nor shall the flame scorch you"
(Isa. 43:1-2).

Daniel's ability was known throughout Babylon.
He was a leader of leaders. In Babylon's ungodly
culture where so many tried to understand dark
sayings and predict the future, Daniel excelled and
was praised for his gift. The following description of
Daniel should fit all vanguard leaders.

There is a man in your kingdom in
whom is the Spirit of the Holy God. And
in the days of your father, light and
understanding and wisdom, like the
wisdom of the gods, were found in him;
and King Nebuchadnezzar your
father—your father the king—made
him chief of the magicians, astrologers,
Chaldeans, and soothsayers. Inasmuch
as an excellent spirit, knowledge,
understanding, interpreting dreams,
solving riddles, and explaining enigmas
were found in this Daniel, whom the
king named Belteshazzar, now let
Daniel be called, and he will give the
interpretation (Dan. 5:11-12).

Like Daniel, vanguard leaders in the coming
twenty-first century should be (1) men filled with the
Holy Spirit, (2) men of illumination, (3) men of
insight, (4) men of wisdom, (5) men of an

extraordinary spirit, (6) men of knowledge, (7) men who can interpret dreams, (8) men who can explain enigmas, and (9) men who can solve difficult problems.

Promotion into new responsibility

Daniel, chapter 6, records Daniel's promotion out of a very unpleasant situation. To Daniel, promotion did not mean greatness; rather it meant new responsibilities. It meant new opportunities to do good and be more useful. Daniel demonstrates the law of life: A man's character should be honored with respect, confidence, success and promotion. Every man finds his place and gets what he's worth. Religion should never hinder a man's success in business, in public life, or on the job. True Christian character is the basis for all promotion. The Bible says that Daniel was promoted over one hundred and twenty of the best leaders in all of Babylon (Dan. 6:2). He was promoted over the whole kingdom (Dan. 6:3). However, Daniel's prominence brought him peril from others' jealousy and envy.

Daniel's promotion was based on his:
• uncompromising personal convictions.
• uncompromising obedience to God and his Word.
• unquestionable loyalty to those over him.
• unsurpassed standard of excellence.
•unsurpassed work ethic and habits.
•contentment.
•excellent character.

Promotion attracts problems including jealousy from others, the exposure of your private world, and inflated pride. Jealousy usually stimulates accusations. Honor and merit always are targets for the malicious arrows of envy. Fault-finding is not a difficult science. A practiced critic will find blemishes in the most beautiful works of men. Envy always follows greatness. It is a price leaders must pay.

A precious stone that falls into the mire does not lose its brilliance. Although Daniel had been dipped into the mire of Babylon and man's jealousy and envy, he never lost his brilliance. He was a man of absolute, impeccable integrity. He had an extraordinary spirit. No corruption was found in him. He held his integrity in public and private, in light and in darkness.

3

The Mission: Fulfilling God's Eternal Purpose

To serve the present age,
My calling to fulfill
Oh may it all my power engage
Do my Master's will.

—John Wesley

When the United States was founded more than two hundred years ago, its population of three million people produced six world-class leaders: George Washington, John Adams, Thomas Jefferson, James Madison and Alexander Hamilton. If the nation's current population of 240 million produced the same ratio of leaders, at least 80 should be living today. Where are they?

In the church about two hundred years ago, John Wesley was a man with a mission achieving great things. A major figure in Christian history, he profoundly influenced the spread of the Gospel in England and America. He once said, "My desire is to be on full stretch for God." In our day, why don't we see more vanguards like Wesley rising to lead the church?

Leaders in the kingdom of God are motivated to move beyond their own concerns and interests.

Every great leader has a mission at the center of his or her soul. The distinction between leadership and mis-leadership is a sense of transcendent purpose. When heading into the winds of adversity, leaders with a mission can move others to follow because of trust established on clear biblical values and principles.

Leaders in the kingdom of God are motivated to move beyond their own concerns and interests. They put the interests of the church and of God's kingdom before their own. They make mission visible, exciting, all-important and reachable for the flock of God. They do not focus on machinery, programs, or statistics. They focus on causes and objectives with a passion for fundamental values and biblical philosophy. It is very important that emerging leaders become kingdom seekers, not empire builders.

Vanguard leaders realize that healthy churches work toward a clearly understood purpose. The purpose captivates and rallies the people. It welds people together and moves them harmoniously in the same direction. Leaders with a mission can move the church from its present condition toward what it should be without being discouraged over its present state.

When people willingly come together to accomplish a mission they create a movement. The movement grows when its members are trained and mobilized to propagate the mission. It is up to the leadership to continually identify and articulate the mission. Leaders must discern what God's mission is. His mission must be our mission. The mission cannot be man's dream or of his own making. Missions may become movements, and movements evolve into machines, and machines into monuments.

God's mission in covenants

God's mission is revealed in a series of eight covenants He formed with man. The Bible records two types of covenants: revocable and irrevocable. In an irrevocable covenant, God promises to act regardless of man's response. He does not require man to fulfill any conditions. In a revocable covenant, God obligates Himself to act only if man obeys. He does require man to fulfill conditions. God revealed His mission originally in the covenant made prior to man's sin in the Garden of Eden.

> Then God said, "Let Us make man in Our image, according to Our likeness; let them have dominion over the fish of the sea, over the birds of the air, and over the cattle, over all the earth and over every creeping thing that creeps on the earth." So God created man in His own image; in the image of God He created him; male and female He created them. Then God blessed them, and God said to them, "Be fruitful and multiply; fill the earth and subdue it; have dominion over the fish of the sea, over the birds of the air, and over every living thing that moves on the earth" (Gen. 1:26-28).

The Edenic Covenant reveals a four-fold purpose of God that becomes the mission of every authentic leader.

1. **Relationship**. God wants man to relate to Him.

2. **Character**. God wants man to be like Him in nature and attributes.

3. **Dominion**. God wants man to rule and to function as king.

4. **Fruitfulness**. God wants man to bear fruit, multiply and fill the whole earth.

The goal of leadership is to produce in the people of God a pure relationship to God, a character that reflects God, a dominion through Christ over sin, hell and the world, and a fruitfulness in helping other people be converted. These four elements of mission find their expression and fulfillment in Christ's church (Matt. 16:16-18).

> to the intent that now the manifold wisdom of God might be made known by the church to the principalities and powers in the heavenly places (Eph. 3:10-11).

God chose His church to be the final instrument to reveal His mission. The new covenant seals the mission to every believer's heart and life. Therefore a vanguard leader's mission is to build the church so that Christ through the church might extend His kingdom, which will conquer the kingdom of hell, ultimately, and have dominion over Satan himself.

The Cross is the source and message of the mission.

Christ's redemptive ministry accomplishes this mission. Jesus' life was completely given to it. He was single-minded in pursuit of his objective. He avoided unproductive effort. He channeled all His effort in one direction: the Cross, which executed or enforced the mission (Col. 1:20-22; 2:14; Gal. 6:14; Matt. 27:42; 20:28; John 10:11,17,18; Heb. 12:1-2; Phil. 2:8).

> The Spirit of the Lord is upon Me, because He has anointed Me to preach the gospel to the poor. He has sent Me to heal the brokenhearted, to preach deliverance to the captives and recovery of sight to the blind, to set at liberty those who are oppressed, to preach the acceptable year of the Lord (Luke 4:18-19).

The Cross is the source and message of the mission. Previous covenants formed a backdrop for the new covenant. At the center of the new covenant stands the Cross, which filters out many Old Testament rituals and sacrifices. Leaders today can build only on the message of the Cross. The Cross is the key to interpreting the covenants and the prophets.

The Cross is the dividing point of the old and new covenants. At the Cross the Jews, to whom previous covenants were given, and the Gentiles, who were strangers from the covenants, were reconciled to God in one body to become the church of the Lord Jesus Christ.

Preaching the kingdom
New Testament theology and practice affirm the mission. Jesus' dominant concern during His earthly

ministry was the kingdom of God. He inaugurated and described this kingdom and went on to demonstrate and exemplify it in His person and work. The mission to which He called His people is best understood as extending the same kingdom (Acts 20:25; 28:23,31).

> From that time Jesus began to preach and to say, "Repent, for the kingdom of heaven is at hand."...Now Jesus went about all Galilee, teaching in their synagogues, preaching the gospel of the kingdom, and healing all kinds of sickness and all kinds of disease among the people (Matt. 4:17,23).

The message of the kingdom of God includes the following basic presuppositions.

• *God is sovereign.* His rule over people and nations is always righteous and just. Whatever He does reflects His character. A loving concern for the best interests of His creatures motivates Him to reveal His power, goodness, holiness, judgment, patience and mercy.

• *God demands personal commitment.* Whoever acknowledges Yahweh to be his or her God must personally commit himself to God and His righteousness. Commitment places them in covenant with Him. He requires people in covenant with Him to love Him with all their heart, soul, mind and strength. He demands righteousness from all who bear His image.

• *God's covenant people become servants.* God extends His righteous influence into families, ethnic groups and entire nations as His community of servants minister not only in the church, but also in the world.

• *The nations, unseen powers and God's own people resist His sovereign rule.* God understands human ignorance, apathy, selfishness, greed and cowardice. Even His own people have opposed His will, squandered His love, and been ungrateful. Although He often bears the shame of His people's failure, God never is overcome by evil.

• *God's direction is always toward the future.* He never is preoccupied with the present. His prophets pointed to a future day when His righteousness will fully triumph and when the earth will be full of the knowledge of His glory. He is the God of hope. He never loses sight of His ultimate goal, therefore, His people face forward. They are sustained by the conviction that His redemptive purpose will be finally realized and that His kingdom will be fully established.

The purpose of God in the world is to reconcile people to Himself, to restore lives to working order in harmony with His design (Rom. 8:18-21; 2 Pet. 3:13; 1 Cor. 15:24).This is the reason for the church's existence. God produced the church to achieve His purpose (Matt. 16:16-18).

The church finds divine energy by pursuing that purpose. His purpose is built into the nature of the church, and the church is built into His purpose. Our mission to accomplish God's purpose requires establishing Christ's church.

Chuck Colson stated in his book *The Body*, "It is hard to imagine...a more urgent or critical task than the recovery and restoration of the biblical view of the church. There is no such thing as Christianity apart from the church. The church is not incidental to the great cosmic struggle for the hearts and souls of modern men and women. It is the instrument God has chosen for the battle."

The people of God need an eternal mindset recognizing the reality of rewards and judgments.

Leaders in the church vanguard, should inspire the grand vision of the church, restore the high view of the church, and expound the great doctrine of the church. Western culture does not really understand the design, nature and work of the church as revealed in Scripture. It is NOT McChurch, just another retail outlet. Faith is NOT just another commodity.

Christ's expected return is part of this mission's message. The people of God need an eternal mindset recognizing the reality of rewards and judgments. Some day every person will actually stand in front of a living, real God (Col. 1:28-29; 1 Thess. 1:10; 2:19; 3:13; 4:17-18; 5:23).

> And everyone who competes for the prize is temperate in all things. Now they do it to obtain a perishable crown, but we for an imperishable crown (1 Cor. 9:25).

> But you be watchful in all things, endure afflictions, do the work of an evangelist, fulfill your ministry. For I am already being poured out as a drink offering, and the time of my departure is at hand (1 Tim. 4:5-8).

Mission theology stands on the New Testament explanation of the eternal purpose of God (Eph. 3:11). Christ is building His church to extend the rule, influence and kingdom of God. Ultimately, Christ will come a second time at the consummation of all things. These are motifs, themes repeated in Scripture for a theology of mission for the church.

All authentic vanguard leaders build upon the eternal purpose of God and not on their own dreams and visions. They must not snatch a few thoughts or obscure Scriptures from the Old Testament to build missions. They must not use personal rhemas or prophecies. Leaders who build on their own vision and dreams end up building for the temporal instead of the eternal. Leaders need to see God's purpose flowing like a river through the covenants and into the second coming of Christ.

Protestant theological understanding of the church's mission has been defined vaguely. The sixteenth century Reformation did not go far enough. Reformers got bogged down with scholasticism and failed to articulate a greater mission. They left succeeding generations no real mission for the globe or for equipping the church to penetrate the world.

The job of a vanguard is to penetrate the culture with the kingdom of God. He needs to recognize that compromise with surrounding cultures produces a diseased Christianity that neutralizes the true power of the Gospel. His mission is to recruit people from the world to become part of Christ's community and movement. Next, these recruits need to be equipped and motivated to serve in their local churches and in the world.

Running the Race

Only free men could compete in Greek athletic games, but even they had to prove they had trained diligently for ten months before the contests. They also had to spend thirty days just prior to the games exercising in the gymnasium. Like an athlete in training, the apostle Paul disciplined himself to fulfill his mission. He ran with a clear goal ahead of him.

> Do you not know that those who run in a race all run, but one receives the prize? Run in such a way that you may obtain it. And everyone who competes for the prize is temperate in all things. Now they do it to obtain a perishable crown, but we for imperishable crown. Therefore I run thus: not with uncertainty. Thus I fight: not as one who beats the air (1 Cor. 9:24-26; see also Acts 9:15-16; 26:19, Rom. 1:1, Gal. 1:1,1:15).

In the Greek games only one runner won a prize, but in the Christian race, all can win the prize. To finish the race and win, Paul states that the athlete needs discipline. Oswald Sanders said, "Any ambition which centers around and terminates upon oneself is unworthy, while an ambition which has the mission of God as its center is not only legitimate but positively praiseworthy."

A church leader can run in vain and not accomplish the will of God.

Paul: Man with a mission

Five words in 1 Corinthians 9:24-26 characterize a man with a mission.

•*Run* is the Greek word *trecho*. It means to run, strive to advance, exert effort, make progress, intellectual striving or spiritual achievement. Every runner could run in vain, potentially. Even a man with a mission can get sidetracked on tributaries, run in circles, or go around the mountain too many times.

> Lest by any means I might run, or had run, in vain (Gal. 2:2).

A church leader can run in vain and not accomplish the will of God. That's why everyone with this great mission must continually seek the source of their vision and the cause of their mission. Is it a God-given mission? Is it found clearly in the Scriptures? Are you accomplishing God-given tasks?

Many potential obstacles lay in the path. Know with certainty that the devil opposes all who are on the Lord's side and will contest every step.

> You ran well. Who hindered you? (Gal. 5:7).

The world, pleasure and the devil make an unholy trinity that try to trap you at every turn and wound you in every war. A leader with a mission must be fully prepared to endure. Endurance is the only real virtue that will guarantee a finish to the mission.

> Let us run with endurance the race set before us (Heb. 12:1).

•*Prize* is the Greek word *brabeion*. It is an award won by the victor in the games. The Bible says a reward awaits believers for overcoming life's conflicts. The athletic prize was awarded in contests involving endurance and suffering. Similarly, some believers will suffer loss and receive greater rewards.

> If anyone's work which he has built on it endures, he will receive a reward. If anyone's work is burned, he will suffer loss; but he himself will be saved, yet so as through fire (1 Cor. 3:14-15).

God gives crowns to the faithful for rewards. Crowns speak of public recognition and honor. The Greek word for *crown* means a chaplet or wreath conferred on a victor in the public games, an honor, a reward, a prize or an adornment. Such a crown had three uses in Paul's day: *(a)* as a wreath of victory in the games (1 Cor. 9:25; 2 Tim. 2:5), *(b)* as a festal ornament (Prov. 1:9), or *(c)* as a public honor granted for distinguished service or personal worth. Believers are often devalued, misunderstood, unrewarded, and even persecuted. But they all will be recognized and given crowns for what they have done and become for Christ's sake. The praise of men will pale in the light of God's glorious recognition. The crowns will demonstrate Christ's approval and His acceptance of their work (2 Cor. 5:9).

Five crowns mentioned in Scripture recognize specific accomplishments: *(a)* the crown of life for faithfulness (James 1:12; Rev. 2:10), *(b)* the crown of glory for undershepherds (1 Pet. 5:1-4), *(c)* the crown of righteousness for loving His appearing (2 Tim. 4:7-8), *(d)* the crown of rejoicing for soul-winning (1 Thess. 2:19-20), and *(e)* the incorruptible crown for self-mastery (1 Cor. 9:25). These crowns motivate believers in this life. God wants believers to invest themselves competing for the prize. Leaders should compete that much more for the prize. They should strive for mastery in all temporal things to attain the eternal.

•*Obtain* is *katalambano* in Greek. It means to take over, seize or obtain; to grasp firmly, comprehend, understand, perceive, catch. It conveys the idea of reaching out and taking by force if necessary to overtake your opponent.

> Not that I have already attained, or am already perfected; but I press on, that I may lay hold of that for which Christ Jesus has also laid hold of me. Brethren, I do not count myself to have apprehended; but one thing I do, forgetting those things which are behind and reaching forward to those things which are ahead, I press toward the goal for the prize of the upward call of God in Christ Jesus (Phil. 3:12-14).

Leaders need to reach out and seize the mission God has set before them. Opposition, satanic attack and harassment will appear. People will withstand believers going forward into the vision. Nevertheless, they are to obtain it, seize it, reach out and take it by force if necessary. A true vanguard leader has a warfare mentality. He does not give up or give in easily.

•*Striving* is *agozonia* in Greek, and it means to strive, contend, enter a contest. It is a warfare term. Lay down your life for the prize.

> Fight the good fight of faith, lay hold on
> eternal life, to which you were also
> called and have confessed the good
> confession in the presence of many
> witnesses (1 Tim. 6:12).

Luke uses the same Greek word to refer to the continual struggle that must take place if one is to enter the kingdom of God by the narrow door (Luke 13:24). Paul uses this word to stress the personal discipline and self-control necessary for a leader to accomplish his goal (1 Cor. 9:25). The analogy of a contest brings out the idea of struggling through life to finish the race.

• *Adelos,* means unclear, unseen, uncertain. It appears in the phrase "not with uncertainty or aimlessly." Paul ran toward a goal. He aimed for it with certainty. The mission-minded leader has a definite target. He fixes his eye on the purpose God put before Him. A mission-minded leader will produce a mission-minded church. Assuming a congregation is doctrinally sound, it can be effective to the degree that:

▼ it has clearly defined its identity.
▼ its people are committed and equipped to function.
▼ it is welded together in fellowship.
▼ it is divinely energized.
▼ it controls hindering tendencies.
▼ its leadership functions are strong, and
▼ every effort is martialed, directed and coordinated in the intelligent, deliberate, strategic effort to accomplish God's purpose for that particular church.

The church that has laid hold of the divine purpose in mission is able to answer the questions:

What are we, Why are we here? Where are we going? How can we get from here to there, and how should we function?

In addressing his students at Dallas Theological Seminary, Howard Hendricks said, "My biggest fear for leadership is not that you will fail, but that you will succeed in doing the wrong thing."

Impart vision, empower people

Local conditions affect how a church accomplishes its mission. Conditions vary between churches, cities and nations. However, every leader must begin by identifying his specific vision and mission rooted in the eternal purpose of God. He must apply it to his own culture and time period. All levels of leadership must adopt the local church mission. Godly mission underlies the dynamic moving of God's Spirit which brings healing in people's bodies, reconciliation to their relationships, reality to their faith, and a fresh meaning to their tradition. Jesus' strategy grew from His kingdom mission.

The mission must be so clear that all leaders understand it and are able to impart it to others.

The time comes when a leader must focus his attention and energy on a few chosen leaders. He has to communicate the local mission clearly and with certainty to all who pastor with him so they can take it as their own. The mission must be so clear that all leaders understand it and are able to impart it to others. Create a team experience. Ownership of mission and vision is vital to keep the leadership team of the church cohesive. Movements dissipate or deviate through mistaken or incomplete understanding of the mission. Not all leaders are in staff positions. Pastors must know who the influential people are. Usually the real movers and shakers compose 12%-17% of the church's population. Pastors must understand group dynamics and know when a leader is withdrawing, alienating himself, becoming critical or polarizing. Every time a ministry leader requests new resources, he or she should explain how the request meshes with the mission to justify the request.

Instruct all levels of the congregation. Every new member's class should devote a significant block of time to present the mission in detail. Preach annually on the mission. Restate it and tie the goals and programs of the church to it. Implement the mission with faith, wisdom, and enthusiasm. Every organization tends to maintain the status quo or—worse yet—to stagnate and deteriorate. The church resists change not only in its traditions, structure, and government but also in its methodology. Use all forms of communication to inspire the congregation with the mission. Use banners, newsletters, bulletins, direct mail, logos, slogans, books, preaching, special meetings. The effectiveness of a leader depends on his ability to stimulate and motivate a church toward the mission. A leader inspires followers to make decisions and take actions.

Leaders with the keenest desire for decision and change fight the greatest temptation to use questionable or unethical methods.

Resist pragmatism—thinking a worthy end justifies any means to achieve it. Pragmatism may achieve a temporary goal, but eventually the leaders lose their credibility. Credibility is far more valuable. Leaders with the keenest desire for decision and change fight the greatest temptation to use questionable or unethical methods.

Authentic vanguard leaders move ahead into God-ordained mission. Steering by God's compass and chart saves leaders from crashing on threatening rocks and hidden shallows. A pure, temperate Christian life is most likely to win real success in any department or activity. Success is a promised result. Consulting God's omniscience secures aid from God's omnipotence. God guides people to true success (1 Chron. 4:10; Josh. 1:7).

> In all your ways acknowledge Him, and
> He shall direct your paths (Prov. 3:6).

In the Living Bible, the last verse above says, "In everything you do put God first and He will direct and crown your life with success."

Twelve *don'ts* for mission success

From my experience in the ministry, I offer the following twelve "don'ts" that guarantee mission accomplishment.

1. Don't move away from a mission mentality to a maintenance mentality. Managers concentrate on doing things right, but leaders want to do the right things. A sense of mission gives a person the feeling that his own contribution has helped to build the world. A person who lives for a cause greater than himself truly lives. Jesus kept His mind on His mission.

> Jesus said to them, "My food is to do the will of Him who sent Me, and to finish His work" (John 4:34; see also Luke 19:10).

2. Don't lose your radical spirit of faith. Reach forward and reach beyond to fulfill your mission. Never give up. Take risks. Move out. Grasp opportunities to stretch your faith. Be adventurous. Great necessities call forth great leaders. Develop faith like Caleb and Joshua had (Heb. 11:1-3).

Faith in God requires boldness to state our desires, unshakable confidence in the trustworthiness of our Father, and a willingness to wait for Him to fulfill our needs. Success requires faith. Anyone in the vanguard of a mission must have great faith. The greater your belief, the greater the degree of your success in fulfilling the mission. Success comes to the person who stays in the race in spite of opposition. Success comes to persistent leaders.

> For a righteous man may fall seven times and rise again, but the wicked shall fall by calamity (Prov. 24:16).

> Do not rejoice over me, my enemy; when I fall, I will arise; when I sit in darkness, the LORD will be a light to me (Mic. 7:8).

The Great Wallenda was a tightrope walker who fell to his death because he became obsessed with failing. He and his family had entertained circus crowds with tightrope shows for several years. However, this time, he planned to walk a high tightrope stretched across a large chasm between two large buildings. For weeks leading up to the event, he led a life of fear. He feared failing. He did fail and paid for it with his life. They call this the Wallenda Factor—concentrating on failing more than succeeding. Concentrate on succeeding and doing the will of God.

> The steps of a good man are ordered by the LORD, and He delights in his way. Though he fall, he shall not be utterly cast down; for the LORD upholds him with His hand (Ps. 37:23-24).

Faith is what you have after everything else is gone. Dare to think big. Faith is maximum use of the God-given power of imagination. Dream up possible ways to reach a desired end. Rid yourself of pessimism and cynicism. Become an incurable optimist. Faith-taking is a risk. Change is natural and challenges accompany every change. Every change invites the unfamiliar and unexpected. Instead of retreating into a shell, become vulnerable. Risk it.

George Mueller faced one of his greatest challenges as he attempted to build the largest orphanage in his ministry. He fasted, prayed and asked himself the following questions. I call these "Guidelines for Faith Leapers and Faith Riskers."

- Would I be going beyond my spiritual capabilities?
- Would I be going beyond my physical or mental strength?
- Have I reached the limits of my faith and mission?

- Am I tempting God, to limit Him in any of His attributes? I do not wish to limit His power or His willingness to give me all the means I need to take this step.
- Would this step cause me to be lifted up in pride? Can I handle promotion?
- Am I violating any principles of wisdom in pursuit of this dream?

3. *Don't allow your cutting-edge vision to be dulled by wrong thinking.* Research shows that the mind processes more than 10,00 thoughts per day. Stop thinking like a victim, preoccupied with the past and things you cannot control. In your mind God places vision for His mission (Acts 26:19).

> I press toward the goal for the prize of
> the upward call of God in Christ Jesus
> (Phil. 3:13-14).

Self-talk about what shoulda-, coulda-, or mighta-been fills people's minds. Victims are fatalistic, pessimistic about the future and feel they can't do anything to change it. Instead, lean on God and go into the future with great faith. Winston Churchill said, "Empires of the future are empires of the mind." Ralph Waldo Emerson said, "A man is what he thinks about all day long. A man's life is what his thoughts make of it."

Stop thinking like a sustainer, preoccupied with present needs and doing only enough to get by. He does what is safe and wants guarantees on everything. He has no faith to reach out, take risks, or push forward.

Stop thinking like a dreamer, preoccupied with the future. He is full of vision but no plans, no steps to reality, no real actions. He says, "I could have done that."

Stop thinking like a controller, preoccupied with controlling every circumstance in life. He can't stand change or surprises. The only One who can control everything is God. We are God's servants. We are not in control.

Get your mind out of its rut where it goes in a circle of routine boredom. Stubbornly it stays on the beaten path without accomplishing anything for God. Conventional thinking runs in deep ruts worn by what everyone else says. It presses people into the negative atmosphere of the culture.

Get your mind out of its rut where it goes in a circle of routine boredom.

Stop thinking like a loser with a prejudiced mindset. Losers make judgments and reach opinions before the facts are in. They also maintain their opinions after facts have changed. Prejudice limits vision and keeps people focused on what exists. Prejudice stifles creativity, insisting on one way to do everything. A stubborn, prejudiced, loser leader will not be flexible enough to allow the Lord to lead him into new realms of faith.

Leaders need to improve their thinking skills. Intelligence does not dictate how a person thinks. The ability to think well is a discipline that can be developed. Lift your mind out of its rut and try new possibilities. Be adventurous. Don't merely react to change; create change yourself. Make things happen by moving in faith and believing God.

4. Don't tolerate jealousy in your spirit. Jealousy is one of the most despicable sins. Not only does it damage others, it destroys the person harboring it.

> Wrath is cruel and anger a torrent, but who is able to stand before jealousy? (Prov. 27:4).

> A sound heart is life to the body, but envy is rottenness to the bones (Prov. 14:30).

Jealousy expresses itself in fault-finding and evil-speaking. When vanguard leaders move in faith to accomplish a God-given mission, they can grow jealous of others who already accomplished similar missions. Jealousy rejoices when others fall. It feeds on ungodly competition and comparison. Jealousy of David was King Saul's root problem.

> So the women sang as they danced, and said: "Saul has slain his thousands, and David his ten thousands." Then Saul was very angry, and the saying displeased him... So Saul eyed David from that day forward (1 Sam. 18:7-9).

Selfish ambition nurtures jealousy. It grows in the garden alongside a desire for fame and recognition.

Genuine leaders have a sense of calling, not a sense of being driven. The strongest leader has been made strong by God who affirms authentic leaders in their personhood and identity. God's affirmation frees the leader not only to lead a cause but also to serve others. A sense of identity is found in servanthood. Security comes from knowing who you are. Jealousy has no place in the heart of a leader at the head of a mission.

God is not concerned with how quickly you build but how well you build.

---

5. Don't lose patience. It produces long-lasting excellence. God is not concerned with how quickly you build but how well you build. Building for excellence is painfully slow. Reject pressures to be relevant, spectacular, and powerful. Jesus told a story about two houses. One was built quickly on sand but it fell (Matt. 7:24-27). If you are working for a year, plant rice. If you are working for a century, plant a tree. If you are working for an eternity, plant a man.

When you deal with God's people, instilling character and God's mission in them, it takes a lifetime. God's purposes cannot be hurried. No step can be left out. Excellence takes time.

6. Don't compromise quality in times of discouragement and testing. Quality will be tested. Depth will be exposed. Quality is revealed over time. You need to ask: Is the dream His vision? Is the method His way? Is the timing His moment? You must become a wise master builder who lays a good foundation using right materials. Building for eternity demands quality.

> According to the grace of God which was given to me, as a wise master builder I have laid the foundation, and another builds on it. But let each one take heed how he builds on it (1 Cor. 3:10).

7. Don't allow distractions from your God-given vision and mission. You have been sent. You have a work to do, a mission to accomplish.

> Therefore we also, since we are surrounded by so great a cloud of witnesses, let us lay aside every weight, and the sin which so easily ensnares us, and let us run with endurance the race that is set before us (Heb 12:1).

The Lord Jesus Christ frequently spoke about being sent to do His Father's will. He had an inner sense of destiny evident from his conversation. "I was sent... I came... My Father's will... My Father's work...To finish His work... The work of God..." Begin to confess and pray that these phrases get into your spirit.

Set your sight on worthwhile things and work continuously toward their fulfillment. People with goals and direction accomplish fifty to a hundred times more in their life than people who wander aimlessly. What are your goals for this year? For the next five years? The next ten years? Jesus saw history as an arrow shot toward a target, a fire cast on earth, a lightning flash across the sky, a door opened to fulfillment, a task to be completed. Jesus' mission-mentality told Him a new time had arrived; a new reality had come. He embodied that new reality and called people to see it and follow Him. His sense of destiny determined His strategy.

8. Don't give Satan any ground in your life. Take a stand. Take control. The devil must be driven out of your conscience, mind, and habits.

nor give place to the devil (Eph. 4:27).

> And do not grieve the Holy Spirit of
> God, by whom you were sealed for the
> day of redemption (Eph. 4:30).

Any disobedience to the known word of God invites the devil to get a foothold into your life. Mission-minded leaders must not give the enemy any room. They must take a stand and take control.

9. Don't avoid difficult tasks or perplexing problems. Go through them. If you avoid them, they will meet you later in life or around the next corner.

> And see, now I go bound in the spirit to
> Jerusalem, not knowing the things that
> will happen to me there, except that the
> Holy Spirit testifies in every city, saying
> that chains and tribulations await me
> (Acts 20:22-23).

Opportunity comes from adversity. Welcome it. It is one of the best friends travelling with leaders. Problems can include the removal of a non-productive leader, the need for a leader to stand by your side, or a personal problem of your own. Face them now. You can go through them. Don't go around them.

10. Don t travel through life alone. Isolation slowly destroys leaders. Cultivate relationships. A person who can master human relationships is priceless. Do for others what you want them to do for you. It's hard to think about David without Jonathan, or Paul without Timothy, or D.L. Moody without Shankey, or Billy Graham without Cliff Barrows or George Beverly Shea.

> Two are better than one, because they have a good reward for their labor. For if they fall, one will lift up his companion. But woe to him who is alone when he falls, for he has no one to help him up. Again, if two lie down together, they will keep warm; but how can one be warm alone? Though one may be overpowered by another, two can withstand him. And a threefold cord is not quickly broken (Eccles. 4:9-12; see also Prov. 17:17).

Special, loving relationships are more than just good. They are essential. A shortage of friends will destroy you.

The Lord God Himself states in Gen. 2:18 "It is not good that man should be alone; I will make him a helper comparable to him." A real friend is a treasure worth more than gold. Friends give you a special place in the world. Relationships confirm personal meaning, value and identity. Solitude casts doubt on them. Special, loving relationships are more than just good. They are essential. A shortage of friends will destroy you. A true friend hears you when you speak your heart, lets you think out loud, supports you when you are struggling, corrects you gently with love when you are wrong and forgives you when you fail. A friend prods you to personal growth, stretches you to your full potential, and celebrates your success as if it was his own.

By God's design, people hunger for contact with others. They want to belong. They want interaction and a sense of community with others. They want to overcome feelings of alienation and do not want to be seen as strange. However, people's need to belong causes anxiety. Unhappy personal relationships create frustration. In an affluent society, self-centered consumers ask for more mobility, privacy and convenience. Those three things cause greater isolation and worse loneliness. Add in the depersonalizing effects of technology and fear of rejection and it is easy to see why people are lonely.

Loneliness is the gut-wrenching feeling that follows being ignored or misunderstood. It knows no limits of class, race or age. It is a permanent condition for millions of leaders around the world. A public person with no personal life is lonely. He can be continually surrounded by people but have no one to share his heart with. Loneliness should not be viewed as a weakness or a character defect. It can be adjusted. Everyone has walls around their lives that should be turned into bridges.

Age tends to complicate personal relationships. Grade schoolers view classmates as a pool of potential friends. They simply pick ones they want to be friends with, like picking ripe, juicy fruit in an orchard. Children never contemplate the odds that the orchard might bear a bad crop or that they might not want to pick or lose the capacity to pick. As years go by friends become rarer, more like gold. Many people are forced to treasure the few they have. Many become skeptical, less optimistic about making new friends.

Baring bruised feelings and memories to strangers is a fearful process, but it is how true fellowship and true friendships are established. Show concern for other people. Talk to them about their interests more than you talk about yourself and your problems. Listen to them.

> The righteous should choose his friends carefully, for the way of the wicked leads them astray (Prov. 12:26).

When building a friendship, never gossip or slander. Be honest in business and personal dealings. Always be quick to praise others with sincerity. Remember their names. Be kind and patient.

11. *Don't allow bad habits to ruin your potential achievement.*
God calls every believer to conquer old habits and sins just like he called Saul to destroy Amalek. Few do. Most pander to their self-interests.

In the beginning you make your habits; in the end your habits make you. Worry is a bad habit. It can paralyze progress. A person who worries also procrastinates, and that's a bad habit, too. Fear is a bad habit. Quit thinking about things to fear and have faith. Laziness is a bad habit. Be an early riser. Start each day with time to get your attitude and spirit on top. Get to work before you have to be there (Prov. 6:10; 10:20; 15:16).

> Do not love sleep, lest you come to poverty; open your eyes, and you will be satisfied with bread (Prov. 20:13).

12. *Don't lose your perspective on life.* Life is a journey, a gradual process. Avoid extremes that damage home, health, friendships, godly character, and biblical values. True success abides in balanced,

stable living. Keep a steady pace. Keep in harmony with the laws of God and nature. Keep your sense of humor. Laugh at life. Laugh at yourself. At times you can even laugh at the devil.

A normal life lasts seventy to eighty years. You don't have three or four hundred years to do unimportant things before you attempt meaningful, significant things. You're running out of time. You may have wasted today, but you haven't wasted tomorrow.

True success is progressive completion of predetermined, worthwhile, godly goals during a lifetime kept stable by balanced, purified belief.

4

The Commission: Advancing God's Army

God always moves His people forward. He leads people to advance, not to retreat. He desires for people to progress to fulfill their destiny. The vanguard leader has a responsibility to encourage the people of God, individually and corporately, to push forward and keep marching on.

The saints need encouragement to keep advancing in spiritual maturity, in their prayer lives, and toward the vision the Lord has given. God is not pleased with those who draw back, fall back or turn away from the straight path. Lot's wife had misgivings about following the Lord and looked back as the angel of the Lord led her family out of Sodom (Gen. 19:26). As she looked back she turned into a pillar of salt.

> Now the just shall live by faith; But if anyone draws back, My soul has no pleasure in him. But we are not of those who draw back to perdition, but of those who believe to the saving of the soul (Heb. 10:38-39).

God's people have to exert self-control to resist thoughts and impulses to look back, fall back, draw back, or go back. Sometimes drawing back is not intentional but occurs slowly. A man's thoughts start drifting, and his focus turns away from the things of God. As his heart drifts away, his willful decisions follow suit and he finds himself slipping backward. In this day and age, the people of God need to be continually exhorted to guard their hearts, their eyes and their feet to make sure they keep moving toward the Lord. Jesus looked forward to "the joy that was set before Him" and warned the disciples to keep the same focus.

> But Jesus said to him, "No one, having put his hand to the plow, and looking back, is fit for the kingdom of God" (Luke 9:62).

From the time Moses led the people of Israel out of Egypt, they continually moved forward until they entered Canaan. The book of Numbers, chapters 9 and 10, describe the manner in which God conducted the movement and the four signals that regulated the journey. The four signals were:
- The lifting of the cloud (Num. 9:15-23; 10:11-13).
- The blowing of the trumpets (Num. 10:1-10).
- The moving of the armies (Num. 10:14-28).
- The prayer of victory (Num. 10:35 & 36).

The Lord directed the movement of His people by the cloud. This was no ordinary cloud. It spontaneously appeared at the completion of construction of the tabernacle, and it became a pillar of fire at night. The cloud dramatically symbolized the presence of the Lord hovering above the tabernacle.

When the mystical cloud moved and the silver trumpets sounded, the congregation moved its armies and offered a prayer of victory.

> At the command of the LORD the children of Israel would journey, and at the command of the LORD they would camp; as long as the cloud stayed above the tabernacle they remained encamped (Num. 9:18).

Today the church follows the vision God has given it. Leaders watch the moving of the Holy Spirit and listen carefully to the blowing of the trumpets. On signal, they gather the people of God and move forward in prayer power. As congregations move forward they encounter obstacles. The books of Deuteronomy and Numbers, especially chapters 11 through 14, contain a permanent record of the movement of the congregation in the wilderness and the obstacles they met. They encountered warfare, leadership controversies over authority, doubts and unbelief, discouragement, murmuring of the people, and mixture.

The people first anticipated moving forward as they prepared to leave Egypt. God had put pressure on Egypt's Pharaoh through plagues and finally through the death of every firstborn to obtain the release of Israel from slavery. The people viewed the trip out of Egypt as a positive step. They moved forward into the wilderness to have a feast and ultimately to move back to Canaan. As they left Egypt, the Lord directed them. As the story unfolds in Exodus chapters 1-13, Israel was delivered by the miracle power of God.

> Now the LORD spoke to Moses, saying:
> "Speak to the children of Israel, that they
> turn and camp before Pi Hahiroth,
> between Migdol and the sea, opposite
> Baal Zephon; you shall camp before it by
> the sea. For Pharaoh will say of the
> children of Israel, 'They are bewildered
> by the land; the wilderness has closed
> them in.' Then I will harden Pharaoh's
> heart, so that he will pursue them; and I
> will gain honor over Pharaoh and over
> all his army, that the Egyptians may
> know that I am the LORD." And they
> did so (Exod. 14:1-4).

When the Lord directed Israel to camp before the
Red Sea, He actually was setting a trap for Pharaoh's
army. For Israel, there was only one way in and one
way out. They were surrounded by mountains and
water. Then the Lord went behind them and stirred
up the enemy and caused the enemy to pursue them.
In this precarious position, they saw the dust of the
chariots coming after them and they began to
murmur, complain and criticize. Moses began to
pray. It looked bad for the Israelites, but God had the
situation in hand. He had a plan to glorify His name
and to show the people of God His miracle power
fighting for them.

Moses himself did not waiver in unbelief. With
the enemy at his back and the people murmuring, he
stood in front of the Red Sea, looked at his obstacle,
and cried out encouragement to the people.

> And Moses said to the people, "Do not
> be afraid. Stand still, and see the
> salvation of the LORD, which He will

> accomplish for you today. For the
> Egyptians whom you see today, you
> shall see again no more forever. The
> LORD will fight for you, and you shall
> hold your peace" (Exod. 14:13-14).

These are words of a vanguard leader. Moses
desired to lead the people forward but encountered
seemingly impossible circumstances. Nonetheless, he
exhorted the people to trust God. Paraphrased, Moses
said, "God did not bring us out this far to leave us. He
will take us on." Then God tells Moses and the
people of Israel to keep a forward-looking attitude.

> And the Lord said to Moses, "Why do
> you cry to Me? Tell the children of
> Israel to go forward" (Exod. 14:15).

Notice the words *go forward*. The word *forward* in
Hebrew expresses the idea of pulling up tent stakes to
move and the idea of taking a journey in stages. The
length of the entire journey was not covered in one
trip. History records Israel's forty-two stops and starts
in the wilderness prior to entering Canaan. The Lord
told Moses to keep his eyes pointed forward and to
give the same message to the people. God first put it
in Moses' spirit, and then Moses imparted it to the
people of God. To lead God's people in stages toward
a vision, the vanguard leader needs a forward-
looking spirit and attitude. The leader needs to instill
the same attitude in the people to keep them moving
forward. A vanguard leader needs a quickened rhema
word in his spirit that will build his faith to speak in
faith to move the people of God forward.

The future belongs to the Lord

The word FORWARD is an acronym for the elements necessary to move a congregation forward into the vision.

F represents the future. It belongs to the Lord and is under His control. Things do not happen by chance. Things happen according to God's will and planning. The Lord already has moved into the future, and we follow Him.

> The Lord your God Himself crosses over before you; He will destroy these nations from before you, and you shall dispossess them. Joshua himself crosses over before you, just as the Lord has said (Deut. 31:3).

Every believer can lean on this faith-building word. God has gone ahead of his followers and prepared their future. Believers need only to move forward and possess it (Deut. 31:6,8).

Christians can face the future because God has prepared it. God guides and directs events to fulfill purposes He has in mind. Believers need faith in the providence and government of God. Providence involves acting wisely and prudently and making preparation for the future. Providence is the continuing action of God preserving the creation He has brought into being and guiding it to His intended purposes (Rom. 8:28-30).

God is good, and He is deeply concerned about His own people. His determination to accomplish His purpose does not excuse people from giving themselves diligently to work toward the same goal. Therefore, believers should press forward toward the goal, believing in the providence of God. The sensitive, obedient believer will be alert to what God is intending and attempting to do even in unexpected, unplanned or unlikely situations.

> There are many plans in a man's heart,
> Nevertheless the Lord's counsel—that
> will stand (Prov. 19:21).

God has predetermined or predestined the future according to His providence. As the church moves forward, it must believe in God's Word and that God has provided everything needed to fulfill the vision He has given. Divinely sent possibilities spark expectancy and excitement in the lives of alert believers. "Accidental" circumstances may in fact be miracles done for believers because God makes all things work together for the good of His beloved family. Sometimes He brings about good directly, and sometimes He counters or deflects the efforts of evil men. He alone determines His plan and knows the significance of each action. It is not necessary for people to know where He is leading. People need to be careful to avoid telling God what He should do for or with their lives.

Before the days of modern navigational aids, boats crossing the Atlantic came equipped with two compasses. One was fixed to the deck where the helmsman could see it. The other compass was fastened to one of the masts. A passenger once asked the captain, "Why do you have two compasses?" "This is an iron vessel," replied the captain, "and the compass on the deck is often affected by its surroundings. Such is not the case with the compass on the masthead. The one is above the influence. We steer by the compass above." Leaders must have a direct line of sight to the compass above. They steer by confidence in God's providence. They cannot be distracted by circumstances seen with the natural eye. They keep their attention on God and His mysterious ways, sovereignty, and providence.

An artist's drawing of a night scene shows a solitary man rowing a little skiff across a lake. The wind is high and stormy. The waves billow and rage around his frail bark. Only one star shines through the dark and angry sky above. But upon that lone star, the voyager fixes his eye and keeps rowing through the midnight storm. Beneath the picture were the words: If I lose that, I am lost.

Ordinary people seek Him

O signifies ordinary people. A man named Celsius in A.D. 178 wrote bitterly against Christianity. He ridiculed Christianity's appeal to ordinary people. "Let no cultured person draw near." he wrote. "None wise, none sensible, for all that kind of thing we count evil. But if any man is ignorant, if any is wanting in culture, if any is a fool, let him come boldly." Of Christians he wrote: "We see them in their own house, wool dressers, cobblers, and fullers, the most uneducated and vulgar persons. Christians are like a swarm of bats or ants creeping out of their nest or frogs holding a symposium around a swamp, or worms in convention in a mud hole." The attitude of cultured and educated people toward Christians in the first few centuries was condescending. The Roman empire had sixty million slaves during the time of Christ. Slaves were considered living tools, things, but not people. Christianity made these "things" into important people. Slaves suddenly were sons and daughters of God with respect and purpose. They were tools in the hand of God. The church consists of the simplest and humblest people.

> For you see your calling, brethren, that not many wise according to the flesh, not many mighty, not many noble, are called. But God has chosen the foolish things of the world to put to shame the wise, and God has chosen the weak things of the world to put to shame the things which are mighty; and the base things of the world and the things which are despised God has chosen, and the things which are not, to bring to nothing the things that are, that no flesh should glory in His presence. But of Him you are in Christ Jesus, who became for us wisdom from God—and righteousness and sanctification and redemption— that, as it is written, "He who glories, let him glory in the Lord" (1 Cor. 1:26-31).

Ordinary people are God's secret weapons. The word *ordinary* means usual, medium, average, unremarkable, commonplace, regular, inferior, second rate, undistinguished. Most people feel just medium or average, and the enemy uses these feelings to beat people down and to heap guilt upon them for not being worthy to be used by the Lord. The enemy is quick to point out sin and weakness. He likes to advertise a Christian's mental lapses and lack of Bible knowledge. The truth is that Christians *are* usual, medium, average and unremarkable, but they are in good company. They are exactly the kind of people God has chosen throughout history to be tools in His hand to accomplish remarkable things. Common folks find themselves standing in the midst of miracles. So-called inferior people find themselves accomplishing mighty exploits for God.

Jesus sent seventy ordinary people into ordinary places to accomplish extraordinary things.

> After these things the Lord appointed seventy others also, and sent them two by two before His face into every city and place where He Himself was about to go (Luke 10:1).

In Romans, chapter 16, Paul mentions twenty-four people. Although thirteen of the same names appear in inscriptions or documents at emperor's palaces in Rome, many of these people were ordinary, common folks. Priscilla and Aquilla made tents and others had jobs working in palaces under the emperor's domain. Six of them were women. Nevertheless, God chose all of them to accomplish His will.

Resiliency holds its ground

R stands for resiliency. When the great missionary William Carey was asked what his key to success was, he simply replied, "I can plod." The church conquers by continuing and by finishing its race. The mighty oak tree started out as a little nut that held its ground. A man who holds his ground can become strong like the oak (Prov. 24:10).

> But the Lord stood with me and strengthened me, so that the message might be preached fully through me, and that all the Gentiles might hear.

And I was delivered out of the mouth of
the lion (2 Tim. 4:17).

Therefore I will look to the LORD; I will
wait for the God of my salvation; my
God will hear me. Do not rejoice over
me, my enemy; when I fall, I will arise;
when I sit in darkness, the LORD will be
a light to me (Mic. 7:7,8).

The world holds three kinds of people: the wills,
the won'ts and the can'ts. The wills accomplish
everything; the won'ts oppose everything; the can'ts
fail at everything. Christians who go forward to
accomplish great things for God, develop resiliency.
They cultivate their ability to endure under pressure,
rise after failure, and push ahead when others fall
back. Ministry is a well-fought fight, a well-run race, a
well-kept faith, and a well-won crown.

Everyone fails; it's a fact of life. Trying to tiptoe
safely to the grave without goofing up is futile. When
failing, Christians should fail forward. At least that
way they promote the will and purpose of God. The
great preacher Charles Spurgeon said, "By
perseverance, the snail reached the ark."

Most successful people in the world have times of
failure. They fail, find themselves, and then pursue
and find success. A man who wants all possible
obstacles removed before he attempts a task never
will attempt it. Sir Walter Scott suffered a childhood
illness that left him with a lame leg, yet he rose to
become a great poet and storyteller. John Bunyan
wrote Pilgrim's Progress while locked in a prison cell.
George Washington led a ragtag army through the
snows of Valley Forge. Born in abject poverty,
Abraham Lincoln rose to the U.S. presidency.

Benjamin Disraeli lost four elections to England's House of Commons before winning a fifth race and eventually becoming England's prime minister, and he did it facing bitter racial prejudice. Theodore Roosevelt was afflicted with asthma and as a boy lay choking in his father's arms. Electrical engineer Charles Steinmetz could not sleep without opiates due to sharp rheumatic pains yet he contributed greatly to advances in electrical science. Walter Chrysler started out in the grease-pit of a locomotive round house. Italian conductor Arturo Toscanini spent time as a second fiddle in an obscure South American orchestra.

Among the students of a well-known college, a young man had to get himself around on crutches. He had an unusual talent for friendliness and optimism and won the deep respect of his classmates. One day a student asked him what had caused his deformity. "Infantile paralysis." he replied briefly, not wanting to elaborate. "With a misfortune like that how can you face the world so?" inquired his classmate. "Oh," replied the young Christian smiling, "the disease never touched my heart." Even with limitations, a man can still dream and accomplish great things. Scripture records how Moses, Gideon, Jeremiah, and other Bible heros accomplished great things for God while struggling through obstacles. Resiliency is the key to finishing the race.

Wholehearted prayer delights God

W represents wholehearted prayer. It moves the hand of God. The final sentence in the following reference contains four key words: "If you seek Him."

> As for you, my son Solomon, know the
> God of your father, and serve Him with
> a loyal heart and with a willing mind for
> the Lord searches all hearts and
> understands all the intent of the
> thoughts. If you seek Him, He will be
> found by you; but if you forsake Him, he
> will cast you off forever (1 Chron. 28:9).

The word *if* poses a question. It requires a decision. It poses a challenge. It also holds potential. Everyone, including the vanguard leader, has to decide *if* he will seek the Lord with his whole heart and if he will move ahead and accept the challenge put before him. If he does, then he can see the vision and accomplish what God has given him.

The word *you* places personal responsibility on the individual. You have to take the responsibility to seek the Lord, and you cannot shift it to someone else. It is not a book you read. It is not a conference you attend. The Levitical priests had to accept personal responsibility to bear the ark on their own shoulders. You have to bend your knees. You have to open your mouth. You have to attune your heart. You have to lift your hands. You have to intercede.

The word *seek* embraces the thought of knocking on doors, pushing down walls, and pursuing a goal or an object until you grasp it. It is an intense word describing a man who will not give up until he finds what he is after. Seeking is not for the lighthearted or for those easily discouraged. It is for the persistent, the overcomer, the resilient one, the one who yearns to accomplish.

The word *Him* focuses attention on the Lord God Himself. Prayer must be to the God of the Bible. He hears; He will be found; He will forgive; He will move by His spirit; if you seek Him.

Consider the following parable given by Christ:

> Then He spoke a parable to them, that men always ought to pray and not lose heart, saying: "There was in a certain city a judge who did not fear God nor regard man. Now there was a widow in that city; and she came to him, saying, 'Avenge me of my adversary.' And he would not for a while; but afterward he said within himself, 'Though I do not fear God nor regard man, yet because this widow troubles me I will avenge her, lest by her continual coming she weary me.'" Then the Lord said, "Hear what the unjust judge said. And shall God not avenge His own elect who cry out day and night to Him, though He bears long with them? I tell you that He will avenge them speedily. Nevertheless, when the Son of Man comes, will He really find faith on the earth?" (Luke 18:1-8).

The words in this parable depict an intense, continual, wholehearted seeking. The woman in this parable was continually coming, making the judge weary. She would not give up. She would not take "No" for an answer. God knows the thoughts of people, yet He wants them to seek Him and submit their requests to Him. He promises to respond to people who seek His face (2 Chron. 7:14).

It is better to have heartfelt prayers even if words do not come easily than to have wordy prayers without heart. When the outlook is bad, people need to try the "uplook," looking up, seeking God for an answer.

Attitudes of faith and courage

A indicates that attitudes of faith and courage are fuel for fulfilling vision. God promised Joshua, a vanguard leader, that He would never fail him, that He would go before him, and that He would fight for him.

> "Be strong and of good courage, do not fear nor be afraid of them; for the LORD your God, He is the One who goes with you. He will not leave you nor forsake you." Then Moses called Joshua and said to him in the sight of all Israel, "Be strong and of good courage, for you must go with this people to the land which the LORD has sworn to their fathers to give them, and you shall cause them to inherit it" (Deut. 31:6,7; see also 1 Chron. 28:20).

Faith sees the invisible, believes the incredible, and receives the impossible.

Christ's followers always are on the winning side. They are not to prepare their minds for defeat but are to march with the assurance of victory. To be strong is to endeavor to go forward and grasp vision God has given. Strength takes a position of faith and determination. Faith sees the invisible, believes the incredible, and receives the impossible. Courage is not the absence of fear, it is the mastery of it. Courage goes forward in the face of severe opposition. Courage says "no turning back; no giving up on the vision; I'm going to be bold; I'm going to go forward; I'm going to lead the people forward." Faith believes that God not only *can* but also *will*. Faith is idle when circumstances are calm. Only when they are adverse is faith exercised. Like a muscle, faith grows strong and supple with exercise.

To accomplish the vision, a vanguard leader must develop his own faith and courage and inspire the same attitudes in people he leads. He must be able to see it, say it and seize it. Faith sees the opportunity that God has laid before the leader and the local church. With words, he commits himself to the vision that has gripped him. The Bible says you have not because you ask not, therefore, speak words of faith and save the dream. To seize the vision, faith becomes a commitment to act on the dream. People follow inward hopes made visible. A vanguard leader doesn't go down to the river's edge; he goes through the river and across it. Joshua didn't go down to the edge of the Jordan River and stand there by faith waiting for something to happen. He stepped in; he had to go over. Faith states the dream, examines all options, uses all resources, removes all nonessentials and then moves forward. A man able to see in faith sees things that do not yet exist in the natural realm and sees the potential to bring to pass something marvelous. Would you have been like the Iowa banker who told Alexander Bell to remove that toy from his office? Would you have been like the Hollywood producer who scrawled "Reject" on the movie screenplay *Gone With The Wind?* Would you have been like Henry Ford's greatest investor, who in 1906 asked that his stock be sold? Would you have been like Mr. Roebuck who sold his part of the

Sears and Roebuck stock for $25,000 and now Sears sells $25,000 worth of stock every 16 seconds? These people could not see future potential. They did not have faith to see what God was doing.

Remember what God has done

R stands for remember. God has done wonderful things, and His people should not let them slip from memory. God never has let His church down. He always will come through. Looking back on my life, I can say God never has let me down. God never has been unjust, and He always has gone before me. God has given when He could have withheld. He has shown mercy when judgment would have fit the occasion.

> Bless the LORD, O my soul; And all that is within me, bless His holy name! Bless the LORD, O my soul, And forget not all His benefits: Who forgives all your iniquities, Who heals all your diseases (Ps. 103:1-3; see also Ps. 77:11-12).

A vanguard leader will show wisdom by continually talking about the goodness, faithfulness, and provision of the Lord. He will not allow negative thoughts or words to flow through his mind or out of His mouth. A leader who doubts God or meditates on things he feels should have happened that didn't happen sows a spirit of murmuring into other people.

The divine blessings that have come as my wife and I have been in the ministry would fill a long list. God has been faithful, and His goodness has beamed like sunshine upon our path. Whenever I have needed answers to prayer, God has provided them.

He never has left me to stumble in darkness and grope through my own natural inclinations to try to find His plan. He has been faithful to make His will known through people, a book, a song, an experience, or a circumstance. God has supplied financially and emotionally. He has supplied friendships and all we have needed in life. Of course, we have had our own trials, tribulations, disappointments, and times of great sorrow, but even in those times God has come to our side as the mighty pillar of strength that He is.

For a number of years my wife and I could not have children. This was a great trial for our faith. We turned to adoption and arranged for our first child. We had been so excited to bring this child into our life, but before it could be accomplished, the child died. We adopted two more beautiful daughters, both of whom have stories and circumstances that were extremely hard and that stretched us beyond our emotional capacity. But in those dark hours, the Lord came through with strength. Later on, my wife bore two children naturally, a son and a daughter. Seeing God answer prayer and put together a family makes me say "Bless the Lord oh my soul, and forget not all of His benefits."

When building programs strained the church's finances, the Lord came through. The down payment on the first building we bought as a pioneering church was due and we were short by $8,000. That Sunday my heart was heavy, my mind was clouded, and I did not know what to say to the people as we began the service. Our small church had raised all the money it could. Everyone had given sacrificially and we were still short. We probably would lose the building the next day. That Sunday, the exact amount of money we needed was collected in the offering. The $8,000 looked like $1 million to me. The financial blessing was there in God's timing. As His people move forward, His faithfulness is new every morning, at every turn and every step of the way. There is no shadow of turning in Him.

Decisions determine destiny
D signifies decisions. Decisions determine destiny. Choose carefully and wisely.

> And if it seems evil to you to serve the LORD, choose for yourselves this day whom you will serve, whether the gods which your fathers served that were on the other side of the River, or the gods of the Amorites, in whose land you dwell. But as for me and my house, we will serve the LORD (Josh. 24:15).

Life is full of decisions. They range from relatively small to major life-changing decisions. The decisions we make turn around and "make" us. The vanguard leader needs to become a wise man to make wise decisions.

> A wise man will hear and increase learning, and a man of understanding will attain wise counsel (Prov. 1:5; see also Prov. 8:33; 9:8,9).

The following ground rules will help guide decision makers in wisdom:
1. Become grounded in basic bible knowledge.
2. Become familiar with Godly principles that govern life and ministry.
3. Be open and sensitive to the Holy Spirit and seek a clear inner witness.

4. Be comfortable with your own gift of common sense.

5. Learn from wise men's lifestyles and decision-making processes and seek mature counsel.

6. Learn from your own mistakes.

7. Ask yourself, "Does this harmonize with my personal desires? What special guidance can I discern?"

8. Pray. In prayer God's voice can be heard, especially if prayer is a daily habit or addiction.

9. Research the subject you are considering and get all the facts. List out potential assets and liabilities.

Hindrances to wise decision making include being hasty, stubborn, self-willed, and double minded. Accounts of wise and poor decision making hold instruction for anyone who reads his Bible. Stories of Bible characters, all of whom made decisions, "were written for our admonition," according to the apostle Paul (1 Cor. 10:11).

Men tend to take matters into their own hands. When this happens, God may let a man struggle in the darkness created by his decisions. Guard against quick decisions and snap judgments. Realize that subjective, personal biases can lead a man to interpret almost anything as a sign of God's approval and blessing on something he wants. Close friends whom you trust the most can lead you astray. Be aware of the subtle influence of your former lifestyle in determining the will of God. Always select methods and strategies that are at harmony with principles and guidelines of Scripture. Sometimes God gives you your request but sends leanness to your soul. The thing received becomes a trial and a constant reminder of the need to yield to God and His way.

God has no policeman walking around, grabbing Christians by the neck, and saying, "Read your Bible, go to church, and give to missions." God created man superior to all other creatures. He gave man the power and privilege of choice. With that privilege comes the terrible responsibility of living with the results or consequences of those choices. There may two sides to every issue, but there also are two sides to a sheet of fly paper, and it makes a big difference to the fly which side he chooses to walk on. The concert violinist at New York's Carnegie Hall said she became skilled through "planned neglect." She planned to neglect everything not related to her goal. Like Mary and Moses, we can choose the best things in life. We can choose eternal pleasures rather than sin's pleasures (Luke 10:42; Heb. 11:25; Prov. 1:29). The essential part of life is the fear of God.

Vanguard leaders are to move the people of God forward. In moving them forward, leaders need to have faith in God's sovereignty, and trust in God's wisdom. They need to keep God's wonderful goodness in mind. They need to allow the wisdom of God to permeate all decision making. Let us move forward.

5

▼

The Strategy: Taking the City

The vanguard leader thinking about missions should shift his attention toward cities in his own country and not think only of countries across the sea. More than half of the world's population today lives in large cities. At least forty-two cities have populations exceeding four million people. Most large urban centers are in Islamic countries in Asia, but in the United States many ethnic groups live together in large cities.

The United States is one of the major mission fields of the world. Los Angeles has 4.5 million Hispanics. It contains the second largest concentration of Chinese people outside of China, the second largest concentration of Japanese outside of Japan, the largest concentration of Koreans outside of Korea, the largest Vietnamese population outside of Vietnam and the largest group of Filipinos outside of the Philippines.

God has a vision for the city. His plan began in the Garden of Eden but ends in the city—the new Jerusalem. Leaders must ask the Holy Spirit to reveal what He wants to do in the city and then partner with Him to accomplish it.

Every city seems to have a personality or a soul with a mind, will and emotions. A minister who ventures into his city will touch its emotions and mindset. In his book *Cities of Destiny*, Arnold Toynbee says, "In order to become a city, it would have to evolve at least the rudiments of a soul. This is perhaps the essence of cityhood."

The word *city* occurs 1,090 times in the Old Testament. In Old Testament times, cities were built with specific purposes. Some were called store cities, treasure cities, lost cities, military cities, cities for chariots and horses, or governmental cities. Today many cities have been built without the purpose of God, yet God has a purpose for them. Christians need to lift themselves out of a self-centered spirituality and see God's vision to reach the city with the Gospel.

> Those from among you shall build the old waste places; you shall raise up the foundations of many generations; and you shall be called the Repairer of the Breach, the Restorer of Streets to Dwell In (Isa. 58:12).

> And seek the peace of the city where I have caused you to be carried away captive, and pray to the LORD for it; for in its peace you will have peace (Jer. 29:7).

Violence, drugs, gangs, prostitution, and poverty fill most large cities. Perversion of all kinds spreads rapidly in cities, but where sin abounds, grace abounds even more (Rom. 5:20). Cities were meant to be dwelling places for the presence of God where His ways are known and His Word is a dominant influence. Christians minister in the city not because it is beautiful or the best place to raise children but because of God's divine call. Believers must see the city and surrounding regions as God sees them and not merely as they appear to the human eye.

> Where there is no revelation, the people cast off restraint; but happy is he who keeps the law (Prov. 29:18).

What do you expect God to do in your city? Is it too small? Is anything too hard for the Lord? Every vanguard leader needs to get to know his city. As he ministers with knowledge, he can believe the Holy Spirit to bring a word of wisdom that will penetrate the darkness in the city.

Here is what I learned by studying the City of Portland. The metropolitan area covers 137 square miles and is home to 1.3 million persons. Portland is the largest city in Oregon and is the state's major center of commerce, industry and transportation. Two rivers run through the city. I believe this is prophetic of the river of God that runs through the midst of the church bringing life and healing to all who come in. One river, the Willamette, flows north. Only two other rivers in the world flow north. More than 2,100 ships sail up the Columbia River to dock at local harbors every year. Portland has 200 parks. A total of 10,000 classes are offered through 11 community centers and 11 community schools. *Newsweek Magazine* identified Portland as one of the top ten cities to live in the 1990s. *Parenting Magazine* said it is one of the top ten cities to raise children in. *Financial World Magazine* names Portland as one of America's best run cities. *USA*

Today put Portland among the six best places to be in the 1990s.

Portland has been criticized for its crime rate, for its growing problem with gangs, and for attracting one of the largest West Coast populations of homosexuals outside of San Francisco, but these facts have made the following Scripture one of my favorites:

> And they shall call them The Holy People, the Redeemed of the Lord; and you shall be called Sought Out, a City Not Forsaken (Isa. 62:12).

Knowledge of the city helps me to pray specifically. Giving this information to the church helped people gain appreciation for the strategy we use to reach out. Christians can love the city while hating its sin, as they love people while hating their sin. Leaders have to guard against their own negative attitudes toward the city. Bad attitudes make it hard to preach to the saints and inspire them with faith and joy to be salt and light in the city's dark places. You need to see your city as "a city not forsaken" in spite of occasional predictions of God's judgment in the form of earthquakes or other catastrophes.

Christ sees a unified church

The Lord Jesus Christ said He would build His church.

> Simon Peter answered and said, "You are the Christ, the Son of the living God." Jesus answered and said to him, "Blessed are you, Simon Bar-Jonah, for flesh and blood has not revealed this to

you, but My Father who is in heaven.
And I also say to you that you are Peter,
and on this rock I will build My church,
and the gates of Hades shall not prevail
against it" (Matt. 16:16-18).

Every city has one or more local, visible assemblies
with bishops, deacons and saints, but when Christ
looks at a city, He does not see the church's different
denominations. He sees one church in each city.
Even though every assembly has its own unique
label, philosophy, and vision, every person in the city
who is a repentant, blood-washed sinner belongs to
the church in that city.

Many elders in Ephesus pastored local assemblies
at different locations, but the church in the city was
considered a unified whole. The apostle Paul
expected the elders of the local church in Ephesus to
"shepherd the church" in that city.

Therefore take heed to yourselves and to
all the flock, among which the Holy
Spirit has made you overseers, to
shepherd the church of God which He
purchased with His own blood (Acts
20:28).

There are a variety of congregations but one
church. The Greek word *ekklesia* refers to people
who are called out to assemble together. The church
is an organism that meets locally and has ministries
that govern or rule. Every congregation that accepts
the New Testament definition of the church belongs
to the universal church. Some call the universal
church the whole body of Christ. (See 2 Cor. 8:1; Gal.
1:2; Rev. 1-3.)

A congregation in Corinth founded by the apostle Paul was troubled by divisions among its members, and Paul mediated the dispute.

> For first of all, when you come together as a church, I hear that there are divisions among you, and in part I believe it (1 Cor. 11:18).

Divisions in one congregation did not fracture the whole church in Corinth. Only the congregation with the divisions needed adjustment. Every congregation is on a citywide team with other congregations praying and working to reap the harvest. There should be a spirit of unity among the congregations. A single church will not be given the entire harvest in any one city. We all need each other.

God gives every local congregation a different destiny, personality, distinctives, and emphasis to influence the city.

Divine destiny. The New Testament speaks of churches in cities like Antioch, Jerusalem, Corinth, and Ephesus. Each church was unique and had distinct destinies to fulfill His purpose (Rom. 8:28).

The Holy Spirit moves upon every local church and sets divinely appointed leaders in place to lead the church into the destiny that God has planned for it.

Unique personality. Local churches are not to be compared against each other or judged because they are different. Every church's personality is shaped by the backgrounds, giftings and personalities of its leaders. As a local church takes on a unique personality in its worship, preaching, or structure, onlookers cannot say that church is wrong and theirs is right.

Dominant distinctives. Each local church has dominant distinctives shaped by its own vision and pastoral ministry and by the Holy Spirit. Even though every church should have Bible truth, each congregation will emphasize or focus on certain distinctives. Some churches might focus on doctrine more than Holy Spirit giftings. Some might focus on structure more than relational small groups. All churches should have certain foundational truths, nevertheless every church has its own dominant distinctives.

Vision and mission. Each local church has its own God-given vision and mission reflecting its doctrinal distinctives, history, and present leadership. One church might concentrate more on the inner city than on the suburbs. One might concentrate more on unchurched yuppies than on street people, drug addicts, and prostitutes. It might be a white-collar, blue-collar, high-tech, or no-tech church.

God's relationship to the city

God has a relationship to every city. With compassion He dispatches ministers who will understand the heart of God toward the city and develop a vision for it.

The cry of the city. God hears the cry of the city, and the church must hear it too if it is going to have influence.

> The dying groan in the city, and the souls of the wounded cry out; yet God does not charge them with wrong (Job 24:12).

> And the Lord said, "Because the outcry against Sodom and Gomorrah is great,

> and because their sin is very grave, I will
> go down now and see whether they have
> done altogether according to the outcry
> against it that has come to Me; and if not,
> I will know" (Gen. 18:20-21).

If you could tune in to the cry of your city, what
would you hear? Would you hear the cry of the
unborn, the abused, the dissatisfied wealthy, the
youth without a father or mother, the homosexual
who hates his life, the alcoholic contemplating
suicide, or the AIDS mother who was violated
through rape and is now dying?

The church's intercessory prayer should be guided
by the cry of the city. Christians should pray with
compassion, "Lord, give us this city. Give us our
inheritance."

God weeps for the city. The Lord Jesus Christ wept
over Jerusalem with great compassion. He was
moved to tears because the city missed its destiny.

> Now as He drew near, He saw the city
> and wept over it, saying, "If you had
> known, even you, especially in this your
> day, the things that make for your peace!
> But now they are hidden from your eyes.
> For days will come upon you when your
> enemies will build an embankment
> around you, surround you and close you
> in on every side, and level you, and your
> children within you, to the ground; and
> they will not leave in you one stone
> upon another, because you did not know
> the time of your visitation" (Luke 19:41-
> 44).

Vanguard leaders need a spirit of compassion for the city that brings tears to their eyes. They must weep over what they see and hear in the Spirit.

God speaks to the city. God can use natural means to get the city's attention and speak into it. He may speak to the city through parachurch ministries with influence or through prophetic voices of local churches that are respected by city authorities and by the general public.

> The Lord's voice cries to the city—wisdom shall see Your name: "Hear the Rod! Who has appointed it?" (Micah 6:9).

> Wisdom calls aloud outside; she raises her voice in the open squares. She cries out in the chief concourses, at the openings of the gates in the city she speaks her words (Prov. 1:20-21; also see Prov. 8:1-3).

God sends ministries to cities. God's desire for the city is revival, not judgment. He wants to save people in the city, not destroy them. So He sends ministers into cities who bring a message of grace, salvation, and hope (Luke 9:51-56).

> Arise, go to Nineveh, that great city, and cry out against it; for their wickedness has come up before Me (Jonah 1:2).

Nehemiah goes to a city

Of all the biblical models of ministries sent to cities, Nehemiah is one of the best to evaluate because of his great influence upon the city he served. Nehemiah carried a deep spiritual burden for the city.

> The words of Nehemiah the son of Hachaliah. It came to pass in the month of Chislev, in the twentieth year, as I was in Shushan the citadel, that Hanani one of my brethren came with men from Judah; and I asked them concerning the Jews who had escaped, who had survived the captivity, and concerning Jerusalem. And they said to me, "The survivors who are left from the captivity in the province are there in great distress and reproach. The wall of Jerusalem is also broken down, and its gates are burned with fire." So it was, when I heard these words, that I sat down and wept, and mourned for many days; I was fasting and praying before the God of heaven (Neh. 1:1-4).

Nehemiah hears the state of his city and responds by fasting, praying, weeping, and mourning four months. He went, spied out the city, and saw the broken-down walls. Out of his burden and through intercessory prayer, Nehemiah develops a vision for restoration of the city. The walls need to be restored and the gates need to be put back into order. As he moved to the city, he received wisdom to rebuild, and other leaders rose up to stand with him to accomplish the goal. Nehemiah was motivated to arise and restore the city when others were motivated only to pray about the city.

Paul worked in metropolitan areas

The leading of the Holy Spirit usually took Paul to great metropolitan areas of Asia Minor to minister and establish churches. In Athens, Paul's "spirit was grieved and roused with anger as he saw this city" (Acts 17:16 Amp). Phillips translation says, "His soul was exasperated at the sight of the city when he saw the city given over to idols." The Holy Spirit stirs up a righteous anger in leaders that brings a season of grief but stirs leaders to set the city free from its idolatrous bondage.

Paul used the power of the Gospel to change people's minds and to establish God's kingdom in cities. Enough churches must be planted in every city to influence and change people's lives. If people's lives do not change, the Gospel will not influence the city. Every city, town, or village has a different personality and slightly different needs, yet the same Gospel, the same Bible, and the same Holy Spirit will penetrate every city.

Keys to taking cities

Every city has pockets of new age humanism, secularism and perversion, yet God holds keys that open cities to the Gospel. Today cities have similarities to fortified Old Testament cities, surrounded by walls to prevent penetration (Num. 13:28). They were "walled up to heaven" (Deut. 1:28). Jericho was a walled city but a shout directed by the Holy Spirit brought the walls down (Josh. 6:5,20). Jericho was humanly impossible to take, but God revealed a key that brought down the walls and gave His people access to march right in. "By faith the walls of Jericho fell" (Heb. 11:30).

The vanguard leader needs to seek the Lord to discover the key to his city. Modern cities have been given over to idols of materialism, violence, and the media, but spiritual walls will fall as the Holy Spirit reveals how to penetrate each city. The following cities were penetrated using various keys:

CITY	THE KEY
Sychar, John 4:28-42	One convert, a personal miracle.
Jerusalem, Acts 1-4	Prayer and a supernatural outpouring of the Holy Spirit.
Samaria, Acts 8:4-21	Philip the evangelist preached Christ with miracles, and Simon the sorcerer was converted.
Joppa, Acts 9:36-42	Dorcas was healed and raised from the dead through a miracle.
Caesarea, Acts 10:44-48	A house meeting and the outpouring of Spirit with signs and wonders.
Antioch, Acts 11:19	Common men preached; lay ministries brought the gospel to that city.

Lystra, Acts 14:8-18	A miracle of the lame man.
Philippi, Acts 16	A house meeting with wealthy business people started the church.
Thessalonica, Acts 17	The teaching and preaching of the Word of God and the power of the Holy Spirit.
Corinth, Acts 18	The demonstration of the Holy Spirit and the preaching of the Cross.

Corinth and other cities mentioned in the book of Acts had needs and problems like cities today. A port city, Corinth was a seaman's paradise, a drunkard's heaven, and a virtuous woman's hell. Education was highly esteemed there. The Corinthians exalted the arts, sciences, and languages and loved sports. The city was known for its pleasure palaces of prostitution. It had a racial mix with large populations of several ethnic groups. Many cities in the United States and around the world can be compared to Corinth.

All who pray for their city can take the following Scripture as a faith-promise.

> Now the Lord spoke to Paul in the night by a vision, "Do not be afraid, but speak, and do not keep silent; for I am with you, and no one will attack you to hurt

you; for I have many people in this city"
(Acts 18:9-10).

The key to open cities is the demonstration and the power of the Holy Spirit.

In 1 Corinthians 2:1-2, the apostle Paul laid out a basic leadership key for penetrating a city.

> And I, brethren, when I came to you, did not come with excellence of speech or of wisdom declaring to you the testimony of God. For I determined not to know anything among you except Jesus Christ and Him crucified. I was with you in weakness and fear and in much trembling. My speech and my preaching were not with persuasive words of human wisdom but in demonstration of the Spirit and of power that your faith should not be in the wisdom of men but in the power of God (1 Cor. 2:1-2).

Paraphrasing, he said, "I did not come with intellectually enticing words. I was not dependent on powerful talent of human origin."

Much oratory today lacks biblical conviction, and much speaking is done without the power of the Holy Spirit. So much training and so many ideas focus on methods and talent more than on the power of the Holy Spirit. People can be trained to speak well, but it is hard to get them to seek God to be anointed by the Holy Spirit to do the works of God. People can be taught to have confidence in their training, but Paul said he had no confidence in the flesh.

The key to open cities is the demonstration and the power of the Holy Spirit. Paul used no philosophical terms, categories, thoughts, or reasonings calculated to captivate his hearers. He demonstrated the power of the Holy Spirit. A demonstration, according to Greek scholar Joseph Henry Thayer, is "a proof by the Spirit and power of God operating in me and stirring in the minds of my hearers the most holy emotions and thus persuading them." Godet, writing on this Scripture says, "a clearness which is produced in the hearers mind as by the sudden lifting of a veil, a conviction mastering him with the sovereign force of moral evidence."

The word *demonstration* does not mean just a display or show, but it means conclusive proof drawn from facts as opposed to theoretical reasonings. The Gospel message has the greatest proof in the world: the resurrection of the Lord Jesus Christ. His body rose out of the grave. That is proof of divine power. The Holy Spirit reaffirms the genuineness of the Gospel message by moving in the hearts of church leaders and their listeners. The message of the foolishness of the Cross is proven by the power of Christ Himself.

The more removed the preaching of the Cross is from a church, the more men must depend upon their own methods, talents and abilities to draw people and keep them. Some critics say that people will be driven from the church rather than drawn to it by preaching the Bible—especially the Cross of Christ and discipleship. They look for quick, easy methods to draw people into the local church. They use advertising, news releases to the media, and many other gimmicks to get people's attention.

Strategize to reach the city

The vanguard leader needs to develop a strategy to reach his city. Here are elements of our strategic plan for city ministry to reach Portland.

1. *Maintain a strong local church with a spiritual armory.*

> The Lord has opened His armory, and has brought out the weapons of His indignation; for this is the work of the Lord God of hosts in the land of the Chaldeans (Jer. 50:25).

To build a church to penetrate an area or to influence an area through prayer, you must have a vision that the local church is a spiritual armory, a place for spiritual powers to be developed to penetrate evil powers over a city.

Bible Temple is a large church, and something about a large church seems to bring negative thoughts into people's minds. People often think a large, metropolitan church cannot have a neighborhood spirit or loving koinonia. Size alone makes large churches suspect. It is a bum rap. A big church is not a bad church. People do not view business, airplanes, or hospitals the same way. Big hospitals have more new equipment and technology to save lives. Big airplanes fly people farther and faster. Big businesses manufacture more products efficiently with economies of scale. Secrets of survival for big metropolitan churches are broad-minded flexibility and small-group participation.

If a person longs for a small neighborhood church, he will be frustrated belonging to a large metropolitan church. He would need a conversion in his own heart to be birthed into a larger church. He would need to see how a metropolitan church can influence an area.

2. Reap the harvest using every means available or necessary.

Harvests can be reaped in a community among different groups through targeted outreach. Portland has many colleges. Thousands of students come from all over the world to attend several colleges in the region. In our city we believe for harvest among students, business people, and inner city residents. We look for harvest through our small neighborhood home cell groups, through radio and television, through music presentations, drama, seeker services, and community services. We also cultivate a worldwide harvest through publications and by sending our ministries abroad.

3. Mobilize members of the local church to penetrate neighborhoods through structured small groups. Small groups are ministry centers where lay people preach, counsel, teach, restore homes and penetrate the powers of darkness through intercessory prayer. They move in the Holy Spirit and let the love of God pulsate through them to their neighbors in creative ways. Leaders need to train and challenge lay people to see themselves as able ministers of the Gospel. Growing neighborhood groups are divided to keep numerical size even. As groups multiply, they penetrate the area, meeting throughout the region.

When we intercede, God intervenes.

4. Penetrate every pocket of darkness by increasing intercessory and corporate prayer in the local church.

Intercession touches the heart of God that moves the hand of God that changes the world.

> He saw that there was no man, and wondered that there was no intercessor; therefore His own arm brought salvation for Him; and His own righteousness, it sustained Him (Isa. 59:16).

An intercessor intervenes between God and man. Prayer by individuals, churches, cities, regions, or nations strikes the winning blow. When the Amalekites came against the Israelites, Moses' hands upheld in intercession brought the victory (Exod. 17:9-11). The real battle was fought by Moses interceding as the armies clashed in the valley. When we intercede, God intervenes.

5. *Restore the inner city by reaching individuals with Christ's forgiveness and redemption and by establishing people in the church.* Dozens—probably hundreds—of different programs and ideas have been devised to reach the inner city. The government has its programs, but the church needs a strategy too.

> And they shall rebuild the old ruins, they shall raise up the former desolations, and they shall repair the ruined cities, the desolations of many generations (Isa. 61:4).

6. *Oppose moral perversity, homosexuality, pornography, prostitution and all moral sins that violate God's Word by being salt and light and through political involvement when necessary.*

7. Train spiritual leaders through our schools. These will be dynamic leaders in business, work, market and church world.

8. Launch more strategic ministry to our metro area: Mission Portland, teams for street ministry, music, drama, concerts, downtown ministry, more intensified city ministry and ministry houses to assimilate the harvest.

9. Radio and TV broadcasts. Broadcast on Christian radio with daily thirty-minute programs of worship and teaching. An annual local television special for Christmas, Easter, or for a prime-time program on the family.

10. Build strong families based on biblical values.

6

The Mandate: Building Unshakable People

Leaders need to be in step with the future, meeting problems and preparing for tomorrow's possibilities and challenges. We live in the last days characterized by perilous times. Leaders should be prepared to lead people who are under pressure. The moral, spiritual and political ground moves beneath our feet. God's people need to be anchored to the rock in the midst of the storms. When Jesus led His disciples into the boat, He said, "Let us cross over to the other side" (Matt. 14:22-34; Mark 4:36-41). They had no idea a life-threatening storm would intercept them before they reached the other side. Although Christ was with them on the ship, the men lost their peace and feared for their lives. Christ invites leaders today to cross over to the other side of the decade without fear. The challenge is to live victoriously in a sin-ridden culture.

Anchored to the Rock
Church leaders must build unshakable people during these shakable times. Jesus said his teaching is

like a rock, and obeying His teaching is like building a house on solid rock.

> He is like a man building a house, who dug deep and laid the foundation on the rock. And when the flood arose, the stream beat vehemently against that house, and *could not shake it*, for it was founded on the rock (Luke 6:48, emphasis added).

The house could represent a believer's personal life and family, or it could represent the church. Storms threaten both.

The word *shake* in Greek means to vibrate, agitate, or unsettle. Unshakable people are firm, stable, and solid. They weather the storm, entrench themselves, sink roots, and refuse to move. They stand riveted, permanent, durable, and indestructible. They take and keep hold (Heb. 6:19).

The Christian believer anchors his life to Jesus Christ, the Solid Rock. Lives not anchored to the Rock will be shaken and unable to handle pressure. A man's only hope is to face the future with the right view.

> For I know the thoughts that I think toward you, says the Lord, thoughts of peace and not of evil, to give you a future and a hope (Jer. 29:11-12).

The future of this world
God knows and sees the future. He creates and controls the future.

Declaring the end from the beginning,
and from ancient times things that are
not yet done, saying, "My counsel shall
stand, And I will do all My pleasure"
(Isa. 46:10).

God is in charge of what man cannot control.
Man's power is fragile, and his wisdom is limited.
The future of the world is under the government of
God. The world belongs to God (Pss. 89:11, 90:2; Heb.
11:3; Acts 17:24,31).

The earth is the Lord's, and all its
fullness, The world and those who dwell
therein (Ps. 24:1).

The world's future judgment

The world is going through astronomical,
complex, and confusing changes. However, nothing
is outside of the government and hand of God.
Believers are being built to face this kind of a society.
Continually return to the Word and you will not be
moved with fear. The Word of God continually lets
us know that we are rooted and grounded in truth.
The world will be judged by God in His time and in
His own way (Rom. 3:6).

Now we know that whatever the law
says, it says to those who are under the
law, that every mouth may be stopped,
and all the world may become guilty
before God (Rom. 3:19).

This world will not sidestep the judgment of God.
All the sin and perversion has filled the earth's glass
to the brim. It will come before the judgment of God,

and God's justice will bring a death blow to it. The world will dwell in deception prior to Christ's coming, according to the Scripture (Rev. 13:3,8).

> So the great dragon was cast out, that serpent of old, called the Devil and Satan, who deceives the whole world; he was cast to the earth, and his angels were cast out with him (Rev. 12:9).

The book of Revelation repeatedly warns the world of an onslaught of horrible deception. The world will be deceived by the dragon, the beast and the false prophet. Only the overcomers in Christ will not fall under the domain and spell of the dragon. They will overcome him by the blood of the Lamb and by the word of their testimony. The world as we know it will be destroyed (2 Pet. 3:10).

This world is not our home. We are only sojourners.

> But when we are judged, we are chastened by the Lord, that we may not be condemned with the world (1 Cor. 11:32).

All the dealings and judgments in a Christian's life now, are designed to save him from total judgment awaiting the world. The world will be purged by fire before it is ultimately redeemed, re-created and inherited by Christ's followers. The meek shall inherit the earth, but not the earth in its present state. They will inherit the earth after the final coming of the Lord Jesus Christ.

The future of western civilization

What is the future of western civilization and culture as we know it? "In the last days perilous times will come" (2 Tim. 3:1). The word *perilous* means to be in danger, high-risk, troublesome, grievous, savage, or perplexing. Francis Schaefer in his book, *How Should We Then Live*, stated, "The American people adopted two impoverished values, personal peace and personal affluence."

Personal peace can be described as the attitude of "just let me alone," or "don't trouble me with your troubles or anyone else's from across the street or around the world." Achieving personal peace requires control over disruptions to individuals' routines. A preoccupation with personal peace ignores the common good. It ignores actions and duties required today to insure peace during the lifetimes of a man's children or grandchildren.

Personal affluence requires overwhelming prosperity. It fills life with things, things and more things. Success is measured in an ever-increasing mountain of material abundance. Chuck Colson in his book, *God of Stones and Spiders*, says "A common thread runs through these images. The notion that life somehow gives us the right to have every whim and desire satisfied." In the United States, society has become miserable as Americans pursue pleasure.

The wrath of God has been dismissed by the same people who have rejected prudence as a standard. No longer are right and wrong moral absolutes. Instead, they are psychological hangups that need to be healed. Society suffers the effects of removing itself from a Bible-based, God-centered standard. It has chosen a self-centered, sin-based framework. It chooses to view morality not in black and white terms but in shades of gray. Oddly, prevalent characteristics of contemporary western culture are rampant narcissism, materialism and hedonism.

The United States often tries to pass itself off as Christian with fifty million Americans claiming to be born-again according to George Gallup. However, it is dominated by relativism and humanism and has been infiltrated by many eastern religions. The do-your-own-thing mindset has liberated us from the absolute structure of faith and set us adrift in a sea of nothingness. Now nothing is more certain than the certainty that there are no certainties. The world is absolutely sure no absolutes exist. All is relative and all is experience. New ethics grow in the fertile soil of a humanistic philosophical base. The only absolute allowed is the insistence that there are no absolutes.

Western man has decided to abolish himself. He creates his own boredom out of his affluence, having educated himself into imbecility, and drugged himself into stupefaction. He kneels over like a weary, battered, old dinosaur and becomes extinct. The sinner that believes in nothing, cares for nothing, seeks to know nothing, interferes with nothing, enjoys nothing, hates nothing, finds purpose in nothing, and lives for nothing remains alive because there is nothing for which he will die. This mentality characterizes a spiritually dead society.

Revival—our hope

Unless a revival of the Holy Spirit brings a genuine taste of Christianity and the Word of God to western civilization, it will head for a complete, disastrous moral breakdown. Already new diseases besides AIDS, which is out of control, maim and kill millions of people around the world. Economic structures continually collapse. Some economists say a depression will shatter the economy, and governments will try to stimulate growth by inflating their currencies.

The last days will be made perilous by a rise in banking crises, environmental crises, increased taxes, rationed health insurance, and cutbacks in workers compensation. The cost of insurance will skyrocket. Prices will rise dramatically, outstripping the normal person's ability to pay. People will try foreign religions and dabble in the New Age movement, which has simply repackaged old eastern religions. Genetic engineering, which tinkers with God's design, and man's new medical technology will heighten people's fears. God and His Bible have no place in man's self-centered, modern morality. More people will live in their own fantasy worlds. Real heroes will disappear, replaced by superheroes and fantasy creatures. Society will continue to deceive itself with the illusion that things are getting better.

The family already has been redefined to consider homosexual and lesbian couples as family units. Trust in social, political and spiritual authority will continue to erode. Uncontrollable violence in larger cities will spread out to small towns. Brutal and senseless killings will plague the nation.

The future of western Christianity and the western church is at stake.

Relativistic philosophy has begun to take its toll on normal people's lives. They approach decision-making with no principles whatsoever. Every moment, questions arise that can be answered only in the context of the situation that created the question. In other words: situation ethics is alive and well. It frees people from having to adhere to consistent principles. Each person is different; each situation is different. For Christians, it is called antinomianism, which is a belief that after salvation by grace through faith, no moral law or standards are in effect.

A vanguard leader who faces the deceived society of the 1990s has his work cut out for him. Things change so rapidly, its difficult to get a hold of the culture because it stays just a step ahead of him. If he went to college fifteen years ago, he was trained to face a culture that no longer exists and people who no longer think the way they did then. If he was trained twenty years ago, he is almost a dinosaur in the ministry.

The future of western Christianity and the western church is at stake. Without revival and the return to Biblical roots, the Christian message and Christian institutions will compromise and blend with their surroundings. The masses yearn to redefine Christian philosophy. The Christian community wallows in confusion over what it believes and what it's function is in society.

Revival of the cross of Christ

Moral, governmental, doctrinal and spiritual issues are all in a state of confusion. Influential voices on TV attempt to establish a pseudo-christianity without substance. The obvious missing ingredient to Christianity in the United States is the cross of Christ. True Christianity and true discipleship are outworkings of the cross of Christ. All morality begins with the cross. Christians who have bought into relativistic philosophy have developed a shallow cross-less, directionless Christianity that has no chance to be salt and light to a relativistic, humanistic, directionless society.

Society follows a hedonistic lifestyle and philosophy, and the church runs parallel with a Christian hedonism. Christian hedonism preaches a message of blessing, prosperity, God-won't-let-me-suffer, and God-gives-me-promotions. Unless the church changes it's philosophy back to the Bible, it will remain directionless.

The country needs a real, bona fide revival. It needs a revival that takes the church back to its roots, to Christ, to the Bible, to the sure foundation. Believers need to rid themselves of shallow pseudo-Christianity without true biblical roots. Within the public church, there will always be a true church enjoying revival and reformation. Even in America the Holy Spirit is moving to build churches upon biblical truth. These churches will last no matter what happens. They are on the Rock, Christ Himself.

> But it is not that the word of God has taken no effect. For they are not all Israel who are of Israel, nor are they all children because they are the seed of Abraham; but, "In Isaac your seed shall be called." That is, those who are the children of the flesh, these are not the children of God; but the children of the promise are counted as the seed (Rom. 9:6-8).

The future of God's kingdom and church

God's kingdom has no end. Vanguard leaders must remind themselves as well as the people that they are being built on the Rock.

Leaders who build people on faulty foundations and on pseudo-Christian philosophies will suffer loss in coming years. Only the churches and people who have been taught properly and built on the Rock of Christ will last. Leaders in the vanguard have the responsibility to teach people an accurate view of the kingdom, the Word of God, Christ's values, and the church.

1. *The church is positioned at the Gate Beautiful* (Acts 3:1-8).

Like the lame man sitting at the gate, unable to walk, the Church needs God's touch. The touch of God strengthens the beggar's feet and ankles and he rises healed. The lame man stood, walked and went leaping into the temple praising God. Likewise, the church needs a touch from God to rise, leap and praise Him with power.

We need a demonstration of the fullness of the Spirit to accomplish the purpose and the will of God. Vanguard leaders understand this and by faith declare it with passion.

2. *The church is victorious in warfare.* The Lord of hosts has spoken. The Lord of hosts is His warfare name. He is Lord over all the hosts of heaven, and He has declared He will shake all nations and He will pour the wealth of the world into the church so the church can accomplish the will of God. The whole earth will be filled with the glory of God.

> but truly, as I live, all the earth shall be filled with the glory of the LORD (Num. 14:21).

> For thus says the Lord of hosts: "Once more (it is a little while) I will shake heaven and earth, the sea and dry land; and I will shake all nations, and they shall come to the Desire of All Nations, and I will fill this temple with glory,"

> says the Lord of hosts. "The silver is
> Mine, and the gold is Mind," says the
> Lord of hosts. "The glory of this latter
> temple shall be greater than the former,"
> says the Lord of hosts (Hag. 2:7).

3. *The church has an unchangeable message.* No matter what happens in society, the church has a great future. The church built on the Rock, busy extending the kingdom of God, will be filled with the glory and the power of the Lord. The church will face a polytheistic and syncretistic culture. Already many gods and religions fill America. Syncretism is the combination of different forms of religion. People take what they see as the best parts of several religions and form new, blended religions. False religions challenge the true Christian church to establish the basic tenets of true Christianity before people are seduced.

Religious consumerism tempts the church to direct its energy to satisfy the expectations of members as if they were simply consumers. Rather, the church should focus its energy on accomplishing God's primary purpose: developing mature believers and reaching the world with the Gospel. Self-centered society will become more materialistic and driven to indulge pleasure. Vanguard leaders must dig in, sink their roots into the Word of God, and teach people how to live a disciplined life.

4. *The church will effect the whole world.* In coming years the church will be victorious as God pours out His Holy Spirit on all flesh. The church will preach the gospel to the whole world and reap a great harvest. The kingdom of God will come to full maturity. God will release true ministries to lead His

people in greater praise and worship. Leaders must face the future with a biblical perspective.

Shaking reminds people of the untrustworthiness of temporal things.

The church strengthened through shaking

During the shaking, the world may suffer, but the church will get better. Shaking will not destroy the true church. It cleanses the true church (2 Thess. 2:2; 3:16).

> See that you do not refuse Him who speaks. For if they did not escape who refused Him who spoke on earth, much more shall we not escape if we turn away from Him who speaks from heaven, whose voice then *shook* the earth; but now he has promised, saying, "Yet once more I *shake* not only the earth, but also heaven." Now this "yet once more," indicates the *removal* of those things that are being shaken, as of things that are made, that the things which cannot be shaken may remain. Therefore, since we are receiving a kingdom which cannot be shaken, let us have grace by which we may serve God acceptably with reverence and godly fear, for our God is a consuming fire (Heb. 12:25-29; emphasis added).

Shaking separates the true from the false. It uncovers instability and reveals what is permanent. Shaking reminds people of the untrustworthiness of temporal things. The earth and the heavenly bodies seem to be permanent, but they are transient, and God will sift everything without solid foundations. The vanguard leader's responsibility is to build people upon the unshakable, immovable Word of God.

Shaking renews people's focus on permanent, immovable, unshakable biblical values. Shaking not only manifests God's truth and principles but also enhances His genuine beauty and attractiveness. It renews the value of faith and relationship with the Lord Jesus Christ. The stability of Christianity is demonstrated best under trial. God has given His people a kingdom that is unshakable and indestructible. It is firm and stable.

The church's unshakable values

Christ's many-membered body, the local church, helps God's people get through seasons of shaking. Believers gather together to nurture each other in Bible truth. In times of shaking, eternal values become more meaningful than temporal things. Vanguard leaders must help people see how they can build lives that are unshakable. Churches must have faith that they can be unshakable. The Word of God teaches that no matter what happens in this world before the coming of Christ, people still can build on the Rock. Here are faith-building scriptures (2 Thess. 2:2; 3:16; Ps. 10:6; Ps. 15:5; Ps. 30:6; Ps. 66:9; Prov. 12:3; Col. 1:23; Ps. 73:2).

> Cast your burden on the LORD, And He shall sustain you; He shall never permit the righteous to be *moved* (Ps. 55:22; emphasis added).

> He only is my rock and my salvation; He is my defense; I shall not be greatly *moved* (Ps. 62:2; emphasis added).

> He will not allow your foot to be *moved*; He who keeps you will not slumber (Ps. 121:3; emphasis added).

> Therefore, since we are receiving a kingdom which cannot be shaken, let us have grace, by which we may serve God acceptably with reverence and godly fear (Heb. 12:28).

The unshakable life

To build an unshakable life means to build it on Christ the Rock, to govern it by biblical convictions, philosophies and values, to adopt kingdom attitudes and an eternal perspective.

• *An unshakable life is built on Christ, the only sure foundation.* Both the wise and foolish builders in Jesus' parable built a house. One builder laid a proper foundation. The other one didn't. The stable house took longer to complete because the builder had to dig down deep (Luke 6:48). He went to the trouble to remove everything between him and bedrock. He got to the bottom of things. He repented of his sin and removed everything from his life to find the rock to build upon. In the flood, one house stood and the other one collapsed. One builder lost more than the other. An unshakable life is built on the Word of God. The Word of God gives a man convictions and a philosophy. It permeates his way of thinking, speaking, and decision-making. It is the last court of appeal for moral questions.

•*An unshakable life is built on Kingdom attitudes.* Viewing events and experiences from a biblical perspective helps shape believers' attitudes. A man's choices will be influenced by whether he has accepted the priorities of the kingdom of God. His lifestyle will reflect the principles of the kingdom of God. Believers build unshakable lives on eternal values and an eternal outlook. Possessions become less important than character (Matt. 5,6,7).

•*An unshakable life is built on the eternal not the temporal.* Vanguard leaders must consistently lift up eternal values and viewpoints instead of temporal. They must guide believers to see the reality of unseen, eternal things. The word *eternal* means without beginning or end, existing forever, everlasting, endless, infinite, constant, immortal, imperishable, deathless, or durable. In contrast, the word *temporal* means temporary, measured or limited by time, lasting only for a brief period, pertaining to this life or this world, secular.

> Therefore we do not lose heart. Even though our outward man is perishing, yet the inward man is being renewed day by day. For our light afflictions, which is but for a moment, is working for us a far more exceeding and eternal weight of glory (2 Cor. 4:16-17).

Inscriptions were carved into three splendid arches over doorways in the Cathedral of Milan. The first inscription carved beneath a beautiful wreath of roses says, "All which pleases is but for a moment." Over the second arch beneath a sculptured cross are the words, "All that troubles us is but for a moment."

Over the central doorway are the words, "That only is important which is eternal."

Years ago, E.M. Bounds sounded a prophetic warning that has been largely fulfilled. "These are materialized and materializing times. Materialized times always exalt earthly things and degrade the heavenly. True Christianity always restrains the earthly and augments the heavenly. If God's watchmen are not brave, diligent, and alert, then Christianity will catch the sickness of the times and think little of and struggle less for heaven."

A vanguard leader takes temporal people and builds them into unshakable people. Temporal people:

• live in a state of decay.
• see only what the natural eye sees.
• live for what is passing away.
• have worldly ambition to please self.
• succumb to man's idea of success.
• think of heaven as material affluence here and now as in retirement.

Are you building people who have been touched by the eternal? Are you building people whose values have been shaped by the message of the Cross? The Cross changes people's perspectives, motivations and lifestyles.

Unshakable people in the making
• Unshakable people see the invisible by faith. They see affliction from a heavenly viewpoint. They look death in the face and rejoice in the future, knowing their bodies will be raised from the dead or that they will meet Christ in the air.
• Unshakable people receive the Holy Spirit who gives them a taste of worlds to come.

•Unshakable people live before the bema seat of Christ, knowing all their thoughts, words, and actions will be judged by Him.

•Unshakable people do not live for themselves but for God.

•Unshakable people view others as eternal beings with eternal destinies. As C.S. Lewis said, "You are seated next to immortal beings."

•Unshakable people engage in spiritual warfare with spiritual weapons. Even though society cannot see spiritual things or believe in true spiritual reality, faith can move God's hand and prayer can resist the devil.

•Unshakable people have a true biblical understanding of God, His nature, His attributes. Every thought of God involves the thought of His attributes, without these He is an unknown and unknowable God. They love doctrine!

•Unshakable people are people of praise. They have developed a capacity of praise God effectively by obedience to His word and trust in who He says He is. They live above the emotions!

•Unshakable people are people of prayer. They have cultivated a prayer attitude that is securely founded in their relationship to the Christ of the bible and the written word of God.

•Unshakable people are people who live life with a sense of purpose. This purpose is established in Christ choosing them and what the word of God confirms as to every believer's future.

•Unshakable people have a sense of right and wrong. They have a firm grasp on righteousness as found in Christ positionally and lived out in their conduct experientially. A life of Godly morality is secured by a proper knowledge and love for God's word and God's character.

•Unshakable people have developed the ability to go on in life when everything goes sour. They persevere in trouble, contradictions, unanswered prayers, and the all around problem of a sin-ruined world. They proclaim God faithfully, His way is right, His decisions just! They do not murmur or criticize God or question His word because it doesn't line up with their experiences. They question their experiences!

▼

7

The Character: Marks of Authenticity

Church leaders periodically need spiritual checkups. They need to pull back from busy lifestyles—the business and burden of ministry—and look closely at who they are and what they are becoming. For leaders to maintain integrity and high levels of biblical productivity, reevaluation is imperative.

Everything left to itself degenerates in this world. Without regular tuneups, car engines clog up with rust, debris and old oil. The same principle works in human nature. Only the power of the Holy Spirit working in Christians' hearts renews and keeps them from spiritual degeneration. If church leaders are willing to evaluate their spiritual condition, their leadership motivation and their ministry, the Holy Spirit will reveal areas that need to be changed or removed (see 2 Cor. 13:5; Amos 6:1).

> They go from strength to strength; each one *appears* before God in Zion (Ps. 84:7; emphasis added).

> Let us search out and examine our ways,
> and turn back to the Lord (Lam. 3:40).

The Hebrew word translated *appear* means to reveal oneself, to open oneself so as to receive new perception, or to come under inspection. This word describes how priests inspected sacrifices brought to the temple. Inspections were detailed, revealing the most minute flaws. Leaders, potential leaders, servants, helpers and workers in the kingdom of God need to appear before the Lord regularly. The Lord desires that we appear before Him for inspection (Ps. 139:23).

> For the Lord *searches* all hearts and understands all the intent of the thoughts (1 Chron. 28:9; emphasis added).

> I, the Lord, *search* the heart, I test the mind, even to give every man according to his ways, according to the fruit of his doings (Jer. 17:10; emphasis added).

The Lord desires authentic leaders in His church. Authenticity of spiritual leadership bears awesome importance as we near the twenty-first century. The word *authentic* means being a genuine original or authority, being what one purports to be, trustworthy, reliable, legally attested and opposing the false, fictitious or counterfeit. It carries the idea of being true, certain, faithful, credible, official and authorized. Authentic biblical leadership is:

Sincere. "...that you may be sincere and without offense" (Phil. 1:10); "with the unleavened bread of sincerity" (1 Cor. 5:8); "serve God with simplicity and godly sincerity" (2 Cor. 1:12).

Trustworthy. "...whose ways thou has come to trust" (Ruth 2:12); "which was committed to my trust" (1 Tim. 1:11).

Truthful. "...men that fear God, men of truth" (Exod. 18:21); "serve God with sincerity and truth" (Josh. 24:14); "that we speak all things in truth" (2 Cor. 7:14).

Honest. "...those with an honest and good heart" (Luke 8:15); "seven men of honest report" (Acts 6:3); "you should do that which is honest" (2 Cor. 13:7; see also Rom. 13:13; 1 Thess. 4:12; Heb. 13:18; 2 Cor. 8:21).

Transparent. "...was of pure gold, as it were transparent glass" (Rev. 21:21); "denouncing the hidden things of dishonesty" (2 Cor. 4:2).

Genuine. "...the genuine faith that is in you" (2 Tim. 1:5).

Credible. "For I have no one like-minded, who will sincerely care for your state. For all seek their own, not the things which are of Christ Jesus. But you know his proven character, that as a son with his father he served with me in the gospel... Hold such men in esteem" (Phil. 2:20-22,29).

All true spiritual leaders wish to have their lives, character and ministries authenticated by God. If you set aside time for your own spiritual checkup and invite the Holy Spirit to work deeply within your heart, you will appear before the Lord. He will inspect and renew you. He will give you a spiritual tuneup and give you His seal of authenticity.

Genuine Christian ministry takes place in an environment of respect and trust. God's grace administered by faithful human servants, softens people's hearts. Changed lives prove that God uses trustworthy ministers to perform His handiwork.

However, the ministry confronts daily challenges to its authenticity. Some challenges come from enemies of Christ. Other challenges arise from within every minister's own humanity. Authenticity can be tested and proven. It cannot be counterfeited. Spiritual leaders need to have and keep their ministries authentic to earn the respect and trust of other people, especially those receiving ministry.

False ministries often hide among genuine leadership ministries in the church. Knowing how to distinguish false from true ministries protects God's beloved children from being deceived, bound and devoured. The apostle Paul, who wrote fourteen of the epistles found in the New Testament, dealt with false ministries and with false accusations against his own ministry. He wrote the epistle of 2 Corinthians to defend himself. In the epistle, he listed criteria that ministries must have to be authentic.

Paul had pastored the Corinthian church for 18 months, and this was the second epistle he had written to the saints there. It exposes his humanity and reveals his pastor's heart. For sure it is the most emotional of all his epistles. He wrote it after his third missionary journey, about A.D. 60, probably from Macedonia. By this time Paul was an elder statesman and had little time remaining until his martyrdom.

According to his own account, Paul was small in stature, maybe not more than five feet tall. Although he had a frail body that groaned under the demands of apostolic ministry, he possessed great zeal, profound teaching and a father's heart. He wrote this epistle with a pen dipped in tears. It was the impassioned, self-defense of a wounded spirit written to erring and ungrateful children.

People whom he had pastored now charged him with pride and suggested that he was deceitfully cunning and manipulative. They bluntly denied his apostleship and his authority over them. They also questioned whether he had the right to threaten them with discipline. Getting personal, they said his outward appearance was base and his speech, contemptible. Paul's enemies tried to minimize his significance and the importance of his teaching. They accused him of indecision, saying he promised to come but changed his mind. They claimed he had capitulated, vacillated and shown weakness.

Paul responded to these charges with the character of an apostle-father. He wanted to reestablish a right relationship between the Corinthians and himself. He wanted to prove his ministry deserved respect and trust. He wanted to show the striking contrast between his and all the false ministries that had invaded Corinth. The Corinthians he loved dearly needed a proper view of his office and work.

False ministries introduced themselves to the Corinthian church apparently through letters of recommendation.

> Do we begin again to commend ourselves? Or do we need, as some others, epistles of commendation to you or letters of commendation from you? You are our epistle written in our hearts, known and read by all men; clearly you are an epistle of Christ, ministered by us, written not with ink but by the Spirit of the living God, not on tablets of stone but on tablets of flesh, that is, of the heart (2 Cor. 3:1-3).

These three verses contain the test of ministry authenticity. A man's ministry or character cannot be authenticated by letters of recommendation. Although Paul himself had written letters to affirm other ministries (Acts 15:25; 18:27; Rom. 16:1; 1 Cor. 16:10; 2 Cor 8:22), letters can be counterfeited. Paul simply stated that the proof of authenticity does not come through some external affirmation.

In the ancient world, as today, written testimonials did not always mean much. A man once asked Diogenes, the cynic philosopher, for such a letter. Diogenes answered, "That you are a man, he will know at a glance, but whether you are a good or a bad man he will discover if he has the skill to distinguish between good and bad. And if he is without that skill, he will not discover the facts even though I write to him a thousand times."

Test of vulnerability

The first test of authenticity is the test of vulnerability. Paul and his companions had opened their hearts to the Corinthians. "You are...written in our hearts" (v. 2). Paul was very conscious of the Corinthians. They were his epistles. They were written on his heart and he could never forget, misunderstand or neglect them.

God's people engrave words or letters upon the hearts of leaders. Sometimes these words are engraved through mistreatment that comes to every leader of the flock of God. One of the greatest apostles of all time, Paul suffered and endured criticism from the people he sought to pastor. Personal attacks often come unannounced and undeserved. False accusations, denials of your authority and questioning of your character write deeply on your heart. Your motives will be tried and tested and yet your heart must remain soft for the people of God to be able to touch it and write upon it.

Any leader can become hardened and shut the people of God out of his life. If you wish to protect yourself from these things, you must leave the ministry and stay out. As Harry Truman once said, "If you can't stand the heat, don't go near the kitchen." Leaders need to watch over their hearts with diligence for from it flow the springs of life (Prov. 4:25). Afflictions and burdens accompany ministry.

> Now if we are afflicted, it is for your consolation and salvation, which is effective for enduring the same sufferings which we also suffer. Or if we are comforted, it is for your consolation and salvation (2 Cor 1:6; also see 2 Cor. 2:4).

Ministry that costs nothing will accomplish nothing. Leaders must be willing to pay the price for their hearts to be changed through the pressures of ministry. Authenticity cannot be counterfeited.

The test of changed lives

The second test of authentic ministry resides in the lives of men and women changed supernaturally by Christ. Evidence of divine, inner spiritual work shows in the way people live. The grace of Christ operates in true ministry and changes lives. Men and women who have words or letters engraved on their hearts by true ministry become living epistles "known and read by all men" (v. 2).

People affected by true ministry experience more than human power and personality. They experience the healthy, penetrating, living ministry of the Holy

Spirit. They become living, pulsating, receptive people. They become living letters, messages of hope to a dying world.

Paul compared living epistles to a public monument. He envisioned a ceremony unveiling the monument, displaying the writing to public gaze. All men who gather around or pass by can read its message. This was Paul's guarantee for apostolic status and authority. He did not depend on a piece of paper, a letter or a title. Observers could plainly see people united with Paul and his companions in heart and soul because they had been treated with respect and sensitive care in authentic ministry.

The spiritual health of the people you lead proves the authenticity of your ministry.

In the 1950s an outbreak of mercury poisoning struck hundreds of people living near Minamata, Japan. Victims suffered progressive weakening of muscles, loss of vision, impaired brain functions, paralysis and, in some cases, a coma followed by death. The cause of the problem was found to be industrial waste containing mercury that flowed from a factory into the bay where fish and shellfish absorbed it. People who ate the fish were poisoned.

The spiritual health of the people you lead proves the authenticity of your ministry. Whatever you are, you will dispense, and whatever you dispense, the people will absorb. If you dispense an unhealthy spiritual diet, the people will become spiritually sick and anemic. Church leaders need time to pull back from ministry to make sure they have not become a poison to the people of God.

Paul states that he had written on the hearts of people under his care and what he wrote was praiseworthy—affirmed by God Himself. Any man can write on paper with ink, but only Christ can write on human hearts by the Spirit of God through another human servant. Writing requires three elements: pen, ink and paper. In this comparison, the pen represents the servant of God, divinely chosen to minister. He is the instrument doing the engraving. The ink represents the divine, golden anointing oil. It flows freely from the pen. Paper represents the human heart. It submits willingly to receive the engraving. Every life is like a white sheet of paper waiting to be written upon. If leaders have authentic character, sealed by God Himself, then holy oil flows from their ministry and what they write on people's lives will have eternal value.

Source of ministry adequacy

God Himself makes His ministers adequate to do the work. He qualifies them and gives them confidence.

> And we have such trust through Christ toward God. Not that we are sufficient of ourselves to think of anything as being from ourselves, but our sufficiency is from God, who also made us sufficient as ministers of the new covenant, not of the letter but of the Spirit; for the letter kills, but the Spirit gives life (2 Cor. 3:4-6).

•*Ministry adequacy is rooted in godly confidence* (see Rom. 4:2-3, and John 16:30). The apostle Paul draws from this Christ-confidence and states it is his only source for ministry authenticity. He and his assistants had sure confidence in their office and the genuineness of its product. This confidence flows through Christ and into His own servants. It comes the same way to leaders today. When we face God and He faces us, we can claim that we speak for God and that God speaks through us because He is our source.

> For we are to God the fragrance of Christ among those who are being saved and among those who are perishing. To the one we are the aroma of death to death, and to the other the aroma of life to life. And who is sufficient for these things? (2 Cor. 2:15-17).

David Livingston, Christian missionary to Africa in the 1800s, said about God:

> He is the greatest Master I have ever known. If there is anyone greater I do not know him. Jesus Christ is the only Master supremely worth serving. He is the only Ideal that never loses its inspiration. He is the only Friend whose friendship meets every demand. He is the only Savior who can save to the uttermost. We go forth in His name, in His power and in His Spirit to serve Him.

•*Ministry adequacy is rooted in godly sufficiency.* Authenticity finds its source there. We are not adequate in ourselves. Our sufficiency is from a higher source (2 Cor. 3:5).

•*Ministry adequacy is rooted in God's choice.*

> God is faithful, by whom you were
> called into the fellowship of His Son,
> Jesus Christ our Lord (1 Cor. 1:9; see also
> Gal. 1:1; Eph. 1:1).

Paul had a conviction of the truth of the Gospel
and of the reality that he received his vocation from
Christ. He did not have a consciousness of superior
excellence. Self-sufficiency is not adequate to achieve
results with eternal value. Self-sufficiency seeks title,
credit and praise but begets a barren epistle.
Dependence upon God begets a living epistle.

The apostle states he felt a sentence of death in his
heart in order that he would rely on the power of
God (2 Cor. 1:9). Grace provides strength for the
adequacy he speaks about. Grace qualifies ministries
and bestows authenticity and confidence in them for
the work they do. Success does not depend on natural
ability or personal initiative but on divine
enablement. Paul's confidence came through Christ
from God. Paul explains this while his opponents
claim to be self-sufficient.

Paul's ministry was not the product of a wish or
imagination. He says he is not even able to form a
competent judgment on results of his own ministry.
He disowns any personal right to claim credit for the
results of what is, in reality, God's work.

> We are fools for Christ's sake, but you
> are wise in Christ! We are weak, but
> you are strong! You are distinguished,
> but we are dishonored! (1 Cor. 4:10).

> So he answered and said to me: "This is
> the word of the LORD to Zerubbabel,
> 'Not by might nor by power, but by My

Spirit,' says the LORD of hosts" (Zech. 4:6).

• *Ministry adequacy is rooted in the new covenant.* The new covenant was not only Paul's message but also the source of his strength to carry that message. This stands true for all authentic leaders today, too. The new covenant was new not only at that point of time but also new in design and quality. The new covenant has power to introduce a fresh element into any situation and produces a relationship between God and man totally different than the old. Leaders ministering through the power of the new covenant are authentic. Their ministries bear lasting fruit in the people who receive them.

The new covenant becomes a mighty fountain of life for all men. God lets us drink and has bidden us to dispense its living waters to others. Here lies our whole sufficiency. Here lies the credibility of authentic ministries. It is Christ who makes us competent administrators of the new agreement or new covenant.

Spirit empowered ministry

The dynamic, pervasive Holy Spirit guides ministry under the new covenant. His grace enables leaders to serve the people of God in humility and simplicity. The test of authenticity reveals whether a leader's attitude and style is birthed by the Holy Spirit or by the carnal man.

> But if the ministry of death, written and engraved on stones, was glorious, so that the children of Israel could not look steadily at the face of Moses because of the glory of his countenance, which

> glory was passing away, how will the ministry of the Spirit not be more glorious? For if the ministry of condemnation had glory, the ministry of righteousness exceeds much more in glory. For even what was made glorious had no glory in this respect, because of the glory that excels. For if what is passing away was glorious, what remains is much more glorious (2 Cor. 3:7-11).

Christ is concerned with the Spirit, not with the letter. The letter of the law leads to death of the soul, but a Spirit-based ministry produces life. The law is a written document that remains external until the Holy Spirit can internalize the truth of it for each man and woman. It can perfectly well tell a man what to do but it cannot help him do it. If a leader moves in the power of the Holy Spirit, there is a release of the Holy Spirit in the lives of the people. However, if a leader moves in carnality and the letter of the law, then tension, anxiety and fear lead to bondage.

The blood of the Lord Jesus Christ gives the new covenant its power. His blood purchased communion between God and man, but communion becomes operative only when the indwelling Spirit imparts new life and enables a person to meet the requirements of the law fully (2 Cor. 3:8; Rom. 7:6, 8:3).

A Spirit-base ministry depends on God to work supernaturally, to do what man cannot do. It depends on the power and grace of God. A ministry that depends on oral and administrative skills and natural talents to bring about the work of the Lord is not birthed by the Holy Spirit.

> Unless the LORD builds the house, they labor in vain who build it; unless the LORD guards the city, the watchman stays awake in vain (Ps. 127:1).

A Spirit-based ministry realizes that God has the ultimate responsibility for house-building and life-changing and relies on God's supernatural flow to affect people's lives.

Law empowered ministry

Letter- or law-based ministry moves people externally with words they have not yet embraced internally. They have not yet received the grace or power to obey from the heart. They have not yet been taught the internal process of change. As a result, they feel great loads of condemnation. Law is bondage, legalism and standards without the Holy Spirit or the love of God.

Letter-based ministry can be deadly. It produces relationships between men and God based on works, fear and daily frustrations. This is not the way of the Gospel. Authentic leaders do not use the law to manipulate people through guilt and condemnation. The law kills hope. It kills life. All the life flowing from the Gospel cannot flow from the law because the law kills joy and strength.

All leaders can slip into a letter-based ministry that will produce death in those who partake of it. A leader can tell that he ministers from a letter-based source when:

•the people of God become more dependent upon a principle than upon the life of the Spirit;

•the people of God are bound to a repetitious formula or tradition even though it is destroying the free expression of the Holy Spirit;

•a code or standard becomes the mark or goal that people are striving for rather than the Lord Jesus Christ;

•we get more concerned about the product than the process. When the soul of the people begins to wither up and there is no expression of joy or zeal, death is the ultimate result;

•the people of God depend more upon what they have learned than upon the powerful, ongoing, life-flow of the Holy Spirit;

•the people of God have a mental determination toward the truth rather than an experience of entering into the truth by the power and grace of the Holy Spirit;

•praying becomes more of a problem and eventually omitted rather than a love relationship with God which comes naturally;

•we perceive as leaders that the house of the Lord is not being built at the pace we want. We begin to become more anxious in ourselves, causing us to rely on fleshly means and carnal traits to bring about the work of God.

Grace does not impose laws on man but encourages a changed heart.

The apostle Paul encourages all authentic leaders to move into a grace-based ministry that produces freedom. Grace ministry has roots in new covenant reality. Grace does not impose laws on man but encourages a changed heart. Grace not only tells man what to do but gives him the strength to do it. Grace focuses on the power and provision in the Cross and the availability of God's Spirit to work in and through men and women.

Transparency of ministry

The veil Moses wore over his face speaks of partial revelation gleaming through a veil, flashing through symbols, and cloaked in types, shadows and obscure prophecies. The veil symbolizes a ministry speaking through clouded revelation.

Authentic leaders under the new covenant unveil themselves and become approachable. They are frank and open. They do not fear exposing their own weakness as they minister. They remove the veil of the carnal man and allow the grace of God to flow. Simplicity and boldness mark their preaching and teaching. They make hard truths easy to understand and deep truths easy to draw from. They use no symbols, types and obscure language to cloud or overlay biblical truth. Leaders who make preaching and teaching sound "heavy" actually hide truth from people's minds.

People under authentic leadership experience liberty. With new focus, their spiritual perception is no longer impaired. No longer do they founder in bondage and condemnation, but they come forth in a spirit of joy and liberty that was not theirs in the past. The oil of God ministered on the minds and hearts of the people brings them new life and new perspective. Where the Spirit of the Lord is there is freedom. Where the Spirit of the Lord is, there is proper use of authority and a presence of Christ that brings release from condemnation. Glory is displayed not outwardly on the face but inwardly in the character of the people. This glory progressively intensifies until the Christian family acquires the ultimate glorious body that comes at the second coming of Christ. The new breed of leadership for the twenty-first century will enjoy this quality of authenticity. Their transparency with humility will allow God to pour out a fresh touch of His Holy Spirit.

8

The Witness: Discerning False Ministry

False ministries always mingle among true leaders in God's flock. Every generation has its share of insidious impostors who pretend to know how to build churches but who in fact weaken them. With cunning craftiness, they pose as legitimate leaders and deceive common folks. They appear to be godly and teach truth but sow mingled seed of false doctrine in church vineyards.

In the last days before Christ's second coming, many questionable and false ministries will appear. False apostles, false prophets, false evangelists, false pastors, false teachers and false leaders will arise. False ministries are unhealthy. They bring winds of adversity and wrong teaching (Lev. 19:19; Eph. 4:14). Jesus Himself prophesied their rise.

> And Jesus answered and said to them: "Take heed that no one deceives you... For false christs and false prophets will arise and show great signs and wonders, so as to deceive, if possible, even the elect. See, I have told you beforehand.

> Therefore if they say to you, 'Look, He is
> in the desert!' do not go out; or 'Look,
> He is in the inner rooms!' do not believe
> it" (Matt. 24:4, 24-26).

The prevalence of deceivers calls for discernment (Deut. 18:2-22; Rev. 2:2). Every saint should be asking, "What distinguishes healthy, true ministry from unhealthy, false leadership? How do you spot them?" The job of discerning will get tougher in the last days as the push to be "relevant" to the culture raises pressure to compromise clear biblical values. False ministries often seem more relevant to a culture but offer no real solutions to its problems.

An onslaught of new, so-called spiritual gimmicks and innovative ideas promise great results but instead produce only pseudo-Christianity. Pseudo-Christianity holds no promise of change for people. Real, true, genuine Christianity is the only hope for a syncretistic society given to pleasure and deception and trying to accommodate an array of attitudes, lifestyles and divergent values in its population.

The mighty move of God in the last days will draw counterfeiters and impostors out of the woodwork. The following diagram shows the positive and negative aspects of the last days.

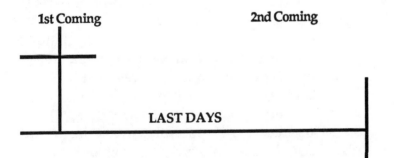

Positive Side	Negative Side
1. Church will be victorious (Eph. 5:27; Isa. 60:13).	1. False church will become more apparent and more wicked.
2. Church will reap great harvest (Matt. 13:39; Rev. 14:15).	2. Love of many shall wax cold (Matt. 24:12).
3. Church will be powerfully moved by the Holy Spirit (Joel 2:28;Acts 2:1-4).	3. Seducing spirits and doctrines of devils (2 Tim. 4:1).
4. Church will preach the Gospel to the whole world (Matt. 24:14).	4. Deception will be prevalent (2 Tim. 3:13; Matt. 24:14,24).
5. Church will see the kingdom of God come to full fruit (James 5:1-7; Rev .22:11).	5. Wickedness will come to full fruit (Rom. 1:18-32; Rev. 22:11).
6. Church will see a greater release of true ministries (Eph. 4:11-12).	6. False ministries will arise (2 Pet. 2; Jude; Acts 20,29,30).
• True Apostles • True Prophets • True Evangelists • True Pastors • True Teachers	• False Apostles • False Prophets • False Evangelists • False Pastors • False Teachers

Every saint and every church has the responsibility to develop the art and science of discerning the spirit of truth and the spirit of error (1 John 4:6). Just as consumer advocates alert the public to false advertising, the church needs Christian consumer advocates to alert believers to false doctrines and false ministries.

Some ministries inspire, yet inspiration alone does not result in building or establishing the house of the Lord. All genuine ministries depend on the anointing of the Holy Spirit, yet the anointing alone will not build the church. Leaders who build successful, enduring churches have genuine spiritual qualities. They have godly character and follow God's principles and methods to reproduce the life of God in His people. Building for permanence requires faithfulness to right principles. Valid ministries must inspire as well as build. Leaders and their ministries can be either true, false or questionable.

TRUE Matt. 22:16 2 Cor. 4:6	QUESTIONABLE Acts 20:30	FALSE Matt. 7:15
Consistent in character, conformable to a standard or pattern, to be without deviation, unswerving loyalty, able to be examined and found to be true.	To drop from a higher place, degrade, sink into disgrace, decline in power, value. To fade gradually.	Not true, nor conformable to fact. Not well founded. Substituted for another. Counterfeit, forged, not genuine. The want of integrity either in principle or in act.

TRUE	QUESTIONABLE	FALSE
Matt. 22:16 2 Cor. 4:6	Acts 20:30	Matt. 7:15
Those who build on the basics of clear biblical revelation of Christ and the church.	Those who give way to carnal impulses, build on questionable, obscure scriptures and methods and confuse results with truth.	Those who deny the basic elements of true Christianity, thus affecting their teachings, morals and practices. Those ministries who hinder and attack the true work of God.

Almost every epistle in the New Testament warns of the peril of false ministries. New Testament writers held nothing back. They exposed false ministries, going after them every way they could to protect the flock of God. They described impostors in derogatory, pointed and dramatic terms. The apostle Peter described the character and ministry methods of false ministries in 2 Peter 2:1-16. Paul identified the bitter fruit of false ministries in the following:

> For such are false apostles, deceitful workers, transforming themselves into apostles of Christ... For you put up with it if one brings you into bondage, if one devours you, if one takes from you, if one exalts himself, if one strikes you on the face (2 Cor. 11:13,20; see also Gal. 1:10-12).

> Beware lest anyone cheat you through philosophy and empty deceit, according

> to the tradition of men, according to the basic principles of the world, and not according to Christ... So let no one judge you in food or in drink, or regarding a festival or a new moon or sabbaths (Col. 2:8,16).

The epistle of Jude deals more with false ministries than any other epistle in the New Testament. It says:

> I found it necessary to write to you exhorting you to contend earnestly for the faith which was once for all delivered to the saints. For certain men have crept in unnoticed, who long ago were marked out for this condemnation, ungodly men, who turn the grace of our God into lewdness and deny the only Lord God and our Lord Jesus Christ (Jude 3-4).

By twisting truth and denying the power of the grace of God, false ministries can produce only false fruit such as:
- False vision (Jer. 14:14; 23:32; Zech. 10:2).
- False witness (Exod. 20:16; Prov. 6:19; Mark 10:19).
- False balance (Prov. 11:1; 20:23; Amos 8:5)
- False tongue (Ps. 120:3)
- False burdens (Lam. 2:14)
- False doctrine (1 Tim. 1:3,10; 6:1-3; 2 Tim, 4:3; Titus 2:1,7; Heb. 13:9; 2 John 1:9; 1Tim. 4:1)
- False report (Exod. 23:1)
- False matters (Exod. 23:7)
- False ways (Ps. 119:104,128)
- False lips (Ps. 17:4)
- False gift (Prov. 25:14)

- False oath (Zech. 8:17)
- False prophecy and prophet's office (Matt. 7:15; Luke 6:26; Acts 13:6; Rev. 16:13; 19:20; 20:10; Matt. 24:11,24; 2 Pet. 2:1; 1 John 4:1)
- False accusers (2 Tim. 3:3; Titus 2:3)
- False christs (Matt. 24:24; Mark 13:22)
- False apostles (2 Cor. 11:13)
- False brethren (2 Cor. 11:26; Gal. 2:4)
- False accusation (Luke 19:8)
- False teachers (2 Pet. 2:1)
- False anointing (Matt. 24:24)

Jesus compared false ministries to wolves in sheep's clothing. They also resemble wandering stars, brute beasts, blemishes and clouds without water, according to the New Testament. Each comparison highlights a dangerous or threatening quality. The Holy Spirit uses the following biblical metaphors to illustrate how false ministries harm believers in Christ:

Hidden Reefs. False leaders and hidden reefs have one thing in common. They are not easily discovered.

> These are spots [hidden reefs (Amp.)] in your love feasts, while they feast with you without fear, serving only themselves (Jude 12).

These hidden reefs are not seen with the natural eye, but are detectable by Holy Ghost "instruments," that through practice can be trained to discern good and evil (Heb. 5:14). Believers are like ships on the sea that risk running into hidden reefs and sinking. Everyone needs to be very careful.

Shipwrecks. Some ships fail to navigate safely and lose their way.

> having faith and a good conscience, which some having rejected, concerning the faith have suffered shipwreck (1 Tim. 1:19).

When the captain himself is not governed by the Word of God, he is not wise or trustworthy. Ships that crash on the rocks sink to the bottom of the sea. Sadly, many of these ships carry precious passengers who do not know the ship's destiny. In a shipwreck, passengers often perish along with the captain.

Clouds without water. Deceptive clouds seem to be charged with refreshing water but drift by, leaving no rain. They are not what they appear to be. They travel around as if carried by the winds.

> They are clouds without water, carried about by the winds; late autumn trees without fruit, twice dead, pulled up by the roots (Jude 12).

> Whoever falsely boasts of giving is like clouds and wind without rain (Prov. 25:14).

Wells without water. Some ministries seem to have such "deep" teaching. They claim to have fresh spiritual insight. They carry on publicly as if they have a very special relationship with God and something very mystical to reveal. As deep as they appear to be, they have no living water to draw from. Really, they are dry wells.

> These are wells without water, clouds
> carried by a tempest, for whom is
> reserved the blackness of darkness
> forever (2 Pet. 2:17).

These ministries take advantage of people's desire to see the power of the Holy Spirit. They point their finger toward the future and spend all their time talking about the coming new "something." They boast of knowing what no one else knows and often claim to be on the front lines of future moves of God.

In this passage, Peter also compares false leaders to clouds driven by a storm. The word *clouds* here refers to a fog or mist. A minister may look impressive but have no substance. His ministry does not give God's people any secure, reliable answers for their questions or help for their practical daily lives. Instead of calming storms, his so-called ministry causes turbulence in groups that receive him. Wherever he goes, he creates tempests or storms in the church.

Wandering stars. Unlike the north star, wandering stars have no fixed place in the sky. They shine for a while and pass into darkness (Isa. 40:26; 45:12; Rev. 12:1; Ps 148:3; Mark 13:25).

> raging waves of the sea, foaming up
> their own shame; wandering stars for
> whom is reserved the blackness of
> darkness forever (Jude 13).

These comets stray at random and without law. A mariner charting his course at night cannot guide his ship by them. They are rebel stars. They do not belong to a predictable system and do not regard the laws keeping other stars in orbit. Scripture uses stars to symbolize both negative and positive things. These wandering stars were created to be under the government of God but strayed into their own self-willed government without any law or restraint.

A bruising boxer. Paul rebukes the Corinthians with irony. He chides them for tolerating leaders who as much as hit people in the face.

> For you put up with it if one brings you into bondage, if one devours you, if one takes from you, if one exalts himself, if one strikes you on the face (2 Cor. 11:20).

The lords and masters in those days struck their servants, occasionally hurting and maiming them. Rarely do false ministries physically hurt and maim people, but they cause spiritual hurts which are far worse. They enslave and devour people with their false doctrine and philosophies. They exalt themselves over people. They smite people in the face spiritually, causing wounds and hurts.

Brute beasts. A brute beast acts only on his own impulses, passions, anger and self-will. He is irrational and lacks higher intelligence. With carefully chosen words, Peter declares that false ministries are driven by fundamental appetites.

> But these, like natural brute beasts made to be caught and destroyed, speak evil of the things they do not understand, and will utterly perish in their own corruption (2 Pet. 2:12).

The word *natural* in Greek refers to creatures of instinct. They possess no common sense. They are similar to wild, ferocious animals who belong behind bars in the zoo or in the wild far away from people.

They have bodies but no rational minds. They don't think about consequences of their actions. They provide for and protect only themselves.

Actors in disguise. Pseudo-prophets, teachers and apostles usually are sincere people, but they try to force themselves into gifts and spiritual positions God never gave to them. Such men are imitators.

> For such are false apostles, deceitful workers, transforming themselves into apostles of Christ (2 Cor. 11:13).

When God has not called someone into an office, he or she produces results from carnal effort. False revelation comes from these great pretenders. Deceiving spirits speak through them. To catch their victims, deceitful workers put out bait. The connotation is that deception kills its victims.

Leaven that corrupts. Leaven, or yeast works silently. Introduce a little leaven into a lump of dough and it quietly penetrates the whole lump.

> A little leaven leavens the whole lump (Gal. 5:9).

Here leaven refers to false doctrine. Secretly and silently, it produces sickness and decay. False doctrine quietly works its way through a church. Many saints do not notice how harmful a false philosophy or teaching can be until they have been injured by it. Leaders need eyes and ears of discernment to detect false doctrines harmful to the flock early, before they spread.

A senior pastor can unwittingly open the door to false doctrine. He may raise someone who holds false philosophies and doctrines into a staff position or support ministry. The Bible calls for a period of testing to discover the true character, doctrine and compatibility of potential support ministers before they are promoted (1 Tim. 3:10). When a leader with false doctrine is exalted, his false doctrine spreads secretly and silently from his office of influence. Raising untested leaders is one of the worst things to do in a church.

Impostors. Impostors prey upon a gift or office.

> But evil men and impostors will grow worse and worse, deceiving and being deceived (2 Tim. 3:13).

Impostors learn spiritual words, cliches and even spiritual looks to win people's trust. They act as if they have a particular gift or office. Knowing it has not been given to them by God, they put on a show, and many people believe the show. Deceived, the people trust in what they've seen rather than in the true discernment of the Holy Spirit.

Swindlers. Money motivates false ministries. They have a spirit of greed. They covet money more than people's souls. They gauge success by how much profit they take in at events. They have sold their gifts for the dollar. They ask, "How much money will the people of God give me for my particular kind of teaching or ministry?" Ministries that use their gifts to produce themselves and earn great sums of money are false and rob the people of God. These ministries should be avoided at all costs.

> By covetousness they will exploit you with deceptive words; for a long time their judgment has not been idle, and

their destruction does not slumber (2
Pet. 2:3).

Sadly, in the United States, millions of gullible
people give millions of dollars to ministries
governed by covetousness. Christians seem to turn
their heads and not notice the extravagant
exploitation practiced by those organizations. We
exalt their gifts so highly and want their kind of
teaching or the supernatural that we ignore the way
they misuse people as well as people's money.

Soldiers who desert. Under pressure, some leaders
will desert. Some front-line soldiers turn to run
because of attacks upon them or because of the lure of
the world.

> For Demas has forsaken me, having
> loved this present world, and has
> departed for Thessalonica—Crescens for
> Galatia, Titus for Dalmatia (2 Tim. 4:10).

At one time Demas belonged on the apostle Paul's
chosen leadership team. However, he chose to turn
and go back into the world rather than live under the
pressures upon leadership. Leaders who have not
really embraced the cross of Christ and the call of God
on their lives collapse under pressure. To them, the
world always is more tempting than it should be.

Stains and blemishes. When they began their
decline into darkness and evil, these ministries
would sin only at night. In the darkness, no one saw
or questioned them. But as they progressed in their
sin, they began to carouse in daytime, in the light,
exposing themselves and displaying their evil
without shame.

> and will receive the wages of
> unrighteousness, as those who count it
> pleasure to carouse in the daytime. They
> are spots and blemishes, carousing in
> their own deceptions while they feast
> with you (2 Pet. 2:13).

These leaders have succumbed to their own habits
and carnality to the point where they are engrossed in
their sin and have no guilt or conviction for what
they are doing. In disgust, Peter says these ministries
are filth spots and scabs.

Dogs and pigs. False leaders also are likened to dogs
that return to their vomit and pigs that return to
their mudbaths.

> But it has happened to them according
> to the true proverb: "A dog returns to
> his own vomit," and, "a sow, having
> washed, to her wallowing in the mire"
> (2 Pet. 2:22).

> As a dog returns to his own vomit, so a
> fool repeats his folly (Prov. 26:11).

Ravenous wolves. Wolves like to eat sheep. When
they are hungry, they hunt lambs. People are like
sheep. Both are vulnerable to cunning hunters
looking for something to devour. The wolf character
in a false leader can be judged by the fruit of their
lives (Acts 20:28-29).

> Beware of false prophets, who come to
> you in sheep's clothing, but inwardly
> they are ravenous wolves. You will
> know them by their fruits. Do men

gather grapes from thornbushes or figs from thistles? Even so, every good tree bears good fruit, but a bad tree bears bad fruit. A good tree cannot bear bad fruit, nor can a bad tree bear good fruit. Every tree that does not bear good fruit is cut down and thrown into the fire. Therefore by their fruits you will know them (Matt. 7:15-20).

Wanting every advantage over his prey, the wolf looks for the following kinds of sheep:
- New converts, the lambs of the flock (Amos 6:4).
- The weak and the immature (2 Pet. 2:14).
- The gullible (2 Tim. 3:6).
- The wounded and vulnerable (Jer. 6:14).
- Sheep who have a lust for the sensational (Acts 8:18-20; 14:11,20).
- Sheep who have a thirst for new things (2 Tim.
- Sheep who love private interpretations of Scripture (Matt. 24:26-27; 2 Pet. 1:20-21; 4:3-4; Acts 17:21,11).

Today in the church, a hireling wants a position not to serve but simply to obtain honor, glory and profit for himself.

Hirelings flee danger. A hireling is a day-laborer. The Greek word *eritheia* originally meant laboring for wages. It was the perfectly respectable and responsible thing to do. Then the meaning of the word degenerated. Now it describes a worker with no sense of loyalty to his employer. He works for pay and nothing else.

> But a hireling, he who is not the
> shepherd, one who does not own the
> sheep, sees the wolf coming and leaves
> the sheep and flees; and the wolf catches
> the sheep and scatters them. The
> hireling flees because he is a hireling
> and does not care about the sheep (John
> 10:12-13).

The hireling has no motive to serve. He has only one question: "What do I get out of it?" Today in the church, a hireling wants a position not to serve but simply to obtain honor, glory and profit for himself. He has a contentious spirit in his life and preaching. The apostle James used the same word in his epistle to describe earthly wisdom which is sensual and devilish (see Rom. 2:8; 2 Cor. 12:20; Gal. 5:20; Phil. 1:6; 2:3; James 3:14,16).

How false ministries develop. Leaders begin the slide down the slippery slope of degeneration by allowing clear biblical principles, values and commands to be violated. When men and women emphasize natural things more than spiritual things, the external more than the internal and the visible more than the invisible, they have violated the clear norm of Scripture.

> Now the Spirit expressly says that in
> latter times some will depart from the
> faith, giving heed to deceiving spirits
> and doctrines of demons, speaking lies
> in hypocrisy, having their own
> conscience seared with a hot iron,
> forbidding to marry, and commanding
> to abstain from foods which God created
> to be received with thanksgiving by

those who believe and know the truth (1
Tim. 4:1-3).

Departing from the faith usually takes place
slowly. In fact, it occurs so slowly that most people
fail to recognize it while it's happening. The word
depart means to stand or step away from, to withdraw
from or to shrink back from. The Bible does not say
believers will reject the faith. Rejection calls for
thoughtful, deliberate action. Departure is slow and
unintentional.

If leaders let down their guard to the tactics of
the enemy and step over boundaries they had
set for themselves, they flirt with self-
destruction.

When cause becomes more important than
character, when a leader justifies all his actions in the
name of the cause, he has begun to slide into
degeneration. When a leader isolates himself in his
ivory tower, he believes he is so important that he
does not need other leaders in the body of Christ. He
will end up in a fog and a mist, blinded by his own
pride. All leaders have to keep alert to the threat
posed by slow degeneration of their spiritual and
moral standards. If leaders let down their guard to the
tactics of the enemy and step over boundaries they
had set for themselves, they flirt with self-
destruction. When they allow a defensive attitude to
develop and start rejecting others, they have set
themselves up for deception.

The devil tries to seduce all believers away from
Christ and into abnormal preoccupation with signs,
wonders, new revelations, supernatural phenomena

and the sensational. Looking for deeper revelation or something more spectacular than what they already have, some believers will follow false leaders and depart from the clear, sound teaching of the Word of God. When a part of the body of Christ exaggerates its own distinctives, heaps praise upon itself and thinks of itself as the exclusive, faithful remnant, it destroys evangelism and begins its own journey into falsehood.

Twelve discernable marks of true ministry

1. Fruits of genuine New Testament salvation that result in the minister being a disciple of Christ. (Matt. 3:10-11; Luke 14:25-35)

2. Handling the Word of God using proper biblical hermeneutics. (2 Tim. 2:15; 1 Cor. 4:1,2; 2 Cor. 4:2)

3. A proven record of sound theology, ecclesiology, pneumatology and eschatology. (1 Tim. 4:6,7; 1 Tim. 6:3; 2 Tim. 1:14; 2 Tim. 4:3; Judges 1:3; Matt. 7:28; Acts 5:28)

4. Proven character encompassing the qualifications of an elder listed in Titus and Timothy. (1 Tim. 3:1-10; 2 Cor. 13:8; 1 Tim. 4:16; 2 Cor. 1:12; 2 Cor. 7:2; 2 Cor. 6:3)

5. Knowing the difference between true biblical anointing and cheap, human hype. (1 John 2:27; 2 Cor. 1:21)

6. Understanding the principles of accountability, authority and submission. (2 Cor. 10:8-9; Acts 13:1-3; Acts 15:2; Acts 13:4)

7. Fixed convictions, principles, and values that have proven to be unchangeable except when found to be unbiblical. (1 Tim. 5:21)

8. Not ruled or led by money. (2 Cor. 11:7-9; 2 Cor. 12:13-15; 1 Tim. 5:17-18; 2 Thess. 3:8-11; 2 Pet. 2:3; 1 Tim. 6:10)

9. A father's heart of genuine concern for the health of the church. (2 Cor. 4:15; 2 Cor. 12:15-16)

10. A strong, godly marriage and a strong godly family. (Acts 21:8-9; 1 Tim. 3:4,5,11)

11. Tangible message that can be watched, evaluated, and examined. Proven to be lasting, biblical and workable. (2 Cor. 3:1-3; 1 Cor. 2:13-14; Matt. 7:17)

12. The cross is the central focus of their preaching. (1 Cor. 2:1-5; Phil. 3:18)

9

The Standard: Moral Purity

The minister most likely to stray into moral impurity is not much different from men in other professions who stray. Research shows he usually is middle-aged and disillusioned with his calling. He has neglected his own marriage and has met another woman who needs him. He is a lone ranger, isolated from his clerical peers. However, his association with God makes his moral failure more serious than immorality among other professionals. The public sees his authority as derived from the Lord, setting him apart even from other so-called professional counselors or therapists.

The Reverend Henry Ward Beecher, the great preacher of the late nineteenth century, was nearly ruined after an illicit affair became known. In the late twentieth century several prominent leaders in the Christian world fell into moral impurity. It occurs in all denominations. Pentecostals fall alongside evangelicals. During rousing rituals, a minister can appear to command great power. One counselor-therapist who works to restore fallen ministries says this power is closely linked to sexual passion. Women may imagine a tremendous benefit in sexual union with the minister, while nearsighted ministers block out thoughts of judgment as they indulge their flesh and fantasies.

Moral impurity is like an infection. An infection puts poison into a healthy body and causes disease. It taints and corrupts. It is a malfunction or sickness that—if not remedied—leads to death. Biblical prescriptions can treat immorality. A diagnosis locates infected areas that need treatment. The prescription for treatment calls for cleansing and proper remedies. Good health depends on good diagnoses and good medicines.

Perversion and filthiness surround people today like it surrounded Lot. Lot lived in a corrupt society vexed by unrestrained evil and moral impurity. It was filthy.

> And turning the cities of Sodom and Gomorrah into ashes, condemned them to destruction, making them an example to those who afterward would live ungodly; and delivered righteous Lot, who was oppressed by the filthy conduct of the wicked (for that righteous man, dwelling among them, tormented his righteous soul from day to day by seeing and hearing their lawless deeds)— then the Lord knows how to deliver the godly out of temptations and to reserve the unjust under punishment for the day of judgment (2 Pet. 2:6-9).

A righteous man purifies his soul and removes filth that causes infection. The Hebrew word for *filth* means stained, dirty, abominable, unclean, and foul. It describes anything that soils or defiles. The Greek word for *filth* means to stain, soil, or smear. It refers especially to sexual or sensual defilements. The word *defile* means to discolor something by painting or staining it, making it unclean. The following verses warn and encourage believers, including leaders, to be avoid filth, defilement and corruption (Isa. 4:4; James 1:21).

> There is a generation that is pure in its own eyes, yet is not washed from its filthiness (Prov. 30:12).

> Therefore, having these promises, beloved, let us cleanse ourselves from all filthiness of the flesh and spirit, perfecting holiness in the fear of God (2 Cor. 7:1).

Joshua is told to remove his filthy garments in Zechariah 3:3-4, and Colossians 3:8 tells Christians to put off all uncleanness. Impurity and sexual misconduct pave the way for future rebellion and disobedience. Societies that fail to restrain moral impurity also run wild with rebellion and disrespect for authority.

> And especially those who walk according to the flesh in the lust of uncleanness and despise authority. They are presumptuous, self-willed. They are not afraid to speak evil of dignitaries (2 Pet. 2:10).

Root causes
Western society has been infected with moral impurity and now suffers the full-blown disease. It's

symptoms include pagan morals and values held by the general public. The symptoms point to the following root causes of spiritual infections:

1. *Stained hearts.* Salvation cleanses man's heart or his inner man. He is responsible to keep his heart clean by walking in the light and applying the blood of Jesus to his daily sins (see 1 John 1:7-9; Ps. 51:10,17; 139:23; Prov. 4:23; 15:28; Matt. 5:8; 2 Tim. 2:12).

> Then I will sprinkle clean water on you, and you shall be clean; I will cleanse you from all your filthiness and from all your idols. I will give you a new heart and put a new spirit within you; I will take the heart of stone out of your flesh and give you a heart of flesh. I will put My Spirit within you and cause you to walk in My statutes, and you will keep My judgments and do them (Ezek. 36:25-27).

2. *Secret sins.* Secret sins are hidden, covered, veiled, concealed, or disguised. When God exposes secret sins, he allows others to see sin's devastating consequences (Ps. 19:12).

> He who covers his sins will not prosper, but whoever confesses and forsakes them will have mercy (Prov. 28:13).

Crafty characters glamorize the pleasures of sin and tempt believers to think like the foolish simple man in Proverbs. He thought the pleasures of sin would last a long time. They don't. The believer should hate sin knowing it undercuts his potential and blocks his achievement of what God has planned for him. He should hate sin as he sees it damaging lives of people he loves. However, he will not hate sin if he does not comprehend its final cost. Unconfessed sin will cause uncontrolled miseries (Matt. 10:26-27).

> Behold, You desire truth in the inward parts, and in the hidden part You will make me to know wisdom (Ps. 51:6).

> Each one's work will become clear; for the Day will declare it, because it will be revealed by fire; and the fire will test each one's work, of what sort it is (1 Cor. 3:13).

Scripture is clear. God's remedy for man's sin is confession. God will reveal hidden things, and man is responsible to confess and forsake them. God gives every man time to repent (Rev. 2:21). It is just a matter of time until a man's sin is revealed. If he repents first, God may be the only one to see the consequences of the sin. If not, the consequences may be seen by all.

3. *Impure thinking.* Christians must not only seek heaven but also think of heaven. They need to expose every thought to God and his Word.

> Set your mind on things above, not on things on the earth (Col 3:2).

Evil thinking leads to evil desires. Evil desires lead to evil actions, that ultimately become enslaving habits. To set an example for others, a vanguard leader needs to immediately cleanse wrong thoughts so they do not destroy his emotions or affections. He needs to turn every one of his thoughts into discussions with God so that God can have His rightful place in the leader's thoughts and cleanse them by Holy Spirit conviction. A man can rebuild his thinking through memorizing and meditating on Scripture (Col. 3:2-5).

Exploiters and manipulators know the basic instincts of man. They know how to exploit the minds of other men to make them lust after ungodly things and enslave them. Stories and advertisements in broadcast and print media engulf the populace with messages aimed at men's basic desires.

4. *Defiling habits.* A habit is part of a person's lifestyle or his habitation—the place he lives. Frequent repetition of an act makes it a habit. Studies show new habits can be established in only six weeks. Likewise, bad habits can be broken in the same length of time.

> Put on the Lord Jesus Christ, and make
> no provision for the flesh, to fulfill its
> lusts (Rom. 13:14).

A person is a slave to whatever he submits to. The apostle Paul exhorts Christians not to present their bodies as instruments of sin, not to let sin reign, and not to obey sin's lusts (Rom. 6:12-14). Believers need to walk in the power of the Holy Spirit and in holiness to make their habits holy unto the Lord.

5. *Modern-day idolatry.* Idolatry is an excessive attachment to or love for something or someone besides God. It has to do with an individual's heart, emotions, and talents. Giving prime time and attention to anything other than God makes a man an unholy idolater. Using resources that God has provided in ways that do not glorify God is a form of idolatry (1 Cor. 10:7; 1 John 5:21).

> You shall not make idols for yourselves;
> neither a carved image nor a sacred
> pillar shall you rear up for yourselves;
> nor shall you set up an engraved stone
> in your land, to bow down to it; for I am
> the LORD your God (Lev. 26:1).

> Put to death...fornication, uncleanness,
> passion, evil desire, and covetousness,
> which is idolatry (Col. 3:5).

6. Defiled conscience. Sensitive to moral pleasure and pain, the conscience can be called man's inner umpire. It distinguishes between right and wrong. It dwells in the spirit of a man urging him to do right and warning him to steer clear of wrong. A clear conscience is essential for success in spiritual warfare. Ignorance of how the conscience does its job can lead to serious spiritual disorders (1 Cor. 1:12; 1 Tim 3:9; 2 Tim 1:3; Heb. 13:18).

> This being so, I myself always strive to
> have a conscience without offense
> toward God and men (Acts 24:16).

> Now the purpose of the commandment
> is love from a pure heart, from a good
> conscience, and from sincere faith...
> Having faith and a good conscience,
> which some having rejected, concerning
> the faith have suffered shipwreck (1
> Tim. 1:5, 19).

Man is comprised of body, soul and spirit. The body houses the five natural senses of smell, sight, hearing, touch, and taste. The soul includes a person's mind, will, and emotions. The spirit is home to a man's intuition and conscience. The conscience is the nerve center of the inner man. It judges the moral quality of a man's decisions and actions. It approves and disapproves his decisions and helps him regulate his choices and wishes

The conscience is a unique, innate faculty put into human beings to hear the voice of God. God created it to guide people to make choices that please Him. If defiled, it becomes unreliable. However, a defiled conscience can be purged and retrained by the Holy Spirit to keep believers on the right track. The conscience is not the supernatural voice of God. A man's conscience delivers a judgment, but his will decides whether to act. When regulated by the Word of God, the conscience grows strong and insists on doing right, condemns wrongdoing, causes remorse over sin, and rewards righteousness with peace.

When not regulated by the Word of God, the conscience grows weak and may become defiled. Defilement speaks of moral corruption in the soul (1 Cor. 8:7,10,12).

> To the pure all things are pure, but to those who are defiled and unbelieving nothing is pure; but even their mind and conscience are defiled (Titus 1:15).

Some people's consciences may never have been strengthened by the Word of God. Some may be weak because of incomplete knowledge of God's will revealed in the Bible. Some may be weak due to unsurrendered wills. And some that were strong may grow weak by ignoring the Word of God. A conscience left in this state of weakness and defilement may become hardened or seared.

God's Word is truth. If a man's actions do not line up with the truth, he lives in deception. When he resists the conviction of the Holy Spirit, rationalizes and excuses his actions, and tries to hide from God, he defiles his conscience. Repeated violation of God's Word produces greater defilement until the man's conscience withers. Lowering his standards continually puts him in bondage to his secret sin.

> speaking lies in hypocrisy, having their own conscience seared with a hot iron (1 Tim. 4:2).

The word *seared* means utterly insensitive or withered up. It describes a plant wilting in the heat. Evil practiced habitually makes a man's conscience insensitive. Repeatedly defiled, it voices no resistance.

God designed guilt to lead people to repentance, not to despair. The Holy Spirit works in man's conscience to make him aware of his guilt. Every violation triggers immediate guilt, which should not be ignored. Man finds help only when he faces reality, admits guilt and repents. When a man tries to blameshift or punish himself, he handles guilt the wrong way. Handling guilt improperly brings no cleansing and further weakens his conscience.

A defiled conscience can change a man's personality. It can make him defensive or depressed. It can make him double minded and unstable in all his ways, causing him to vacillate on every decision. A defiled conscience often makes a man talkative, nervous, and unable to concentrate. It can drive away his friends. He must ask the Holy Spirit to apply the blood of Jesus to cover the sin and cleanse his conscience (Heb. 9:9-14). In response to a man's faith, the Holy Spirit applies the power of the blood of Christ to his conscience.

> Let us draw near with a true heart in full assurance of faith, having our hearts sprinkled from an evil conscience and our bodies washed with pure water (Heb. 10:22).

The sacrifice of the red heifer, spoken of in Heb. 9:15 and alluded to in Heb. 10:22, always was available and accessible. It could be taken at any time to cleanse violators of the law. God looks for the sinner to respond to conviction like King David. When confronted with his sin, David quickly said, "I have sinned against the Lord" (2 Sam. 12:13).

To live in moral purity, a man must restore his conscience. Memorizing portions of Scripture will allow a fresh flow of the Holy Spirit to cleanse his mind and strengthen his character. The Scripture gives him God's thoughts to apply in areas of weakness. He can keep his conscience clear by limiting his daily exposure to known temptations. With the removal of the dead weight of past sin, his soul will soar like a lark with a song, released in its native element. The Holy Spirit delights to help men live free of offense toward God and man.

7. *Absence of moral standards.* Moral standards influence a person's attitude toward God and toward life. Unfortunately, what people say and what they do are miles apart. A recent survey showed eighty-six percent of the United States population believes extramarital sex is always or almost always wrong. Only three percent say infidelity is not wrong at all, however, Washington, D.C., newspapers recently

reported that more than half of the members of Congress are involved in extramarital affairs.

The land is full of adulterers, and the truth of Jeremiah 23:9-17 is being fulfilled in our lifetimes. Sex saturates society. Fidelity is out, and adultery is in. Books, magazines, billboards, and movies promote it ceaselessly. Television shows it in color. Soap operas and talk shows continually send the message: "Sex is good in or out of marriage. Get all you can, any time you can." A prominent sexologist recommends "healthy adultery" for couples, arguing that it rejuvenates romance.

Immorality in society threatens church purity. Permissive attitudes tend to infiltrate the church. Some Christian leaders act as if anything goes. Love covers all. They accept everything. They don't preach against immorality in the church body. It's a touchy area. They don't mention the word *adultery*. They use the word *affair*. They don't emphasize the holiness and purity of God.

In the past thirty or forty years, some church leaders have loosened their standards hoping to make the church relevant to society. However, their efforts to make their churches so relevant have instead made them irrelevant. Mona Charen, a syndicated columnist and consultant in Washington, D.C., chided one church group for its misdirected efforts in the following article taken from The Oregonian newspaper, Portland, Oregon, April 21, 1991.

Today's Churches Found Wanting in Spiritual Cure

There is a school of thought which says the solution to America's worst ills, rising violence accompanied by a total lack of conscience among criminals, unwed mothers and infant mortality, poverty and drugs, is a return to religion. For sickness of the soul, nothing less than a spiritual cure will do. But what if the churches aren't there to go back to? The question is prompted by news last week that a national committee of the Presbyterian church has issued a recommendation that the church disregard its traditional teachings on sexual morality and, well, loosen up. The head of the committee, John J. Carey, told the Washington Post, "The history of Christianity is to regard anything from the waist down, the stirring of the loins, as demonic. That's all baloney. We think it is time to affirm the eros." That is both unhistorical and ridiculous. But these eros-affirming Presbyterians are messianic. Rather than inquiring whether sexual activity is pre-marital, marital or post-marital, the report advises, we should be asking whether the relation is responsible, the dynamics generally mutual and the loving full of joyful caring. This report is full of something, but it ain't joyful caring. For teenagers, the Presbyterian committee offers that maturity, not marriage, should be the guide to whether sexual intercourse is appropriate. If the report's recommendations were adopted, gay men and lesbians would be ordained into the ministry and homosexual couples would be considered every bit as much a family as the traditional heterosexual version. The hip Presbyterians don't think adultery has been given its day in court. Provided the relationship is mutually satisfying and not exploitive, the new

dispensation would permit or even encourage
it. To suggest that what America needs right
now are looser standards of sexual morality is
like saying the Kennedy family is altogether
too straight-laced. Come on, where do these
people live? In my America, thousand of
teenage girls are walking around pregnant,
potentially ruining two lives at once, precisely
because no one taught them that premarital
sex was wrong. Where I live millions of
couples have divorced, spinning the lives of
their children out of control, often because one
or both parents elected to have a joyful
relationship with someone else. This is a
culture where it seems at least half of all
television talk shows, magazine covers and
best selling books are about sex. These hip
Presbyterians may think they are
revolutionaries, but in fact they are
reactionaries. Sexual permissiveness is the
norm. Did they sleep through the sexual
revolution of the past thirty years? Has the
AIDS epidemic gone unnoticed? But here is
the real point. The churches make a fatal error
when they assume that in order to staunch the
hemorrhaging of members (the Presbyterian
church has lost one million adherents in the
past twenty years) they must sex up their
message. People don't leave churches because
the rules are too strict. They both need and
expect those standards to remain firm.
Particularly in a fast paced, transient society,
only a church that remains true to its
principles can provide solace and meaning for
people's lives. The reason people are leaving
the churches in droves is precisely because of

reports like this one. The mainline Protestant churches, reformed Judaism and liberal Catholicism have all attempted to transcend the merely religious role of their churches to become politically relevant. But as libertines, churchmen can never compete with the pros. Why do we need Presbyterian advice on Christian sexuality when we've already got the Playboy philosopher. The sad part is if these trends continue and the churches contort themselves beyond recognition and pursuit of illusive relevance, there will some day be no standards left to repair to when the society at large has tired of license. (By permission of Mona Charen and Creators Syndicate)

This article should have been written by a Pentecostal historian, pastor, or television personality who speaks to millions of Christians. Instead it was written by a journalist who lives in Washington, D.C., and sees the ill-advised actions of struggling, well-intentioned churches. The unbelieving world mocks Christians who compromise biblical standards. When a church leader lowers his standards to improve his image in the public eye or to be seen as "in touch" with the philosophies of the day, he actually destroys the distinctives of the church. He destroys the essence of his own ministry.

As the church moves into the twenty-first century, vanguard leaders must draw lines. They must exalt the faithful, consistent standards of the Word of God, and those standards forbid moral impurity. It cannot be swept under the carpet or ignored. It will be judged by God. Fallen leaders must repent of it. Vanguard leaders must lift their voices like trumpets and declare that premarital sex and adultery are wrong.

Understanding the wrath of God

People need to see that immorality in the church and in the world draws the wrath of God. The wrath of God is not fiction or a figure of speech but is a terrible reality. It is the constant, unchanging reaction of God's holiness and righteousness to sin. It is not a passion for revenge or just a display of anger as human wrath tends to be. Within the framework of covenant theology, the wrath of God is an expression of rejected and wounded love. God has the last word when man indulges in human perversion. Man cannot escape. God's wrath is revealed (Rev. 6:16; Ps. 76:7).

> For the wrath of God is revealed from heaven against all ungodliness and unrighteousness of men, who suppress the truth in unrighteousness (Rom. 1:18)

> Let no one deceive you with empty words, for because of these things the wrath of God comes upon the sons of disobedience (Eph. 5:6).

God judges the righteous, and God is angry with the wicked every day (Ps. 7:11). God's wrath has fallen on society because impurity has become a way of life. Society has indulged in almost every form of sexual immorality mentioned in the Bible, and people have become callous to guilt.

Sexual sin

The Bible uses the following words to define sexual immorality:

Sensuality is a planned appeal to the physical senses for personal gratification. It is a preoccupation with bodily or sexual pleasure. It means to be governed by appetites and passions of the flesh (1 Cor. 2:14; 15;44,46; James 3:15; Jude 19).

Lasciviousness is a tendency to excite sexual desires that cannot be righteously fulfilled. It refers to unbridled lust, shameless, filthy words, and indecent bodily movements (Mark 7:22; Rom. 13:13; 2 Cor. 12:21; Gal. 5:19; Eph. 4:19; 1 Pet. 4:3; 2 Pet. 2:7,18; Jude 19).

Fleshly lusts are strong cravings, longings, or desires for what is forbidden. People with fleshly lusts have strong, abnormal sexual desires or appetites.

To *defraud* someone means to obtain something from him or her by deception. It means to take advantage, overreach, cheat, deceive (2 Cor. 2:11; 7:2; 12:17-18; 1 Thess. 4:6).

Fornication is sex outside of marriage or voluntary sexual acts between an unmarried man and woman. Fornicators prostitute their bodies outside of a marriage covenant (1 Cor. 6:13, 18; 1 Thess. 4:3; Heb. 12:16).

Adultery is sex between a married person and a partner other than his or her spouse.

Homosexuality is sexual intercourse between two people of the same sex. The Bible calls it sodomy and rejects it as an acceptable lifestyle because it perverts God's natural order for sexual identity and fulfillment. Referring to homosexuals as *gay* or as *consenting adults* and defending their behavior as protected by a right to privacy is misleading and deceptive.

People who have committed immoral acts often demonstrate telltale signs. They frequently appear argumentative, resentful, and nervous. They reject standards from the Word of God, wear provocative clothes, and redefine their moral convictions. They may lie, drop close friends, and avoid getting near people. They may not be able to engage in normal conversations. Moral bondage exists when human desires conflict with God's nature, but moral freedom reigns when God's desires become our desires.

Stages of adultery

Like other men, godly leaders must deal with temptations to commit adultery. Even Elijah was a man "with a nature like ours" (James 4:17) and had to contend with temptations "common to man" (1 Cor. 10:13). The Bible says, "Thou shalt not commit adultery" (Exod. 20:14), and adulterers in the Old Testament fell under the death penalty (Lev. 20:10).

Adultery slips quietly into a person's life. Men and women do not usually wake up one morning and decide it's a good day to commit adultery. They progress into a state of mind that leads to the hideous sin. Here are adultery's four phases:

1. Mental infidelity occurs first. Adultery begins in the inner person, the mind and the emotions.

> For out of the heart proceed evil thoughts, murders, adulteries, fornications, thefts, false witness, blasphemies (Matt. 15:19).

These wicked designs come from the center of a man's being, from his heart and mind (Mark 7:21; 2 Cor. 10:4-5). The apostle Peter warns that our eyes are not to be full of adultery because we will not be able to cease from sin (2 Pet. 2:14). Jesus said whoever looks on a woman has already committed adultery (Matt 5:28). The Greek word translated *look* means a continual habit of life. It refers to a man's thinking being continually dominated by an evil fantasy with a particular person. A glance does not equal adultery. Mental infidelity occurs when a man's mind repeatedly previews the desired action in a fantasy. Jesus condemned the practice of centering your attention on a particular person with the intent to commit adultery.

Christians cannot just shift their brains into neutral and hope for good thoughts. They must discipline their minds and fill their minds with righteous thoughts concerning the person they are thinking about (Phil. 4:8).

2. *Feeding the flesh magnifies adulterous thoughts.* Vanguard leaders need to be careful about what they fill their eyes with. Any reading material that excites sexual desire, lust, or fantasy should be eliminated. The Bible exhorts believers to cast off all the works of darkness and not to walk in wantonness (Rom. 13:12-13).

Some television and video shows dramatize and sensationalize immorality, illicit sex, and nudity. Immoral scenes feed fantasies into people's imaginations, which need to be cleansed and disciplined.

Thoughts steer actions. A man's thoughts will shape his character. The mind is like a garden. It can be cultivated to produce a harvest you want. The mind is like a workshop where important decisions for life and eternity are made. The mind is like an armory where weapons are forged to win victories. The mind is like a battlefield where decisive battles of life are won or lost.

3. *Temptations appear.* Hidden thoughts will be revealed through a temptation to the flesh. Temptation is not sin, but yielding is.

> Every man is tempted when he is drawn
> away by his *own* lusts and enticed [by his
> *own* lusts] (James 1:14).

> Abstain from fleshly lusts which war
> against the soul (1 Pet. 2:11).

Carefully monitor friendships with the opposite sex. Hugs that last too long excite amorous emotions, and having too many intimate conversations can be dangerous. Avoid flirting with adultery. Your mind and body are your servants. You must discipline them and bring them into order. Keep aloof from fleshly lusts. They campaign against your soul. The body is the servant of the mind.

4. *A single act or a planned program?* There is a difference between a person who stumbles in a single adulterous act and one who repeatedly sins following a planned program and shows regret only when he is caught.

King David committed adultery although he was not an adulterer. He stumbled; he repented; he was cleansed; and he had to live through the consequences of his sin. He was overtaken in a trespass.

> If a man is overtaken in any trespass,
> you who are spiritual restore such a one
> in a spirit of gentleness (Gal. 6:1).

If a man stumbles and does something foolish in an act of weakness and falls into sin—even if it is adultery—he can be restored. Certain walls of restraint broke down that need rebuilding. However, an adulterer is habitually involved in immoral acts. He is not stumbling. He uses deceit and strategic, evil planning. It is his lifestyle. An adulterer feeds on the emotions of weak women, understands their makeup, and goes out of his way to seduce them. He looks at members of the opposite sex and fantasizes about acts of adultery with them. He seduces them while counseling, while involved in ministry, or while traveling on business. This person has sold himself and his body to the pleasures of immorality.

Adultery exacts a high price from its participants. It carries great consequences. Esau sold and could not retrieve his birthright because he was a profane man—a fornicator (Heb. 12:16-17).

Reuben forfeited his birthright because he was a fornicator and had committed incest (Gen. 49:3-4). David committed adultery and murder. He was pardoned but also was punished. The sword never left his house. The Lord raised up evil against his house. David was openly rebuked and humiliated. Amnon committed incest and was assassinated for it. Absalom had lain with his father's wives in his rebellion and died for it. Solomon had many wives who turned his heart away from the Lord. Once that happened, he could not find satisfaction or enjoy life. Numbers, chapter 25, records a period of immorality between the Israelites and Midianites. God brought judgment upon them. Phinehas, who was zealous for the holiness of God, tried to stop it, but God brought the consequences of their immorality upon the whole nation.

Sin may be enjoyable, but it is never successfully covered. No amount of prayer or pious living is going to undo the damage caused by undisciplined actions of infidelity.

> He will accept no recompense, nor will
> he be appeased though you give many
> gifts (Prov. 6:35).

An adulterer shall not go unpunished for his sin.

> Immediately he went after her, as an ox
> goes to the slaughter, or as a fool to the
> correction of the stocks, till an arrow
> struck his liver. As a bird hastens to the
> snare, he did not know it would take his
> life (Prov. 7:22-23).

He is snared like a bird and the end of his snare will be death. The Beck translation of Hebrews 13:4 states, "Those who sin sexually, whether single or married, God will judge."

The adulterer receives the following consequences, according to Proverbs, chapter 6:
- He destroys his own soul.
- He shall not be innocent.
- He receives a wound that shall not be healed.
- He will be dishonored.
- He receives a reproach that will not be wiped away.
- He ruins his friendships.
- He sins against his own body.
- He could possibly be judged with a death penalty.
- He may experience broken fellowship with God's people and excommunication.
- He may give himself to immorality so completely that he becomes reprobate.

Vanguard leaders must see hope for change. They must experience genuine conviction, confession, repentance, and cleansing from any sin of immorality or impurity. They must rebuild moral restraints in their lives and break off any immoral relationships. They need to be alert to friendships that could lead to immoral or adulterous relationships.

Quit rationalizing. Quit thinking divorce is the answer to your own marriage problems. Rebuild your marriage carefully. Ask other leaders to stand with you. Become accountable. The best advice is useless against strong temptation unless it is thoroughly taken to heart and translated into habits for right living.

Therefore let him who thinks he stands
take heed lest he fall (1 Cor. 10:12).

10

The Authority: Holy Spirit Anointing

The practice of anointing has deep roots in the Old Testament. A priest would anoint kings, prophets and other priests by pouring holy oil on their heads. In ceremonies, the anointing publicly authorized a man's leadership. It set him apart for service to the Lord and gave him divine enablement to carry out his mission (1 Sam. 10:1; 16:1; 1 Kings 1:29; Isa. 61:4; Acts 4:27; 10:38).

Costly sweet and bitter spices blended into the oil symbolize the sweet and bitter experiences God's followers go through to receive the true power of the Holy Spirit. The holy oil was not poured on anything unclean. It was not for strangers or anyone who was not already separated unto service for the Lord. If a person substituted, imitated, or counterfeited the holy oil he was cut off from the priesthood and from the leadership of Israel.

The anointing bestows God's divine enablement—the strength to take dominion over the enemy.

The anointing of God still is very sacred and protected by Christ Himself. Principles that apply to Old Testament anointing hold significance for New Testament believers. New Testament anointing does not involve oil poured on the body, but it resembles Old Testament anointing because it is poured upon dedicated believers who have set themselves apart for service just as prophets, priests and kings did in the Old Testament. The anointing bestows God's divine enablement—the strength to take dominion over the enemy. It empowers blood-washed believers to exercise authority to establish God's rule.

Christ, the Anointed One, calls people whom He can anoint with His Spirit to do what He had done. He presses men and women into challenges and opportunities beyond their talent, training, and skill. His anointing imparts authority and strength to accomplish those tasks.

Many false ideas about the anointing circulate, especially in Pentecostal and charismatic circles. Some people equate the anointing with emotional reactions or with noise, movement, and physical activity. The power of the Holy Spirit is part of Pentecostal theology and experience, but the word *anointing* still has not been well defined.

Hebrew words for anointing are: (1) *balal*, which means to overflow with oil, (2) *dashen*, which means to be fat, symbolically healthy and satisfied, (3) *yitshar*, a noun for oil used to produce light or anointing salve, (4) *mimshach*, which means to apply or to rub with oil, especially in medicinal applications, and (5) *masah*, to apply oil by pouring or spreading. The Greek words for anointing are: (1) *chrio*, which means a special appointment to set a person apart, (2) *aleipho*, a literal rubbing of oil upon the body, and (3) *chrisma,* a metaphor for the oil itself and the unction it imparts.

True anointing is the power and influence of the Holy Spirit saturating and permeating a person. It is imperative that leaders move into the future with true Godly anointing, not with a false, questionable, or man-made anointing. The anointing of the Holy Spirit makes ministry effective. As in the Old Testament, when someone imitates, substitutes, or counterfeits the anointing the guilty person will be adjusted by God or be cut off from ministry.

The foundation of holiness

The Gospel of Luke, chapters 3 and 4, record foundations for the anointing in the life of the Lord Jesus Christ.

> Now when all the people were baptized, it came to pass that Jesus also was baptized; and while He prayed, the heaven was opened (Luke 3:21).

Jesus was baptized by His cousin, John, a prophet in the wilderness waiting for the Lamb of God to appear. As John's eyes were fixed upon Christ, the revelation came to him that he was meeting the Messiah for the first time. John baptized the Messiah in the Jordan River. At first, John would not baptize Jesus, but Jesus said, "We should fulfill all the righteousness of the Law." Jesus was baptized not because He had sin, but as an example and as an announcement of the beginning of His public ministry. John knew Jesus had no sin but he also knew he would fulfill the Law by obeying Christ's command.

John's baptism was a baptism of repentance. Repentance is the first step to cleansing lives from known and unknown sin. One of the first foundations that should be put into our life to receive the pure oil of God is a pure holiness that we must experience. Holiness has not been a major doctrine or emphasis in the twentieth century. But leaders need to embrace this doctrine and experience it, too. God cannot anoint what is unholy. A person might have charisma, but he might not have the true holy oil of God.

The dove principle

The dove symbolizes the Holy Spirit. The Holy Spirit came down upon Christ like a dove.

> And John bore witness, saying, "I saw the Spirit descending from heaven like a dove, and He remained upon Him. I did not know Him, but He who sent me to baptize with water said to me, 'Upon whom you see the Spirit descending, and remaining on Him, this is He who baptizes with the Holy Spirit'"(John 1:32,33).

The dove represents purity, innocence, meekness, and the graciousness of Christ's ministry. The dove's chief characteristic is the ability to focus. Although the dove has two eyes, it sees only one thing at a time. The Holy Spirit moves into leaders' lives to help them focus on responsibilities and avoid distractions. Peripheral things can sidetrack leaders into the activities of the flesh and the carnal mind. Keep your eye on your goal the way Jesus set His compass toward the mark He wanted to hit. His goal was the cross—the redemption of all mankind through Calvary. He would not give up His focus. Although others would prophesy and try to stop Him, He had a single passion.

The father's affirmation

When a Jewish son had come of age, his father would acknowledge the son by saying, "This now is my full, recognized son." Then the father would give his son the keys to his estate, his name, his wealth, his power and his seal that was like a checkbook or credit card to draw out all the resources needed from the father's bank account.

> And the Holy Spirit descended in bodily form like a dove upon Him, and a voice came from heaven which said, "You are My beloved Son; in You I am well pleased"(Luke 3:22).

At His baptism, Christ experienced The Jewish right of sonship. The Father confirms the Son's incarnation and proclaims this humble man is truly the Son of God. The Father affirms the Son by saying, "I am well pleased with you, I am well pleased in choosing you." This statement refers back to the moment God selected His Son to do the redemptive work on earth and the Son accepted. The Father elected the Son for the great task, and the Father showed His approval of the Son's obedience. Jesus showed His obedience through the incarnation and thirty quiet years of submission to His earthly parents waiting for the time to show Himself.

Wilderness temptations

The active ministry of Jesus began in Galilee. His temptations took place near the Jordan River. The enemy tried to derail Christ's budding ministry just as he tries to nip every good thing in its bud, to blast its fruit, to spoil it. The enemy watches for budding leaders, rising prophets, vanguard leaders who will have an effect on the body of Christ. He tries to discourage them as quickly as possible and make the work of God tedious, dangerous and seemingly impossible. He would like to bring leaders under his bondage and enslavements and to ruin their ministries. He brings seasons of conflict and trial immediately after times of gladness and spiritual victory.

New oil from God comes upon ministries that pass through temptations. The enemy always prowls around looking to tempt leaders, but wilderness testings always lead to fresh anointings. Temptations come to vanguard leaders as they came to Christ. They appeal to basic appetites. Satan knew Jesus had experienced divine abundance, and tried to arouse in Jesus the painful sense of contrast between the abundance He knew in heaven with the miserable poverty He knew at that moment.

The devil appeals to a leader's ambition to provoke him to try to win universal empires by sudden exhibitions of divine power rather than by patient manifestation of divine character. The tempter appeals to men to misuse faith and to presume upon God's power, favor and love, which the voice from heaven confirms. However, God will not suspend established natural or spiritual laws when we break them.

Satan adapts temptations to every individual based on his observations of men. He watches where the streams of men's affections run, and how their relations, callings and opportunities make them most vulnerable to sin. Accordingly, he lays traps and spreads nets. When Satan sees what is prominent in any man, he takes advantage of it and fashions suitable tests. Temptation comes to the holiest saints. It never ceases but it does change forms. As a man grows in moral strength or refinement his temptations just become more refined and harder to detect. But they remain just as deadly.

Temptation usually tries to isolate people in solitary places. This is dangerous. Unite yourself to others. Do not let the tempter separate you from the flock. Wolves separate wounded sheep for the kill. Temptation can be conquered by using the same weapons that Christ used: the Word of God, integrity of heart and prayer. Christ won the battle over temptation, and so can his undershepherds.

> No temptation has overtaken you except such as is common to man; but God is faithful, who will not allow you to be tempted beyond what you are able, but with the temptation will also make the way of escape, that you may be able to bear it (1 Cor. 10:13).

The devil chooses seasons to surprise men with temptations. After he tempted Jesus in the wilderness, he left him with an eye on the future—thinking about the next opportunity he would get. After Satan had exhausted his efforts, he departed from Jesus. Satan intended to attack Jesus again at a time that promised better success. Temptation has a way of springing up and surprising a man after he has coasted for a season on the power of past spiritual strength. The absence of temptation can lead a man to put down his shield of faith and take off his breastplate of righteousness because he senses no apparent threat. When lukewarmness has nurtured self-confidence, the devil will return. It will be a suitable season to hurl a death blow into the man's life.

The Holy Spirit baptism

The Gospel of Luke refers to the Holy Spirit's interaction with the Lord Jesus in several ways. At Jesus' baptism, the Holy Spirit *descended upon* Him (Luke 3:22). On His way to the wilderness to be tempted, He was *filled* with the Holy Spirit (Luke 4:1). Leaving the wilderness, He returned *in the power* of the Spirit (Luke 4:14). Reading the scroll of Isaiah, He said the Spirit of the Lord *"is upon* Me because He has *anointed* Me" (Luke 4:18). These could be indications of growth in the Holy Spirit as leaders who need to experience the anointing of God.

Many times the Spirit of the Lord can come upon us but not remain upon us in power. All who believe in Christ and accept the doctrine of the Holy Spirit as personal truth have been filled with the Holy Spirit. The baptism of the Holy Spirit is distinct from and subsequent to regeneration. It imparts power to believers for Christian service. The Holy Spirit baptism was not exclusively for the apostles or for their age but for all who are far off even as many as the Lord our God shall call (Acts 2:39). It is for every believer of the church age.

D.L. Moody was filled with the Holy Spirit. He wrote the following account:

> I began to cry as never before for a greater blessing from God. The hunger increased. I

really felt that I did not want to live any longer. [He had been a Christian, not only a Christian but a minister, and in charge of a mission for sometime. He was getting conversions, but still he wanted more.] I kept on crying all the time that God would fill me with the Spirit. Well, one day in the city of New York, oh what a day, I cannot describe it. I seldom refer to it. It is almost too sacred an experience to name. Paul had an experience of which he never spoke for 14 years. I can only say God revealed Himself to me. I had such an experience of His love that I had to ask Him to stay his hand.

To move in the true power of the anointing of God we need be filled with the Holy Spirit as Christ was filled. Believers need to cry out to God for the baptism of the Holy Spirit. We need the Holy Spirit not only to come upon us, but also to fill, permeate, and saturate us.

Oswald J. Smith wrote a song titled *Lord Anoint Me With Thy Spirit*.

Lord anoint me with Thy Spirit; Fill me with Thy power divine
Take away the love of sinning; Make O, make me Holy Thine.

Lord anoint me with Thy Spirit; As I wait and watch and pray
Grant a pentecost from heaven; Send O, send Him today.

I am hungry for the fullness; I am thirsting Lord for Thee

Fill, O Fill me with Thy Spirit; Holy Thine I want to be.

I am praying, waiting, trusting for the power of Pentecost
Lord anoint me with Thy Spirit; Send Him now at any cost.

Savior cleanse and make me holy; Burn out every base desire
Fill, O fill me with Thy Spirit; Lord anoint and send the fire.

Lo He comes the Holy Spirit; Now with joy my soul is thrilled
Glory, glory Hallelujah; All my heart with Love is filled

Worldly things no longer lure me; I am Thine and Thine alone
All I have is on the altar; And my heart is now Thy throne.

These words were penned by a man truly hungry for the Holy Spirit. Early Pentecostals in their tarrying meetings had a passion for the Holy Spirit. We should take another look at the doctrine of the baptism of the Holy Spirit, the way we minister it to other people, and how we as leaders have received it. Did it really come as a life-changing experience? Was it really a passion of our heart to be filled with the Holy Spirit? Charles Wesley wrote the following song titled, *Pentecostal Gifts*. It captured his passion.

Come Holy Spirit, raise our songs to reach the wonders of that day,

When with Thy fiery cloven tongues Thou didst such glorious things display.
Lord we believe to us and ours the apostolic promise given.
We wait the Pentecostal power, the Holy Ghost sent down from heaven.
Assembled here with one accord, calmly we wait the promised grace,
The purchase of our dying Lord; Come Holy Ghost, and fill this place
If everyone that asks may find; If still Thou doest on sinners fall
Come as a mighty rushing wind; Great grace be now upon us all
O, leave us not to mourn below or long for Thy return to pine
Now Lord, the comforter bestow and fix in us the guest divine.

In 1935, another song was written by Daniel Iverson, called *Spirit of the Living God*. I have used this song for many altar calls and prayer meetings. It contains a presence, a substance, a passion. These words move the heart:

> Spirit of the Living God, fall afresh on me
> Spirit of the Living God, fall afresh on me
> Melt me, mold me, fill me, use me
> Spirit of the Living God, fall afresh on me

Iverson wrote this song during the early Pentecostal movement when people stayed up all night praying for the power of the Holy Spirit. More than ever, we need the anointing that breaks yokes, heals diseases, penetrates people's hearts as the Word is preached. If we are going to receive such an anointing, we need to have the Spirit come upon us and fill us.

The greatest need today for every individual and church is to be filled with the power of the Holy Spirit. The Word of God reveals that every believer should live entirely and unceasingly under the control of the Holy Spirit. An old Puritan preacher declared that the Holy Spirit was the least known, loved and worshiped of the three persons of the Trinity.

To be filled with the Holy Spirit, is to experience Christ as He unselfishly shares with us the same power for living and serving that He experienced Himself. To be Spirit-filled is to have the Holy Spirit, the oil of heaven, poured from God's throne into our own being. According to Jack Hayford, in his book *Spirit Filled*, "To be Spirit-filled is an expansion of our capacity for worshiping, an extension of our dynamic for witnessing, and an expulsion of the adversary through our spiritual warfare."

To be Spirit-filled is to have your heart filled with God's love, your mind filled with God's truth, and your soul filled with God's life. Pentecost is the gift of power. The Spirit fills, vitalizes, and energizes with the power of God. Efficiency in service and effectiveness in witnessing are given with the fullness of the Pentecostal blessing. Power to move the world for God and to win souls is in the Spirit of God. It is not intellectual or social power. Pentecost wakes people up. It vitalizes latent powers and makes the utmost of every faculty and gift.

Pentecostalism has become a movement of worldwide importance, reckoned as a third force in Christendom alongside Catholicism and Protestantism. Therefore, Pentecostals need to live up to their name. They need to have individual pentecosts. They need to experience the power of the Holy Spirit.

Those who would have life—abounding life, victorious life, satisfying life, glorious life—must get to pentecost. The fullness of the Spirit holds an abundance of wisdom, resources and power. If this generation tried pentecost, the face of Christianity would change. Jesus' church should receive the same power He received. (See Luke 4:14,36; 5:17; 6:19; 8:46; 9:1; 10:19; 19:37; 21:26,27; 22:69; 24:49).

God is sovereign. He anoints anyone He wishes. Leaders want the anointing that abides in their ministries for a lifetime and can be passed to the next generation. They want their own personal experience of the Spirit of the Lord coming upon them, filling them, giving them power, anointing them to do particular tasks.

The Holy Spirit filled and came upon Christ's servants.

- John the Baptist "will be filled with the Spirit" (Luke 1:15).
- Elijah, "...the Spirit and power of Elijah" (Luke 1:17).
- Mary, "the Holy Spirit will come upon you and the power of the Most High..." (Luke 1:35).
- Elizabeth "was filled with the Holy Spirit" (Luke 1:41).
- Zacharias "was filled with the Holy Spirit and prophesied" (Luke 1:67).
- Disciples, "the Holy Spirit will come upon them and remain upon them"(Acts 1:5,8; 2:4,17,18).
- The first deacons were filled with the Holy Spirit (Acts 6:3).
- Saul (Paul) "be filled with the Holy Spirit" (Acts 9:17).

• Believers today, "The promise of My Father is upon you and will clothe you with the power from on high" (Luke 24:49. See Eph 5:18, Luke 11:3).

Entering the twenty-first century, vanguard leaders must be powerfully anointed by God. So many religions, ideas, philosophies, and false anointings abound in this century that we need the true power of God to break through. The church cannot remain in its traditions. It must move out as a mighty warship. Sailors a century ago discovered a vessel among icebergs in the Arctic ocean. The captain was found frozen making the last entry in his log book. The crew was discovered—some in their hammocks and some in the cabin—all frozen to death. The last date in the log book showed that for thirteen years the vessel had moved among the icebergs, a drifting sepulcher manned by a frozen crew. Some churches are in similar conditions. Leaders with the fire of God must thaw the church out. Fire symbolizes the Holy Spirit in Scripture (Acts 2:3,4). The anointing of God moves through church leaders like a fire to penetrate people's hearts in the church today.

The anointing is not a fitful emotion, a wayward impulse, or a rapture of excitement. It saturates the recipient with a calm, constant, settled conviction. The character of Christ formed in the believer becomes the evidence of true anointing.

The anointing is not mere natural ability or talent. It is not skillful oratory in the pulpit. It is not the direct result of religious knowledge or training. It is not the released power of human emotions. It is not merely the right voice tones. It is not for the personal, selfish enjoyment of the saints. Gifts, callings, and anointings are to build Christ's church.

Biblical anointing differs greatly from natural charisma. A certain singer, politician, or speaker can have charisma. He can have charm, attraction, and personality. He may have the ability to draw people to himself. He may have an aura about him. Anointing is not mere charm, attraction or personality. It is not a matter of looks, voice tones, or an ability to articulate or communicate.

Charisma does not give anyone power over the enemy or over sin. If charisma and anointing were the same, we would see greater separation from the world's views, philosophies and values. We would see real steadfastness and growth in faith in the Scriptures. We would see real miracles, real healings and real lives delivered from fear and depression. We would see true soul-winning, true burdens for the lost. We would see true sacrifice in extending the kingdom of God. We would see less exaltation of self. Charisma can do many things without God but produces pitiful results. We need a biblical anointing that will bring deliverance to the church and extend the kingdom of God in the twenty-first century.

Proofs of the anointing

Several forms of the words *anointing*, *Christ* and *antichrist* appear in 1 John 2:15-27. These words stem from the same root word, *Christos*. This portion of Scripture offers several ways to validate whether the anointing abides on a ministry.

1. He cannot love the world system. Cravings of the flesh, the lust of the eyes, and the pride of life conflict with the anointing of God.

> Do not love the world or the things in the world. If anyone loves the world, the love of the Father is not in him. For all

> that is in the world—the lust of the
> flesh, the lust of the eyes, and the pride
> of life—is not of the Father but is of the
> world. And the world is passing away,
> and the lust of it; but he who does the
> will of God abides forever (1 John 2:15-
> 17).

The cravings of the flesh expose a man's love for
the world. Flesh speaks of a self-centered outlook,
independent of God and fellow Christians. The lust
of the eyes is attraction to outward visible splendor,
greed and illegitimate sexual desire. The pride of life
describes a pretentious hypocrite who glories in
himself or in his possessions. Pride allows things or
positions to define a person's identity. Identifying
yourself by your job, salary, size of house, degrees,
experience, how many books you've written, the size
of your church, etc., is the height of pride.

2. *He commits himself to a local church and
refuses to withdraw or live independently.* The
apostle John wrote the following warning about
people with a false anointing.

> Little children, it is the last hour; and as
> you have heard that the Antichrist is
> coming, even now many antichrists
> have come, by which we know that it is
> the last hour. They went out from us,
> but they were not of us; for if they had
> been of us, they would have continued
> with us; but they went out that they
> might be made manifest, that none of
> them were of us (1 John 2:18,19).

The word *antichrist* means against-the-anointing, or false anointing. Many antichrists, or falsely anointed leaders have come into the body of Christ. Leaders with a false anointing break fellowship with the church. They leave the church with a proud independency. They feel they need nothing but knowledge. Gnostics claimed superior knowledge because they had received an exclusive, ritual anointing that gave them special knowledge, insight and revelation into deep mysteries. Ministers claiming to possess deeper truth always have a way of breaking fellowship with local churches and roaming around doing their own thing. The anointing they have received is not the same anointing that the Holy Spirit of Christ gives. It is a fake anointing, a pseudo-anointing. It is birthed by man not by God. They hurt the body when they break fellowship and choose to esteem and serve their own gift more than they serve the church. They leave the church, drop their responsibilities, and put pressure on other people as they leave just because they were confronted or crossed on an opinion or doctrine. They clearly do not have a love for the body of Christ. Christ loves His body, and when a person takes advantage of the body, they cannot be doing it in the Spirit of Christ's anointing. They move in a false, antichrist anointing.

> God sets the solitary in families; He brings out those who are bound into prosperity; But the rebellious dwell in a dry land (Ps. 68:6; see also 1 Cor. 12:12-18).

3. *He discerns between truth and error.* He opposes heresy and withstands Satanic attack.

> But you have an anointing from the
> Holy One, and you know all things. I
> have not written to you because you do
> not know the truth, but because you
> know it, and that no lie is of the truth.
> Who is a liar but he who denies that
> Jesus is the Christ? He is antichrist who
> denies the Father and the Son. Whoever
> denies the Son does not have the Father
> either; he who acknowledges the Son
> has the Father also. Therefore let that
> abide in you which you heard from the
> beginning. If what you heard from the
> beginning abides in you, you also will
> abide in the Son and in the Father. And
> this is the promise that He has promised
> us—eternal life. These things I have
> written to you concerning those who try
> to deceive you (1 John 2:20-26).

When the anointing abides, a person has a love for
the truth. The nature of truth is simple, not complex.
The Word of God already has laid out truth in
simplicity and consistency. When a person abides in
the anointing of God the basics of Christianity
become his meat and bread—his sustenance for
living. When a person abides in his own spirit or in a
false anointing, he makes truth complex, obscure and
absurd. He twists truth into unrealistic doctrines that
lead people astray and ultimately into deception. A
person who abides in the true anointing of Christ
makes truth applicable to life and keeps the simplicity
of the Gospel central to his ministry.

4. *He grows in truth with a teachable spirit and a
cultivated, open heart.* When Jesus gave his disciples
the Great Commission, He commanded them to

"make disciples . . . teaching them" (Matt. 28:19,20). In the following verse, John does not contradict Jesus' instruction.

> But the anointing which you have received from Him abides in you, and you do not need that anyone teach you; but as the same anointing teaches you concerning all things, and is true, and is not a lie, and just as it has taught you, you will abide in Him (1 John 2:27).

John does not say the anointing makes teaching and Bible knowledge superfluous. John is saying the believers do not need deceivers who teach false doctrine. The Spirit of Christ will teach the believer and help him distinguish truth from error. Jesus had instructed all who profess the Word, to teach learners. Effective preaching of the Word, faithful teaching in Sunday school or catechism class and daily reading of the Scriptures are necessary for a Christian's spiritual growth. Believers have the gift of the Holy Spirit to lead them into all truth.

A person who is stubborn, reactionary, or disobedient to the written or preached Word of God is not moving in the anointing of God. The anointing nurtures a humble spirit and helps believers receive truth humbly and receive correction easily. An anointed leader is quick to hear correction, easily penetrated. If someone points out a harmful teaching or one that leans toward heresy, this leader will correct his mistake. If a public apology is needed, this leader has no problem making it because he abides in the anointing. When a person has a false anointing, pride takes hold of his heart and he will not relinquish any position he has taken even if it is heresy. He will maintain his stance in his own stubborn way because he never can be wrong.

5. *When the anointing abides in us we abide in Christ.* True anointing does not come through specialized revelation. It comes through abiding in Christ.

> And now, little children, abide in Him, that when He appears, we may have confidence and not be ashamed before Him at His coming (1 John 2:28).

False teachers offer to Christians a new and different anointing available only to those who submit to the secrets and special teachings of the teachers. Young Christians are tempted because they want more spiritual authority and strength if there is more to be had. Christians do not need to seek out other anointings to be equipped. Abiding in Christ comes through embracing the message of the Cross. If a person is going to abide in the true pure anointing of Christ, he must abide in Christ Himself. (See 2 Cor. 1:21,22, Eph. 1:12,13, John 15:1-11.)

The word *abide* in the Greek is *meno*. It means to dwell or rest in. Jesus uses this word in the promises He makes in the deeply personal discourse: "Abide in Me and I in you" (John 15:4). The word is practical and warmly personal. It is definite and understandable. It is too common for the religious or ideological elite. It is a word for amateurs who may not know the ways of ritual or avant garde privilege, but who know how to settle into a genuine relationship and enjoy the fellowship.

Most Christians go astray in life when they lose the basic truth of abiding in Christ. Then superficial and secondary themes take over. The counterfeit starts to look appealing, not because it is good, but because the people are confused. The exhortation to abide in the true anointing is to learn Christ, live in Christ, and rest in Him.

6. He practices righteousness. A man cannot abide in the anointing of God and practice sin.

> If you know that He is righteous, you know that everyone who practices righteousness is born of Him (1 John 2:29).

> In this the children of God and the children of the devil are manifest: Whoever does not practice righteousness is not of God, nor is he who does not love his brother (1 John 3:10; see also 1 John 3:5-8).

When a known leader falls into deep and perverted sin, an alarm goes off in the hearts of believers. How is it that someone so highly esteemed, preaching and singing the Gospel, counseling, teaching and writing can fall into gross sin? When a person practices sin as a lifestyle, when his life is governed by a habit more than by Christ, he cannot abide in the anointing of God. He might have charisma; his gift may be counterfeited so well that it seems the Spirit of the Lord is speaking and leading, but it is a false anointing. The true anointing abides upon the righteous. Christ, who is the model for all leaders, led a lifestyle above reproach. He had an impeccable life filled with righteousness and holiness that God validated. Leaders who practice unrighteousness yet move in a so-called anointing actually entertain deceiving spirits.

7. He has spiritual power to destroy the works of the enemy.

> He who sins is of the devil, for the devil has sinned from the beginning. For this purpose the Son of God was manifested, that He might destroy the works of the devil (1 John 3:8).

8. He has the ability to preach the good news of hope to the hopeless.

> The Spirit of the Lord is upon Me, because He has anointed Me to preach the gospel to the poor. He has sent Me to heal the brokenhearted, to preach deliverance to the captives and recovery of sight to the blind, to set at liberty those who are oppressed (Luke 4:18).

The Gospel is good news. It is a message of victory, a word that causes joy. The Gospel is a message of hope, encouragement, deliverance and the power of Christ to change lives. It is not a message of condemnation, legalism or disappointment. The Gospel is not to beat down, intimidate and bind people with fear. The Gospel brings hope to people who face insurmountable odds. The Gospel brings hope for people who already have a lagging spirit and have lost all desire for life (Eccles. 9:4). The Gospel brings hope for people who are smoldering spiritual wicks (Matt. 12:20,21). The Gospel brings hope for those who have failed in ministry as John Mark did (Acts 13:13; Col. 4:10). The Gospel brings hope to prodigal sons (Luke 15:11-32). A person who is anointed of God will preach the true Gospel with the

Spirit of Christ. When the anointing abides, love and compassion heal crushed hearts and shattered emotions.

9. *He has a spiritual passion and zeal for the house of the Lord.*

> Then His disciples remembered that it was written, "Zeal for Your house has eaten Me up" (John 2:17).

One translation reads: "Concern for God's house will be my undoing. The jealousy for the honor of Thine house shall burn in me" (see also Ps. 69:9).

> For He put on righteousness as a breastplate, and a helmet of salvation on His head; He put on the garments of vengeance for clothing, and was clad with zeal as a cloak (Isa. 59:17).

The Lord Jesus Christ was clothed with zeal. His zeal focused on the house of God. The word *zeal* means to burn with strong feelings. Zeal is hot, not lukewarm. It means to be passionate with a cause. It is a motivating force and is warlike. Zeal could also be called passion, enthusiasm, or fervency. A zealous person concerns himself with something so much that he takes it up as a goal and strives after it energetically. Zeal is passionate intensity. It is an eager desire to accomplish or attain something. The anointing of God produces zeal, not lukewarmness.

The carnal mind prefers lukewarmness. It lets circumstances dictate attitudes. It results in spiritual paralysis, profession without substance, and mediocrity in service. Lukewarmness abides in indifferent, cold hearts, complacency, idleness, reluctant sacrificing, and burdenless, passionless, neglect of spiritual things (Rev. 3:16).

The anointing of the Lord encourages zeal toward God's house. When a person abides in a Christlike anointing, he will love Christ's church more than anything else. Loving God's purpose encompasses loving God, His Word, and His people including our families. This is loving God's house.

The focus of Christ's zeal is God's house. His fervency concentrated on God's purpose, His church. We are also anointed with the same anointing, and the zeal for God's house should eat us up as well. For further study, refer to the following:

- A zeal of loving God's house. Ps. 28:6, Eph. 5:25, 2 Cor. 4:7-12, 6:1-10, Ps. 132:13-18.
- A zeal in going to God's house. Ps. 42:4, 122:1; Heb. 10:25; Ps. 127:4, 55:14; Isa. 2:1-4.
- A zeal in building—not tearing down— God's house. Prov. 14:1; Ps. 127:1; 2 Cor. 11:1-4; 1 Cor. 14:12; Prov. 24:3.
- A zeal in finding satisfaction in God's house. Ps. 36:8, 87:7; Ezek. 47:3-6; Ps. 42:1-2, 63:1-5; Col. 3:1-3.
- A zeal in being planted and rooted in God's house. Ps. 92:10,13; Ps. 84:10; Eph. 2:20-22; Ps. 1:1-3.
- Zeal in keeping unity in the house. Ps. 133:1-3; Acts 1:14, 2:1, 2:46, 4:32, 5:12.

The zeal of the Lord shows in the enthusiasm of the servant of God ministering in the house of the Lord. Any obstacle or stronghold in his life that stops the flow of zeal should be torn down. Complacency, carnality and cooling off spiritually can be mistaken for balance. Negative thinking and speaking kills zeal. Self-imposed isolation kills zeal. Zeal weakens under an independent spirit and lack of commitment to the church of Jesus Christ. Refusal to sacrifice—even from fear—obstructs the anointing of God.

10. *He lives a lifestyle of unselfish and sacrificial serving.* True anointing cultivates a servant's heart in a leader. Christ contrasts His kingdom with the gentile kingdom. Christ's idea of greatness is inverted, upside down. The pyramid rests on the apex. The great man sits below the lesser man, not above him. Greatness in the kingdom is measured by sacrificial service. Whether the servant is rewarded and exalted or not makes no difference. Christ served without position and gave without asking for a fee.

> Then James and John, the sons of Zebedee, came to Him, saying, "Teacher, we want You to do for us whatever we ask" (Mark 10:35).

Today believers still bring the same request to Jesus that James and John brought. When the human heart lives for itself, its prayers emphasize its own needs, dreams, and desires (Mark 10:36-45). Jesus points out how authority becomes a stumbling block for many in leadership positions. Rulers over the Gentiles lord it over their subjects, and men instinctively follow the Gentile spirit. Gentile rulers maintain their high positions to be considered great in the eyes of the world. Unredeemed man has the Gentile spirit, unable to serve unselfishly. He protects his ego, position and image. He finds security and fulfillment in his position, not in serving. The thought of serving others makes him feel more insignificant, and an insecure man cannot cope with that.

Anyone who does not serve or sacrifice cannot be anointed with Christ's anointing. The world's mentality seeks two things: to be great and first. Everyone has to deal with these desires. The way of the world is to fight to become first in line. The way of the kingdom of God is to become a servant, a willing slave serving others, putting others first.

To achieve true greatness, men must first disregard their own ideas of what it is.

A servant serves people to please God. He remains humble before others and stands by his commitment to help them, willing to pay the price of personal suffering. He draws strength from God alone who promises to uphold the humble (Isa. 42:1-9, 49:1-16, 50:4-10, 52:13).

Serving focuses attention on meeting needs of others. The natural man thinks this type of service is shameful. To subject his will and surrender his time and effort for the sake of others is intensely distasteful—even humiliating. Unregenerate man thinks he should achieve his natural potential for himself. Jesus transforms His followers' value systems. In Christ, serving is the highway to greatness. A person's full potential is reached by giving, not grasping. Christ surrendered His life for our sake, demonstrating the ultimate servanthood. Greatness is not a goal to be sought after. It is a by-product of learning how to serve. To achieve true greatness, men must first disregard their own ideas of what it is.

A servant spirit is not defensive when confronted. It has nothing to prove and nothing to lose. A servant has an authentic desire to help others, being sensitive and spontaneous. Servanthood means:

•Leading by relationship, not by coercion. Servants don't demand obedience or submission. They demonstrate consistent concern for their followers.

•Leading by support not control. They give from themselves. They do not take for themselves.

•Leading by developing other's potential.

•Leading by motivating, not manipulating.

•Leading from a love that never domineers.

•Never seeking position, but seeking kingdom productivity.

•Having a life full of crosses, towels and basins.

•Leading out of brokenness not bossiness.

•Being abused, insulted, and never appreciated to the full depth of their worth.

•Leading by trusting people not fearing people. Fearful leaders likely will either dictate their wishes to people or avoid others completely.

> Most assuredly, I say to you, unless a grain of wheat falls into the ground and dies, it remains alone; but if it dies, it produces much grain (John 12:24).

Man's way to greatness focuses on his own power, freedoms and gain. The carnal man desires immediate fulfillment and yearns for the praise of other men. God's way to greatness is through submission and accepting responsibility. He insures lasting achievement rather than immediate fulfillment. Leaders with true anointing yearn for God's approval rather than approval of men.

> Let nothing be done through selfish ambition or conceit, but in lowliness of mind let each esteem others better than himself (Phil 2:3).

The greatest obstacle to becoming a servant is self-centered living. A me-first attitude and an age of gross selfishness fights a running battle against the servant spirit. Looking after one's own interests is the way of life in the world. Advice such as "Feather your own nest" and "Take care of number one" rules the day. Advertisers openly target self-interest with mottos like: Have it your way; Do yourself a favor; You owe it to yourself; You deserve a break today; Please yourself.

The Greeks said, 'Be wise; know yourself.' The Romans said, 'Be strong; discipline yourself.' The Epicureans said, 'Be sensuous; enjoy yourself.' Education today says, 'Be resourceful; expand yourself.' Psychology says, 'Be confident; assert yourself.' Materialism says, 'Be satisfied; please yourself.' Humanism says, 'Be capable; believe in yourself.' But Jesus says, "Be a servant; give yourself; deny yourself; don't live for yourself; give your life away."

> For all seek their own, not the things which are of Christ Jesus (Phil 2:21).

> Then Jesus said to His disciples, "If anyone desires to come after Me, let him deny himself, and take up his cross, and follow Me" (Matt. 16:24).

The words of the Gospel direct God's servants to take up their crosses. Bearing the cross is simply the death of your own will in preference to God's will, the death of your self to God's purpose. If you are going to abide in the anointing of Christ, you need to abide in these words.

For you died, and your life is hidden with Christ in God (Col. 3:3).

Or do you not know that your body is the temple of the Holy Spirit who is in you, whom you have from God, and you are not your own? For you were bought at a price; therefore glorify God in your body and in your spirit, which are God's (1 Cor. 6:19,20).

This reminds me of a saying I once heard:

I would like to buy $3 worth of God please. Not enough to expose my soul or disturb my sleep, but just enough to equal a cup of warm milk or a snooze in the sunshine. I don't want enough of Him to make me love a black man or pick beets with a migrant. I want ecstasy, not transformation. I want the warmth of the womb, not a new birth. I want a pound of the eternal in a paper sack. I would like to buy $3 worth of God please.

Lukewarm people like to find the easiest, cheapest way that requires the least effort to do any job. They look for a way that costs as little as possible and would like to get it for free. Sacrifice is God's way, not man's way. Sacrifice means to surrender or suffer, to give up something for the sake of something else or someone else. A leader sacrifices his ideas and plans on the altar of God to get God's ideas. A leader sacrifices his desires so he can live by God's desires. A leader sacrifices his image so that he can take on the image of Christ, who "did not come to be served, but to serve" (Matt. 20:28). A leader sacrifices his will, time, money and resources to become a recipient of divine resources. King David gave up money to buy a field to build an altar. He said he would not offer a sacrifice on ground that cost him nothing. "I will surely buy it from you for a price; nor will I offer burnt offerings to the Lord my God with that which costs me nothing" (2 Sam. 24:24).

A.E. Whitham, the sensitive Methodist preacher from an earlier era, mused in one of his books on the possibility of a museum in heaven exhibiting tokens of spiritual leadership. Moses' staff and Aaron's rod (the one that budded) surely would be in such a museum. Alongside these might be the ink pot Luther threw at the devil, John Wesley's saddle and stirrups, praying Hyde's knee patches, and Billy Graham's airline tickets. But two items would surely not be there yet; the servant's towel and basin are still being used on the earth today.

The anointing of God abides upon those who abide in Christ and allow serving and sacrifice to be their way of life. God does not anoint a selfish, egotistic, sin-ridden leader. Let all true leaders aspire toward a higher goal. Let them hunger for the pure anointing oil of God.

▼

11

The Motivation: Divine Blessing

To strive for greatness is not sinful. God put a desire for greatness in people, and the yearning will always exist. God wants people to enjoy success and has called people to achieve and accomplish great things in their lifetimes, but the vast majority stumble trying to achieve it. Few people know the price they would have to pay for greatness or the procedure God established to achieve it.

True greatness is measured in Godly character, wisdom, self-control, patience, love, service, and purity. Temporal success is deceitful. We have to discard the notion that wealth, houses, jobs, cars, clothes or good looks are signs of greatness. In ministry, the size of church buildings and congregations are all temporal and do not necessarily testify to great leadership. The desire to achieve something lasting, authentic, and godly motivates all leaders. Achieving it without using carnal, ungodly means is the goal.

No one can understand the secret of success or appropriate God's abundance until God reveals it to him. True success comes by revelation—

understanding the godly principles and secrets that bring godly success.

He favors and promotes leaders to places where they can achieve great things for His kingdom.

> "For my thoughts are not your thoughts, nor are your ways my ways," says the Lord. "For as the heavens are higher than the earth, so are my ways higher than your ways, and my thoughts than your thoughts. For as the rain comes down, and the snow from heaven, and do not return there, but water the earth, and make it bring forth and bud, that it may give seed to the sower, and bread to the eater" (Isa. 55:8-10).

God's thoughts and ways are different than ours. They are higher than ours. He favors and promotes leaders to places where they can achieve great things for His kingdom. Biblical success is defined using the following Bible words:

Prosperity. The Hebrew word means to succeed, become profitable, thrive, flourish, finish well, accomplish satisfactorily what is intended, to be successful in everything you put your hand to, to be raised to great honors and receive promotion (Ps. 118:25). The Greek word means to grant a prosperous and expedient journey, to lead a direct, easy way, to grant a successful issue (Rom. 1:10; Matt. 25:21; Eph. 6:3). The dictionary meaning for prosper is achievement, having a favorable result, getting wealth, fame and position.

Abound, Abundant and Abundance. The word abound in Hebrew means to have enough, sufficient, with surplus, to enlarge what you have (Prov. 28:20; Gen. 45:28). The Greek word means to exceed a fixed number and measure, to have more than you need, to receive something overflowing, to increase, without lack, to have access (Luke 15:17,29-31; John 6:12,13.). Abundance is having all you need, plus enough to give others. It is the opposite of living in want, lack and frustration. Abundance lifts a person above the level of his need, enabling him to reach out to others (John 10:10; 2 Cor. 8:2,14; Gen. 1:20; Ps. 36:8; 132:15).

These words link success and achievement. To prosper or live abundantly is to succeed and receive promotion in your life and ministry. God grants His leaders success. He puts His favor and honor upon them and promotes them to high levels and great honors. It does not just involve money or things. Godly success for church leaders is the favor, blessing and hand of God on their lives. He promotes us to allow us to achieve great things for His Namesake.

Psalm 127 holds truths concerning the blessing of the Lord and Godly success. The chapter clearly emphasizes the need for divine blessing on all undertakings. This section holds special meaning for ministers helping to build God's house, the church, the people of the Lord.

> Unless the Lord builds the house, they labor in vain who build it; Unless the Lord guards the city, the watchman stays awake in vain (Ps. 127:1).

Without the true blessing of the Lord upon their lives, builders of houses, cities, fortunes, empires and churches labor in vain. But under divine favor they find sweet and restful success. Finding success that brings rest and peace is the point of this chapter, and it should be the goal of our ministry. The Psalm clearly points out man's need for a genuine blessing of the Almighty. Charles Spurgeon calls this Psalm the builders psalm, or the Psalm directed against self-reliance. Commenting on this passage, a German commentary states, "Everything depends on God's blessing. This Psalm can represent our life, our family, our church or our ministries. All of us are building something." Solomon wrote this Psalm. He built the great Temple of the Lord and built a large family as well.

Everyone builds a house in this life. Some build on the rock that will be blessed. Others build on the sand that will be destroyed. One is going up and one is going down. Both builders do the same thing. Both look successful at first, but storms will expose what the builders have done. Storms also will expose what leaders have truly done with their ministries and lives (See Matt. 16:18; 1 Kings 3:5-15; 1 Chron. 28:20; 2 Chron. 2:1,3,5,9; 3:1; 5:1; 5:13; 6:40,42; 7:11-16; Heb. 3:1-6; 1 Cor. 3:5-15).

> Therefore whoever hears these sayings of Mine, and does them, I will liken him to a wise man who built his house on the rock: and the rain descended, the floods came, and the winds blew and beat on that house; and it did not fall, for it was founded on the rock. Now everyone who hears these sayings of Mine, and does not do them, will be like a foolish man who built his house on the sand: and the rain descended, the

floods came, and the winds blew and
beat on that house; and it fell. And great
was its fall (Matt. 7:24-27).

Notice three words from Psalm 127: house, city
and family. The *house* built by a person can
symbolize his or her life, family or ministry. What he
builds with the materials God gives him is his house.
It is the work of his lifetime.

The *city* represents what a person rules over. The
level of authority God trusts him with is his city.
Authority given by God is a sign of God's approval as
He authenticates a leader's ministry and pours out
His blessing. No man can honor himself. Only God
can put this honor on a ministry that is recognized by
the people and will be blessed by God Himself.

Family represents what a person reproduces. It is
his ministry reflected in other people's lives. The
unmistakable spiritual offspring of a leader is his
family. Solomon built a house, a family and a city. He
was beloved of Jehovah. But Solomon failed with his
family, his house was destroyed and his city was
captured by the enemy and annihilated.

What you build with your gift, you may destroy
with your character.

Psalm 127 should catch the attention of all leaders
who seek the blessing of God and sweet, restful
success. Every house is built by someone and every
house will be tested by storms. The house is spiritual.
The natural-minded man does not understand and
never will because it is a spiritual revelation.

What you build with your gift, you may destroy
with your character. What you build with your

charisma, may be destroyed by your lack of integrity. God wants HIS church built—churches that are spiritual and biblical and that challenge people with true Christianity.

Every vanguard leader wants to build something that outlives him and that lasts until the second coming of Jesus Christ. God doesn't guard what He doesn't build. A leader can be involved in the work of ministry yet not be building what God wants built. If he is not building God's way with God's materials then God is not committed to protect what he builds. The work of a lifetime can be destroyed within a few minutes or a few weeks. After your lifetime the work does not continue because it was carried by your own talents and energy, not by the divine energy of God.

An earthquake in Mexico several years ago revealed the faulty foundations in the city. In forty seconds parts of the city were completely destroyed. San Francisco was destroyed in sixteen seconds by an earthquake. Building without the proper foundation and materials, is like flirting with sudden destruction.

God doesn't guard what He doesn't build.

Building without blessing

A few years ago in a time of prayer, the Holy Spirit quickened a thought to my mind. *"I built it, but was it worth building?"* The thought would not leave me for days and weeks. It became almost an overbearing, haunting thought: "I built it, but was it worth building?" We had pioneered a church and ran building programs to erect sanctuaries to house the people and the vision. After we finished our second building program and the church had grown to a large number, I felt we had success. But this haunting thought kept coming back: "I built it, but was it worth building?" This thought actually led me to Psalm 127. I began to pray and consider what it truly means. I wanted success. I wanted to achieve. I was not dishonest with myself or with the church. I had stated it several times to the church. I had stated it to God in prayer and fasting. I felt my motive was pure and I wanted to achieve for the Name of the Lord and for the kingdom of God. I felt that all of the energy put into building the church and building the kingdom was truly a pure divine energy that God was using me to do. But now this thought was weighing on my mind and spirit daily: "I built it, but was it worth building?" Anyone can ask that about his own life, career, church, marriage, or ministry.

Churches can build without the blessing of the Lord. That is why the first verse of Psalm 127 begins with *unless*. Unless. The word stands as a warning. It causes the reader to stop and ponder. *Unless* in the Hebrew language is called a signal word. It signals that something may not happen if a condition is not met. "*Unless* the Lord builds the house, they labor in vain who build it. *Unless* the Lord guards the city, the watchman stays awake in vain." It does not say that unless the Lord consents and is willing that the house be built and the city be kept; but *unless* the Lord build—*unless* the Lord keep; not only His consent, but His working with us is required. God doesn't guard what God doesn't build.

> Not by might, nor by power but by the
> Spirit saith the Lord (Zech. 4:7).

The word *unless* allows readers to stop, ponder and pray. Unless the Lord initiates, governs, and carries through the ministry we have, we will labor in vain. Our work will be futile, empty and destroyed. It will not live long.

•*The Tower of Babel.* The Tower of Babel was built without the blessing of the Lord (Gen. 11:1-8). The following passage sounds a divine warning about building without God's blessing.

> And they said, "Come, *let us* build *ourselves* a city, and a tower whose top is in the heavens; *let us* make a name for *ourselves*, lest we be scattered abroad over the face of the whole earth." But the *Lord came down* to see the city and the tower which the sons of men had built. The Lord said, "Indeed the people are one and they all have one language, and this is what they begin to do; now *nothing* that they *propose* to do will be withheld from them. "Come let Us go down and there confuse their language, that they may not understand one another's speech." So the Lord *scattered* them abroad from there over the face of all the earth, and they *ceased* building the city (Gen. 11:4-8; emphasis added).

A number of phrases in the Tower of Babel account run parallel to Psalm 127. "Come let us build ourselves a city." The word *ourselves* stands out as a negative motivation. They wanted to build something reaching into heaven, but they wanted their own names on it. They wanted to build a city, but they had no idea the Lord would come down and inspect what they were building. They realized that with the momentum and unity they had, nothing would be impossible for them. Even though man felt it was possible, man felt that their goal was godly and should be attained. Verse 8 simply says "the Lord scattered . . . and they stopped."

How many churches do you know the Lord has scattered and stopped? We want church growth and multiplied church planting all over the globe, but how many times does the Lord need to come down and scatter what we have put together and stop what we are trying to build? Many church programs, church splits, and churches themselves have been scattered and stopped, not because man did it but because God Himself did it.

Lessons from Babel

Five points stand out in the Genesis passage on the Tower of Babel:

1. *The reach of human ambition.* In all of us is a carnal reach for human ambition to achieve for ourselves, to make a name for ourselves. "Let us build for ourselves... let us make a name for ourselves" (v. 4).

2. *The pride of religious reputation.* "Make a name for ourselves" also speaks of ownership. It speaks of taking the glory and taking the praise from the lips of man and putting it upon ourselves. The pride of religious reputation is dangerous. We can build our own church structures, our denominations, or our worldwide ministries with pride as a motivation. We have a name. Our name is stamped on everything that goes out all over the world. If we are not careful, our own name will be greater than the name of the Lord.

3. *The surprise of divine interruption.* "God came down." These words should weigh heavily on our minds as we plan any activity in the kingdom of God.

The Lord inspects, the Lord comes down, the Lord gets involved. God surprised them by coming into their building program. God surprised them by interrupting what they thought was impossible to stop.

4. *The awesome reality of reaching goals and plans never ordained of God.* Verse 6 says, "Nothing that they propose to do will be withheld from them." How many times do we as religious leaders go to our boards and our planning committees to plan great dreams and visions that never were initiated by the Holy Spirit—never ordained by God? With all the modern technology, fund-raising techniques, and good ideas we get from books and magazines we can build for ourselves and make for ourselves a ministry, a church or a worldwide activity. But we need to consider the awesome reality of reaching goals and plans never ordained of God. We could pour our life energy into something for years that God never said to do. How wonderful it is to finish your life and hear the words, "Well done thou good and faithful servant." How haunting it is to think that when you stand before the great throne of God that the Lord would only say to you "Well? Well? Well, why did you do that? Well, what did you do? Who told you to do that? Why did you use so many people's lives and energies and monies? I never initiated it; I never ordained it; and yet you gave your whole life to it."

5. *The fragmentation of divine origin.* The Lord scatters and stops. The Lord actually sends confusion into the work so the people could not continue on. He fragments a ministry if it hurts His people. God will not let a leader or a work continue for years destroying thousands of lives.

The Jeroboam Warning

The life of Jeroboam sounds another warning (1 Kings 12:25-33). The books of Kings and Chronicles explain how Jeroboam also tried to build without the blessing of the Lord. Immediately following Solomon's death, the disruption of the kingdom took place. And from this point on the fortunes of the two kingdoms and the two lines of kings become history.

Rehoboam who took the throne from Solomon dealt a grievous blow to the people because of his own stupidity. In 1 Kings, chapter twelve, the people of Israel requested, "Your father made our yoke heavy; now therefore lighten the burdensome service of your father, and his heavy yoke which he put upon us, and we will serve you." Rehoboam's response lacked wisdom and destroyed his own leadership. He came back to the people saying he would rule more severely than his father. His senseless threat to outdo his father's severity toward his subjects was the last straw. The ten tribes that had been loyal renounced their allegiance to the house of David and took Jeroboam as their king.

So Jeroboam devised a plan to take the heart of the people away from Jerusalem and woo them to Shechem.

Jeroboam was as shrewd and unscrupulous as he was energetic and forceful. He knew that although he had fortified Shechem to be his capital, Jerusalem still would be regarded as the united center of all the tribes unless he took drastic steps. He realized people worshiped at the Temple in Jerusalem where the ark of the covenant and other sacred symbols of Israel's religion resided. "If the people continue going to

Jerusalem to religious festivals," Jeroboam thought to himself, "sooner or later it will prove fatal to my throne. The people's loyalties will be where they worship." So Jeroboam devised a plan to take the heart of the people away from Jerusalem and woo them to Shechem. He built a false religious system around the worship of golden calves at Bethel and Dan. He built shrines, instituted religious festivals and appointed priests who were not Levites.

Lessons from Jeroboam

Six things to consider stand out in 1 Kings, chapters 13 and 14.

1. Jeroboam had wrong motivation. Fear of failure motivated him. He feared the people would turn their hearts back to Rehoboam if they went to Jerusalem to worship. He built his vision out of fear, competition and greed. A leader who begins to build a church or ministry adding certain things so that people will not go to another church or ministry is building based on fear, competition, and greed. It will lead his own ministry into confusion. Building things out of competition will destroy a man's ministry.

> If these people go up to offer sacrifices in the house of the LORD at Jerusalem, then the heart of this people will turn back to their lord, Rehoboam king of Judah, and they will kill me and go back to Rehoboam king of Judah (1 Kings 12:27).

2. Jeroboam was self-initiated. We must be careful as we read materials and hear testimonies that we do not devise a plan or strategy in our hearts that never was blessed by God, ordained by God, or given to us by the Holy Spirit, especially when competition, fear, or greed are already at work in our heart.

> And Jeroboam said in his heart, "Now the kingdom may return to the house of David" (1 Kings 12:26).

> So he made offerings on the altar which he had made at Bethel on the fifteenth day of the eighth month, in the month which *he had devised in his own heart*. And he ordained a feast for the children of Israel, and offered sacrifices on the altar and burned incense (1 Kings 12:33, emphasis added).

Jeroboam's offerings, feasts, and sacrifices were not ordained or initiated by the Holy Spirit. His own mind and heart devised them.

3. *Jeroboam was a master counterfeiter.* He took the semblance of truth and perverted it to make it look real. But it lacked Godly substance. It lacked the blessing of the Lord.

> He made shrines on the high places, and made priests from every class of people, who were not of the sons of Levi. Jeroboam ordained a feast on the fifteenth day of the eighth month, like the feast that was in Judah, and offered sacrifices on the altar. So he did at Bethel, sacrificing to the calves that he had made. And at Bethel he installed the priests of the high places which he had made (1 Kings 12:31-32).

Jeroboam understood that praise, worship, and sacrifice brought the blessing of God upon a nation. However, Jeroboam did not covenant with God, nor was he directed by God to offer these kinds of sacrifices, nor did the Lord ever tell him to build an altar. He used priests who were never ordained of God, blessed of God, or birthed in the ministry to offer the sacrifices. He understood a truth but went about it the wrong way.

Today many books and materials have been written on praise, worship, prayer and church growth. We can begin to counterfeit a truth. We can begin to act out something never birthed by the Holy Spirit. We can have the sound of praise and not have praise. We can have the noise of prayer and not have prayer. We can have the structure of eldership and not have leaders. Many areas in the body of Christ can be counterfeited. Truth must be birthed in the heart of the people for God, not for our own goals or visions or dreams.

When leaders use principles that seem to work for a while and receive temporary blessing, they feel they have received the authentication of God upon their dream, vision and work.

---

4. *Judgment did not come immediately.* The judgment of God upon Jeroboam's vision, his house and his leadership was delayed. But it did come. When leaders use principles that seem to work for a while and receive temporary blessing, they feel they have received the authentication of God upon their dream, vision and work. When God delays consequences and judgment, people often think—mistakenly—God is blessing. Look at the

longevity of the blessing of the Lord. Has God's hand been on it for a long time? Longevity proves the authentic blessing of the Lord, not just a week or a year or even a few years.

> therefore behold! I will bring disaster on the house of Jeroboam, and will cut off from Jeroboam every male in Israel, bond and free; and I will take away the remnant of the house of Jeroboam, as one takes away refuse until it is all gone (1 Kings 14:10).

5. Jeroboam had superficial repentance. When exposed, Jeroboam worried only about his reputation and his hand, which withered as he reached out to arrest the prophet pronouncing God's judgment (1 Kings 13:4). Jeroboam did not repent for building a false altar or for establishing a feast on the wrong month or for profaning the priesthood by bringing in non-priests to offer sacrifices. His only concern was about his own physical hand until he asked the prophet to "please pray and ask God to heal my hand." The prophet did pray for his hand but rebuked him for such folly. "Why would you be concerned about your hand when you are going to lose your house, your temple, your city and your own life and all your family will be judged with you."

6. The harsh judgment of God upon Jeroboam. God judges what is not built at His direction or initiated by His Holy Spirit. 1 Kings, chapter fourteen, describes the judgment on Jeroboam's house, city, and family.

> I will bring disaster on the house of Jeroboam, and will cut off...every male... cut off the house of Jeroboam... the Lord

> will strike... He will uproot...and will
> scatter...and He will give up Israel (1
> Kings 14:10,14,15,16).

Much can be done by a man. He can labor and
watch, but without the Lord he can accomplish
nothing, and his wakefulness has not warded off evil.
Without God, human labor is possible but fruitless.
The Lord knows with whom He will build and with
whom He will not build. Vanguard leaders learn
what to avoid from biblical models like Babel and
Jeroboam. They take the judgments of God seriously
and know at any point that God can stop and scatter a
work that He never ordained.

Laboring in vain
Builders can labor in vain, according to Psalm
127:1. If the Lord does not help the builders, then
building serves no useful purpose. Success depends
on more than hard work. It depends upon the
unseen but all-important blessing of God. God
Himself must be the builder. If God is not the builder,
men labor in vain, with wearisome toil, fruitlessly,
aimlessly, and without any divine purpose, eating
the bread of sorrow (1 Cor. 3:7,8).
Laboring in vain means to work:
- long and continuously with great effort, without
  a thought for the need of divine blessing.
- in projects, tasks, and responsibilities, with a
  measure of human success but leading nowhere.
  The house, or the city may survive, but were they
  worth building? Were they worth all your life
  and toil? Did you end up with kingdom fruit,
  kingdom satisfaction, and kingdom affirmation?
  Did you ever hear the words, "Well done, thou
  good and faithful servant"?

- hard but seeing no productivity. Increasing your labor and working harder doesn't change end results. It's only a new enslavement. I call this 'hamster philosophy.'
- without deep spiritual and moral satisfaction.
- with wrong attitudes, placing undue confidence in your own working and watching.
- busily on important issues as if God were not involved. The way you busy yourself, you leave no more room for God than if He were asleep in heaven, uninterested in your affairs.

God gives success to those who trust Him, abide by His principles, and do not try to manipulate those principles.

Success without tension

Psalm 127:1 contrasts vain labor with blessed enrichment. Some builders enjoy success without strain. They sleep at night with trust instead of tension. It's the sleep of contentment without craving. In the natural, when a person sleeps, his brain becomes inactive. Consciousness and volition are idle. The expending of energy by the body is curtailed. The system takes time to build itself up after the wear and tear of the day. This could signify the blessing of God, the blessing God gives, or the time and way in which He gives it. What a contrast between fruitless toil and effortless enrichment. What a contrast between two attitudes toward God: dependence or independence. The mention of sleep in this passage implies a contrast between fruitless strain of self-effort and the relaxed, fruitfulness of the Godly. We enter into a proper spiritual sleep when we cast ourselves upon God's way with trust and confidence that He will honor His Word and His principles. We abandon our selfish methods energized by the flesh. It's not a sleep of passive fatalism but true rest as we do our part, our work, and leave the results to God. God gives success at a time when man's participation is ruled out, so to speak. Therefore, it is apparent the success is purely a divine gift. Solomon was asleep when the Lord appeared to him in a dream (1 Kings 3:5-15). He dreamed. God spoke; and God gave him success. God gives success to those who trust Him, abide by His principles, and do not try to manipulate those principles. They trust God to give what is right, and they leave the timing and the measure of success entirely in His hands.

> And He said, "The kingdom of God is as if a man should scatter seed on the ground, and should sleep by night and rise by day, and the seed should sprout and grow, he himself does not know how. For the earth yields crops by itself: first the blade, then the head, after that the full grain in the head. But when the grain ripens, immediately he puts in the sickle, because the harvest has come"(Mark 4:26-29).

Jesus connected sleep with success. He said, the man does not know how the seed sprouts and grows. It's a mystery. God intertwines His blessing with the sprouting seed apart from the methods or energies of man. When Adam slept, God was able to bring forth Eve. When we are asleep, God gives us not only our food and houses but also better things. Some of my sweetest friendships that make my life better and brighter came when I was not looking for them. I didn't plan them, somehow they just dropped into my life. When man gives himself to be guided by God, the best things come to him.

In Matthew 6:25-34, Jesus speaks on the lesson of trust versus anxiety. Do not be anxious for your ministry. Do not be anxious about church finance. Do not be anxious about church growth.

> But seek first the kingdom of God and
> His righteousness, and all these things
> shall be added to you (Matt. 6:33).

Leaders desire happiness and stability in their churches and ministries, but are unable to secure it by their own endeavors. Everyone is dissatisfied with their lot to some extent. We see trees as being not tall enough, the grass not green enough. The sleep of faith rests in God's ability to satisfy us in whatever state we find ourselves, so we are content. God's truth draws us away from excessive labors and anxious cares and excites godliness and faith in us. Therefore, those who fear Him receive the blessing of God because He gives prosperity with even lighter labors. It is man's duty to put a limit to his labors and cares.

> When a man's ways please the LORD,
> he makes even his enemies to be at
> peace with him (Prov. 16:7).

Strain and tension in the ministry brings a higher sense of inadequacy and a haunting consciousness of the lack of spiritual resources. Continually comparing yourself with others opens the door to condemnation. Anxiety grows. Worrying over things that are beyond your power to control paralyzes the nerve of your spiritual endeavors and sets up dangerous inner tensions. Fear paralyzes the spirit of faith. Then ministries find themselves driven by fear of new responsibilities, fear of doing the wrong thing, fear of failure, fear of man, and fear of the past.

A wrong perspective toward others will grow—bad attitudes, which strain relationships with other leaders and brothers and sisters in the body of Christ. Spiritual depression sets in and you end up with what I call *promotion confusion*. Promotion comes from the Lord. It is not what we do that really brings the blessing of the Lord. This does not negate obedience, faith, good conduct and Godly character. But with all those we still need the divine hand and blessing on our lives.

Understanding the word *blessing*

> He shall receive blessing from the LORD, And righteousness from the God of his salvation (Ps. 24:5; also see Ps. 3:8; 67:1; Gen. 49:25).

> The blessing of the LORD makes one rich, and He adds no sorrow with it (Prov. 10:22).

> And all these blessings shall come upon you and overtake you, because you obey the voice of the LORD your God (Deut. 28:2).

> Blessed be the God and Father of our Lord Jesus Christ, who has blessed us with every spiritual blessing in the heavenly places in Christ (Eph. 1:3).

The word *bless* in Hebrew means to endue with power for success, prosperity, longevity, provision, protection, glory, honor, and favor. Every leader on the face of the earth would joyfully embrace such a promise upon their own life, family, ministry and church. Old Testament believers saw God blessing people who entered a uniquely defined relationship with Him. People entered this relationship through covenant and maintained it through obedience.

Attaining and maintaining blessing

Attaining and maintaining the blessing of the Lord is the main point of interest for leaders. Abundant life, enriched by God, is found in the Lord's covenant of grace. Practical experience teaches us to obey His Word and walk in His ways.

1.*Blessing is attained in grace origins and grace emphasis.* It's all in Christ, of Christ, and by Christ. A ministry, a church or a future must be built in Christ. Our emphasis to attain the blessings of God is found in our position in the covenant of grace, the covenant that brings us together with Christ in forgiveness and redemption. The cross and the blessings that are found in Christ are our emphasis (Eph 1:3).

> that the blessing of Abraham might come upon the Gentiles in Christ Jesus, that we might receive the promise of the Spirit through faith (Gal 3:14).

2.*Blessing is attained through integrity, transparency and a pure focus.* Character is the foundation for the blessing of the Lord. God honors and favors integrity in the lives of leaders.

> He who has clean hands and a pure
> heart, Who has not lifted up his soul to
> an idol, Nor sworn deceitfully. He shall
> receive blessing from the LORD, And
> righteousness from the God of his
> salvation (Ps. 24:4,5).

> Blessed are the undefiled in the way,
> Who walk in the law of the LORD!
> Blessed are those who keep His
> testimonies, Who seek Him with the
> whole heart! (Ps. 119:1,2).

3.*Blessing is attained by rejecting human power and wisdom as the source of success.* The apostle Paul succeeded in his ministry and was blessed because he did not depend on his own human power or wisdom. He said, "I came not with great oratory. I did not come to you with superiority of speech, not persuasive words" (1 Cor. 2:1-3). Paul did not plant the church in Corinth with plans and strategies he learned through the flesh or his carnal mind. He simply came to their city with fear, trembling and weakness. In his weakness, the demonstration of the Holy Spirit came forth.

4.*Blessing is attained when we cultivate a healthy fear of God.* The fear of the Lord is the beginning of His blessing. Living in the fear of the Lord is the continual awareness that you are in the presence of a holy, just and almighty God. You are conscious that every thought, word, and action is open before Him and being judged by Him (Ps. 128:1).

> Praise the LORD! Blessed is the man
> who fears the LORD, Who delights

greatly in His commandments (Ps. 112:1).

By humility and the fear of the LORD are riches and honor and life (Prov. 22:4).

5. *Blessing is attained when we guard harmony with a passion.* The unity of vision, philosophy, doctrine, policy and spirit must rest upon our ministries and churches. We are to avoid divisions. We are to avoid disloyalties. The kingdom of God cannot be divided. The Lord blesses that harmony and people who flow in unity (1 Cor. 1:10; Mark 3:24,25).

Behold, how good and how pleasant it is For brethren to dwell together in unity! It is like the precious oil upon the head, Running down on the beard, The beard of Aaron, Running down on the edge of his garments. It is like the dew of Hermon, Descending upon the mountains of Zion; For there the LORD commanded the blessing — Life forevermore (Ps. 133:1-3).

6. *Blessing is attained by treating disunity as devilish.* Anything that causes disunity—attitudes, actions, or philosophies—does not come from the Holy Spirit. Daniel, chapter two, records the vision Daniel had of the man that represented the kingdoms of this world. The feet of the image were iron and clay, two elements that do not mix. Mixture of iron and clay speaks of fragmentation, which is the spirit

of humanism. Man's human nature seeks independence and solitude.

> Thus says the LORD: "As the new wine is found in the cluster, and one says, 'Do not destroy it, for a blessing is in it,' so will I do for My servants' sake, that I may not destroy them all" (Isa. 65:8).

The blessing of the Lord rests in the corporate gathering that flows in unity, that treats the body of Christ with respect. In that cluster, the blessing of the Lord is maintained.

7.*Blessing is attained through a liberal spirit.*

> The best of all firstfruits of any kind, and every sacrifice of any kind from all your sacrifices, shall be the priest's; also you shall give to the priest the first of your ground meal, to cause a blessing to rest on your house (Ezek. 44:30).

> "Bring all the tithes into the storehouse, that there may be food in My house, and prove Me now in this," says the LORD of hosts, "If I will not open for you the windows of heaven and pour out for you such blessing that there will not be room enough to receive it" (Mal. 3:10).

8.*Blessing is attained when we exalt faithfulness not flashiness.*

> A faithful man will abound with blessings, but he who hastens to be rich will not go unpunished (Prov. 28:20).

God honors faithfulness. Leaders in His house ought to exalt the virtue of faithfulness more than talent and flashiness. Trying to get God to bless flashiness only weakens churches. God has already committed Himself to bless only faithfulness. He looks for faithfulness in prayer, in support, in loyalty, and in just being there.

9.*Blessing is attained when root attitudes are dealt with.* The need for proper root attitudes—not just surface actions—are the premise of the Sermon on the Mount given by Jesus, recorded in Matthew, chapter five and Luke, chapter six. To see blessing on your house, your family and your ministry, you must work on your character. You must deal with your root attitudes of life, not just surface actions. Blessings are attained through cultivating kingdom attitudes. By shaping attitudes, not just demanding desired action.

> Then He lifted up His eyes toward His disciples, and said: "Blessed are you poor, for yours is the kingdom of God. Blessed are you who hunger now, for you shall be filled. Blessed are you who weep now, for you shall laugh. Blessed are you when men hate you, and when they exclude you, and revile you, and cast out your name as evil, for the Son of Man's sake" (Luke 6:20-22).

10.*Blessing is attained by cleansing offenses often.* When offenses fragment people's spirits and minds, the blessing of the Lord is not able to flow. Free of offenses and relational conflicts, a church can have a properly observed communion table.

> The cup of blessing which we bless, is it
> not the communion of the blood of
> Christ? The bread which we break, is it
> not the communion of the body of
> Christ? (1 Cor. 10:16).

The early church had the communion table every
time they met together to maintain unity of heart in
the house of God. We might consider having the
communion table open more often than it is. The
spirit of the communion table and a time to cleanse
offenses should be part of our corporate gathering
and leadership meetings.

11. *Blessing is attained through the prayer of
brokenness.*

> And Jabez called on the God of Israel
> saying, "Oh, that You would bless me
> indeed, and enlarge my territory, that
> Your hand would be with me, and that
> You would keep me from evil, that I
> may not cause pain!" So God granted
> him what he requested (1 Chron. 4:10).

God granted Jabez what he requested. Hear the
prayer of a broken man, a humble prayer where the
blessing of the Lord was honored. Humility and
brokenness is not something we hear a lot about in
this day and age. It is more exciting to tune in to the
executive leader and all the principles, strategies and
plans on how he builds. But the true blessings of God
are found in brokenness rather than in strength.

12. *Blessing is attained by acquiring wisdom from
above for our leadership style.* Seeking and finding
the wisdom that God respects will bring the favor and
blessing of the Lord upon our life. The word *favor*

means to be pleased with, delight, show bias toward and be blessed.

> Now therefore, listen to me, my children, for blessed are those who keep my ways. Hear instruction and be wise, and do not disdain it. Blessed is the man who listens to me, watching daily at my gates, waiting at the posts of my doors. For whoever finds me finds life, and obtains favor from the LORD; but he who sins against me wrongs his own soul; all those who hate me love death (Prov. 8:32-36).

The book of James contrasts wisdom from above with earthly, sensual and demonic wisdom. All leaders in ministry should have a good dose of wisdom from above. We need the wisdom of God in all leadership decisions. We need it in budget decisions, staffing, missionary endeavors, preaching and counseling (James 3:13-18).

Wisdom from above is pure, peaceable, gentle, reasonable, unwavering, full of mercy, good fruits, and without hypocrisy. Earthly wisdom is jealous, arrogant, natural, selfish, demonic, and disorderly. If we would judge ourselves by these two lists, we would immediately see what kind of wisdom we draw from. If we draw from the wisdom from above, we will have peace, mercy, reasonableness in all of our decisions and a transparency in our lifestyle. If we draw from earthly wisdom, that is from the pit of Hell or from the carnal mind, we will always be jealous, arrogant, disorderly, and selfishly ambitious.

13. *Blessing is attained by learning true spiritual dependence.*

> And He said, "My Presence will go with
> you, and I will give you rest" (Exod.
> 33:14).

> Therefore I take pleasure in infirmities,
> in reproaches, in needs, in persecutions,
> in distresses, for Christ's sake. For when
> I am weak, then I am strong (2 Cor.
> 12:10).

An authentic leader in the vanguard of Christ's church understands his own weakness and draws his strength from the Lord. Learning true spiritual dependency is a mark of humility. God Himself promises to lift up the humble. It is pride that allows us to think we can do on our own what we really can do only with God's power. If we look to God for vision, strength and wisdom, we will find the source inexhaustible, flowing freely into our mind and our spirit.

14. *Blessing is attained by following God's pattern for building His house.* Leaders must promote the divine pattern from Scripture. Finding and following God's divine plan is prerequisite to enjoying His divine blessing. God has given patterns in Scripture for church structure, worship and leadership training. If we follow the divine pattern the blessing of the Lord will rest upon it and we will not have to exert extreme carnal energy to accomplish things on our own. All we have to do is follow the principles God already has laid down.

> According to all that I show you, that is,
> the pattern of the tabernacle and the
> pattern of all its furnishings, just so you
> shall make it (Exod. 25:9).

The Scripture testifies that following divine pattern leads to the glory of God.

> Then the cloud covered the tabernacle of meeting, and the glory of the LORD filled the tabernacle (Exod. 40:32).

Solomon followed the plan given to David by the Holy Spirit.

> Consider now, for the LORD has chosen you to build a house for the sanctuary; be strong, and do it (1 Chron. 28:10).

God will guard and bless what He has built, and He builds according to His own pattern. We want the Lord to build His house. Let us be wise builders, exacting in our application of Scripture as we exalt the Lord in the church in these last days.

12

The Commitment: Covenant Relationships

People in every culture need relationships of intimate trust. Everyone needs friends with whom they can be open and reveal their deepest feelings. God created everyone to want to belong, to accomplish, to understand and be understood. He made us to need love, self-respect, meaning and purpose.

People enter our lives. Some stay for a moment; some a lifetime. We meet hundreds of people but only a few become intimate friends. Who do you love and respect? Who has influenced your life most in the past year, five years or ten years? Who brings the most joy and meaning to your life besides the Lord Jesus Christ? What attracts you to these few precious people?

Alvin Toffler, in his book *Future Shock*, says "ours is a throwaway society where even friendships are temporary. Commitments to friends, job, community, country and family are on the decline." In the United States, the ideal man stands alone, self-sufficient, autonomous. He is the Marlboro man. He is the strong, quiet type from the wild West. He has no friends, no roots and he disappears into the glow of the desert. He enjoys his solo journey through life. This is *not* the way of vanguard leaders in the twenty-first century. God calls His leaders to be joined to Himself and to His people. Men and women called to the ministry are called to involvement with people. We are called to love not only God and His Word but also the people we serve.

Many leaders cannot handle the process of loving, being hurt, forgiving, being repaired and restored, and making themselves vulnerable in relationships again.

In his writings on the "four loves," C.S. Lewis said, "To love at all is to be vulnerable. Love anything and your heart will certainly be wronged and possibly broken. If you want to make sure of keeping it intact, you must give your heart to no one, not even to an animal. Wrap it carefully around with hobbies and little luxuries. Avoid all entanglements. Lock it up safe in the casket or coffin of your selfishness. But in that casket, safe, dark, motionless, aimless, it will change. It will not be broken, instead it will become unbreakable, impenetrable, irredeemable."

Many leaders cannot handle the process of loving, being hurt, forgiving, being repaired and restored, and making themselves vulnerable in relationships again. The leader who suffers deep hurts and does not handle them biblically isolates himself. He needs to find the source of strength and mending that only God can bring to his life or else he becomes vulnerable as a loner in the kingdom. To isolate yourself from people is dangerous and God will do all that is possible to prohibit this. You are called to serve and in serving you face the possibility of being misused, abused, offended and hurt.

More than one hundred people are mentioned in Acts and the Pauline epistles as Paul's co-laborers, partners, comrades, or fellow-workers in the Gospel. He lists twenty-six of these people in Romans, chapter 16. Again in Colossians, chapter 4, he lists another ten people he loved and respected and who worked with him. The apostle Paul's writings reveal that he related to other people, not only to leaders of churches but also to members of the congregations. He loved people dearly and was hurt deeply by some he loved.

A person who fell into relationship with the apostle Paul improved, became better, and fulfilled his destiny in God.

• *Tychicus*, whose name means fortunate and dependable, ministered to Paul at Paul's most vulnerable time. He was called a dear brother, a faithful minister, a loyal servant, a trusted assistant, a fellow servant (Col. 4:7). Tychicus travelled with Paul on this third missionary journey and spent time in prison voluntarily to be with Paul. A man of spotless integrity, he was trusted to carry the Jerusalem offering. He also delivered letters written in prison by Paul to churches, and he hand-delivered the private letter about Onesimus to Philemon.

• *Onesimus*, whose name means profitable, helpful, reliable, and dedicated, had been a believer a short time but had earned Paul's respect. A runaway slave, Onesimus had met Paul in Rome and turned to Christ. His life was now in the Lord's hands, and he was willing to do right. Paul sends him back to his hometown with no mention of his past except he is now "one of you."

•*Philemon* was a member of the church of Colossae. Onesimus was his slave. Paul sent Onesimus back to his master with a high recommendation. By standing Onesimus beside Tychicus as a witness of events in the church in Rome, Paul tells the Colossians—including Philemon—that he regards Onesimus as reliable. By God's transforming grace, Onesimus lived up to the meaning of his name.

A person who fell into relationship with the apostle Paul improved, became better, and fulfilled his destiny in God. Paul was a "people-person," reaching out, discipling, helping, encouraging, praying and training people to work in the church of Jesus Christ.

•*Aristarchus* had experienced storms, shipwrecks, brutality, riots and prison. He did not look for an easy way but looked for the right way. He never ran out. His name means best ruler, commitment and loyalty, and he stuck to it. From Thessalonica he went on Paul's third missionary journey. He was caught by the mob at Ephesus and beaten. He also was with Paul on his dangerous voyage recorded in Acts, chapter 27. He was shipwrecked with Paul and imprisoned at Rome. He volunteered his imprisonment to aid Paul without any thought for himself. For a man to throw away his life in prison to serve someone else shows what a remarkable ability Paul had to draw out people's strength and build loyalty into them.

Vanguard leaders have the ability to build relationships with people. Without relationships, a minister suffers loneliness, burnout and possibly shipwreck. For friends to give themselves to a leader as these men gave themselves to Paul is a very sacred trust. This trust must be handled very carefully and wisely.

It's easy to use people to build things rather than using things to build people.

•*John Mark*, out of fear, quit and went home in the middle of an early missionary journey with Paul and Barnabas. They were headed into dangerous territory and John Mark left. Thank God for Barnabas, the Son of Encouragement, who picked up John Mark and led him through these terrible months of failure. He encourages all who fail to get up, press on, and go forward in God. Through encouragement, John Mark got up again. He didn't sulk and feel sorry for himself. He persisted after failure. John Mark probably needed the discipline Paul gave him by refusing to take him on a second missionary journey. Nevertheless, John Mark was restored to Paul and they ended in a great relationship. In Paul's last letter, 2 Timothy, Paul refers to this man as a dear friend.

Leaders need to develop friendships with people they can pour their lives into and receive from. As a pastor, one of my greatest challenges has been developing and maintaining friendships. It's easy to use people to build things rather than using things to build people. Our vision should always be to build big people. Never sacrifice people on the altar of your big dreams or for the temporary buildings and things you use to accomplish your dreams. People are more important than any program, project or building you ever will be involved in. To minister life, you must maintain a close relationship with God's people and treat them with respect.

Four levels of relationship

Four levels or types of relationship occur in the body of Christ: fellowship, relationship, partnership and friendship.

The entire body of Christ enjoys *fellowship* because each member is in Christ (2 Cor. 5:17; John 17:23). The Holy Spirit pulls together all who are washed in the blood of Jesus. Nationality and distance create no barriers to fellowship. Believers can travel to Russia, Cuba, New York or Spain and have immediate fellowship with Christians there. They do not have close relationships or intimacy with each other, yet the Holy Spirit places a love and an identification between them because they are in the body of Christ.

Relationship refers to a more structured koinonia. It develops as people work with each other in a church department or activity such as choir, music groups, home meetings, or full-time staff duties. Responsibilities in the kingdom of God get people working together and allows them to become close. People who never choose to be close to each other develop relationships because of their responsibilities.

The word *partnership* refers to fellow-workers who have the same vision, values, heart, and kindred spirits. They join each other as partners in the work of the ministry. They share a common commitment to extend the kingdom of God. In full time ministry, these people walk with the senior pastor to accomplish the dreams and goals God shares with them. They are like Timothy, Barnabas and Silas who partnered with Paul and like the partners Priscilla and Aquilla. They are elders, deacons and staff ministry God has joined with the senior pastor to accomplish the vision God has given them.

Friendship is shared by people who have common ground, common love and appreciation for each other that draws them together. Friends choose to be with each other. They choose to socialize and work together on things away from their job responsibilities. Their relationship grows in transparency, responsibility, accountability and vulnerability. These are not necessarily people on the church staff or in a department with me, although they could be.

Grasping the word *friend*

The word friend refers to a partner, comrade, mate, companion or sidekick. The Northern American Indians called a friend "one who carries my sorrows on his back." Friends feel safe with each other without having to measure words or weigh thoughts. Aristotle said, "A friend is a single soul dwelling in two bodies." When two people become so involved with one another that their thoughts and emotions are intertwined, they are truly vulnerable. Vulnerability means exposure. You can be hurt. You can choose, as C.S. Lewis pointed out, to hide your heart and guard it so nothing will ever happen to it, but you will become hard, impenetrable and not useful in the kingdom of God.

"A friend is a person with whom one can be sincere," said Ralph Waldo Emerson. Socrates said, "Be slow to fall into friendship, but when thou art in, continue firm and consistent." Abraham Lincoln said, "The better part of one's life consists of his friendships."

Men in Western cultures have chosen isolation and autonomy as a way of life. Women seem to make friends and develop deep friendships more easily than men do. Women seem to have the ability to be open, vulnerable, and transparent and talk about more than just superficial, daily talk. Among those I pastor and counsel, men are more lonely.

The definitions of masculinity and manliness have been distorted in western culture. Masculinity here is detached, unemotional and uninvolved in relationships. Our culture says men should not be emotional or vulnerable because it is dangerous. A set of laws for men state:

- He shall not cry.
- He shall not display weakness.
- He shall not need affection or gentleness or warmth.
- He shall comfort but not desire comforting.
- He shall be needed but not need.
- He shall touch but not be touched.
- He shall be steel, not flesh.
- He shall not be vulnerable in his manhood.
- He shall stand alone!

Men must be liberated! These destructive definitions prevent healthy personal relationships from developing. Pastors and leaders who take responsibility in the church are among the men who suffer most under these conditions. As their time goes into ministry to accomplish the work of the kingdom, they find it difficult to reserve time to nurture healthy relationships. Yet God has given men a desire for relationships and uses them as a safety device for men.

Vanguard leaders adopt a biblical manhood able to express emotion, love and a need for friendship. It is not wrong for a man to be seen crying or to show that emotion to another man. The increase of homosexuality has aggravated the problem for men willing to show emotion and be seen together. A true friendship demonstrates a pure emotion that can be seen between two men who allow the Holy Spirit to use their friendship to strengthen their lives. Two women can experience the same thing.

We need to break through the bondage of talking only about superficial subjects like sports, politics, and the weather. We need to ask for help. We need to count on others. We need to get our priorities right. Developing relationships, especially for people in the ministry, is very important and may be the key to longevity in ministry.

Physical things are not more important than spiritual and soulish relationships. Wealth and success are great accomplishments, but friendship is greater. Someone once said, "A man must get friends as he would get food and drink for nourishment and sustenance."

Friendship foundations

Strong friendships stand on solid foundations built of shared attitudes, commitments and principles. Here are ten fundamentals that must underlie intimate, lasting, Christian friendships.

A God-centered basis of belief. Intimate friendship develops when two individuals share a basic frame of reference—common beliefs. Christians share a world view and a respect for the Word of God. They share values of the kingdom of God and the urgency to see the harvest reaped for Christ. A believer cannot share his life with someone who does not have a strong, God-centered basis of belief.

A personal commitment to another. Relationship is based on a nurtured bond of love. Love desires to express itself in commitment. Covenant love is faithful and loyal. God is a covenant-making and a covenant-keeping God. The Bible is a covenantal book. Jonathan and David's friendship recorded in 1

Samuel demonstrates covenant love. They shared a set of values and were drawn to walk together. Jonathan was committed to David unto his own death. Moses had covenant relationship with Joshua. Paul had Timothy. Jesus had his twelve disciples.

> Two are better than one, because they have a good reward for their labor. For if they fall, one will lift up his companion. But woe to him who is alone when he falls, for he has no one to help him up. Again, if two lie down together, they will keep warm; but how can one be warm alone? Though one may be overpowered by another, two can withstand him. And a threefold cord is not quickly broken (Eccles. 4:9-12).

Ruth 1:14-18 and 1 John 3:16 encourage believers to lay down their lives for their brothers. Ben Franklin once said, "Be slow in choosing a friend, be slower in changing one." Lasting friendships are one of the joys of life but they take commitment. A friend will not always please you or be where you think they should be. Friends need to forgive and continually be open and transparent.

Faithfulness in adversity (Prov. 14:20; 19:4; 18:24; 27:10; 17:17; Ps. 55:12). Adversity proves true friends. It sorts out people who hang around for what they can get from those who hang in there because they are committed. Faithfulness is the sign of true friendship. If a person is not faithful during the time of trouble, when you are down and making mistakes, that friendship will not last.

> A friend loves at all times, and a brother
> is born for adversity (Prov. 17:17).

The cloudy day disperses the crowd that delights in the sunshine.

The old saying goes, "Laugh and the world laughs with you; cry and you cry alone." If you really want to know who your friends are, just make a few mistakes.

Straightforward honesty with sensitivity (Prov. 17:10; 29:5). Friendship calls for speaking the truth in love and sensitivity. Straightforward honesty is absolutely necessary with friends.

> Faithful are the wounds of a friend, but
> the kisses of an enemy are deceitful... As
> iron sharpens iron, so a man sharpens
> the countenance of his friend (Prov.
> 27:6, 17).

Giving personal respect always. Familiarity breeds contempt. The closer people get to each other, the easier it is to pick each other apart. Every person is unique and has his own ways, habits, problems and weaknesses. Friends accept and protect each other instead of expose each other. Friends show respect continually to ones they love.

> Seldom set foot in your neighbor's
> house, lest he become weary of you and
> hate you (Prov. 25:17).

Think about this. Everyone can give respect. We all like to receive it, but we are slow in giving it. Thoughtlessness and taking advantage of others does not build friendship. When respect is shown in a friendship there is something holy and sacred about it. Something real can be built on it.

Unquestionable acceptance. We all want to be accepted by others whose opinion we value. Everyone feels pain when they are not accepted. The Bible teaches us to love and accept one another. We are not to reject someone because of what he has done. My children, when caught red-handed, ask, "Do you still love me? Do you love me anyway?" They need to hear my acceptance again because they fear I may reject them for what they have done. When people make mistakes and reveal their weakness, that is really the time to be a good friend and accept them in their weakness.

> Hatred stirs up strife, but love covers all sins (Prov. 10:12).

Empathy instead of judgment. Empathy is the ability to show feeling when others want to show judgment. It means to understand and feel the thoughts and experiences of others. It is an opportunity to identify with someone going through hard times. Some of the deepest friendships develop in sorrow. Empathy has its source in humility, because you realize without God you could be in the same spot. You reach out to hurting people and walk through the grief or sorrow or the mistake with them. It means to treat people as equals. It means to listen more than you talk.

> Rejoice with those who rejoice, and weep with those who weep (Rom. 12:15).

Loyalty over time. Loyalty is the ability to stand with someone, even when they do not accept or esteem your opinions highly. Loyal friends tolerate each other's idiosyncrasies. They keep secrets. An Arabian proverb says, "A friend is one you may pour out all the contents of your heart to, chaff and grain together, knowing that the gentlest of hands will take and sift it, keep what is worth keeping, and with a breath of kindness, blow the rest away."

> He who covers a transgression seeks love, but he who repeats a matter separates the best of friends (Prov. 17:9).

> A perverse man sows strife, and a whisperer separates the best of friends (Prov. 16:28).

Loyalty is opposite of being two-faced. Gossip destroys friendships. Immature people gossip to gain attention. Loyal friendships endure the test of time and gossip.

Willing to ask for help. Asking for help is hard because it shows vulnerability. But how can you have close friends if you never ask for help or show weakness? If you must always have the upper hand or be the one who gives counsel instead of receives it, you are a stingy receiver. When a friend feels needed, he feels important. Too many of us withdraw from people who seem self-sufficient. True friendship is built with both parties giving one to another that which they need.

> A man who has friends must himself be friendly, but there is a friend who sticks closer than a brother (Prov. 18:24).

Forgiveness, love and compromise. Both sides make concessions to reach compromises. Neither side always gets his way. Friends compromise on matters of personal convenience but not on values or principles. Commit yourself to a friend, resist judgmental attitudes and accept love given by the friend. You will find fulfillment in true committed friendship, although it grows slowly.

> A brother offended is harder to win than
> a strong city, and contentions are like
> the bars of a castle (Prov. 18:19).

Some leaders find it hard to compromise. Many men think being firm and unwavering in their decisions is a sign of strength, but how can being sensitive to others be weakness? Have convictions and express them but do not disregard the convictions and feelings of others. Don't be a doormat but don't be a dictator!

Laws of relationships

Relationships operate successfully on the basis of principles, keys or laws. These laws make relationships work. The following elements develop and maintain deep relationships:

1. *The law of initiation.* Nothing begins without a beginning. A concrete and specific act begins the process. A person initiates relationships by presenting himself to others in a recognizable way.

> A man who has friends must himself be
> friendly, but there is a friend who sticks
> closer than a brother (Prov. 18:24).

I encourage pastors and leaders in full-time ministry to initiate relationships and friendships. Many times I have said to myself, "I wish so-and-so would make me his friend" or "I wish that couple would be more friendly. I would like to develop a relationship with them." I wait to see if they will initiate and they do the same thing. After years of waiting, I found that someone has to start. Both of us are waiting for someone else to show some interest. No one wants to be rejected.

People are slow to initiate toward leadership. People are a little intimidated by pastors. Most people think leaders are too busy and don't really need friends.

2. *The law of response.* Recognize the person who initiated the contact. "We love Him because He first loved us" (1 John 4:19). Reply to people when they initiate a friendship. Respond to them in a concrete, specific way. Be very careful you respond positively. Don't act as if you are too busy. Don't brush it off.

These two laws form the cycle of relationship development. They need to be applied to all growing relationships. Not everyone is good at initiating; not all are good at responding. Almost everyone needs to work on both.

3. *The law of faith* (Heb. 11:1,8). Relationships require faith that God will help us love and forgive. They require faith that God will heal hearts that get broken. All intimate relationships go through times of hurt and brokenness. Those are times that can deepen a relationship or destroy it. If we pray, God will give us faith to go through these times. He will build our character and our ability to be more loving and sensitive. Faith believes what a person is and does are acceptable to God. And faith believes people grow in relationship (Eph. 5:29; Prov. 15:19).

4. *The law of love* (Prov. 17:17; 19:4-7; 1 Sam. 2:17). Love covers a multitude of sins. Love holds all relationships together like glue. Love has a language—a vocabulary. Love has a smile. We must pray and speak the Word of God in our relationships. Love and forgiveness build strong relationships.

5. *The law of toleration* (Eph. 4:2; Col. 3:13). Everyone has idiosyncrasies, weaknesses and irritations. Good friends tolerate each other's tastes, opinions and idiosyncrasies. Anyone unable to tolerate other people's quirks will not have many friends. He will try to legislate friendships according to his own taste, likes, dislikes, values and opinions. If you have a dogmatic belief, don't impose it on others while you are trying to develop friendships.

6. *The law of sacrifice* (Heb. 13:16; Gen. 22:2; Matt. 16:25). All friendships are built upon the sacrifice of time, taste, and opinion. The sacrifice you make will determine the return you receive. If you never sacrifice to make time to get together for talk, prayer, recreation, then your friendships will suffer. Many people go through life with only one or two friends. Some people have no friends. Why? They make no time. They spend too many hours on the job, building their career and climbing the ladder only to find they crawled up the wrong ladder. Success in life enriches people. It does not isolate them. Therefore, some sacrifice must go into making and keeping close friends.

7. *The law of confidentiality* (Prov. 17:9; 16:28; 11:13). You may be transparent and tell a friend your weaknesses, but you don't expect your friend to take your dirty laundry next door and show the neighbors. No one wants a friend who would expose them in a time of weakness. Therefore, when you learn secret information, be careful with it. Carelessly exposing

another's weakness has ended countless relationships. It is not healthy to lose friends. When we lose a friend, we die a little. A Russian proverb says, "An old friend is better than two new friends." We want old, lifelong friendships.

13

The Legacy: Passing The Baton

Replacing senior pastors exposes a church to peril but does not have to lead to grief. It can be exciting. A change in leaders can move a church forward to new horizons. The church replaces its spiritual leaders as needs arise. Pastors and elders may move away to accept new assignments, go to the mission field, shipwreck spiritually, or just get old and retire. As older leaders near the end of their service in the kingdom of God, younger leaders need to be ready to carry heavier responsibilities.

Training leaders for the future is a challenge in a complex, ever-changing, society. When the founder of a great church departs, retires, dies or is removed, the church faces a minefield of potential problems. Training and installing his successor demands utmost care and wisdom. Adhering to biblical patterns increases the likelihood of success. This is God's best and His desire for every transition. Ignoring scriptural patterns leads to almost-certain destruction.

My personal Journey

For twelve years, my wife and I pastored a church we pioneered. We never entertained the thought of leaving it. The most traumatic experience of my life occurred one Sunday morning as I stood before the congregation to announce our resignation and plans to move to another city. I passed the leadership baton of the church to another man who had labored there with me from the beginning. I wrote the announcement ahead of time and read my notes to make sure I said it correctly.

• *The announcement*:

> *Pastors Frank and Sharon Damazio have accepted the invitation of Pastor Dick Iverson to be his successors and take the church in Portland, Oregon. The move will take place by September 1. My successor here will be Gary Clark whom I have appointed and the eldership has confirmed to be my replacement.*

The announcement caught the congregation off guard. No one in the congregation knew this transition was in the works. I had met with the two associate pastors, each one of the fifteen elders and their wives individually, and our entire leadership team of about 150 people prior to the Sunday announcement to the whole congregation. I tried to answer questions I knew they wanted to ask: Why should I succeed Pastor Iverson? Why now? Why did I say yes? Where was my commitment to the church we had founded? What about the vision we had started? I told the congregation about my deep spiritual roots at Bible Temple. Since my days in Bible college and leadership training there, I had felt it was my home church. Pastor Iverson had been like a spiritual father to me.

• *The mixed emotions.* I explained our mixed emotions. We felt sorrow at leaving the church we founded. It was difficult for us to leave a vision unfinished. It was hard for us to leave friends with whom we had labored in leadership. It was hard to leave the staff and the people who had come to Christ under our ministry, however, it is extremely important for leaders to keep themselves and the congregation mindful of God's sovereignty during times like this.

• *The bond between church and leader.* A bond grows between a pastor and a congregation, especially in a pioneer work. The bond was being broken and we were being moved by the leading of the Holy Spirit. The congregation had a strong foundation, and now needed to rise to the challenge of accepting a new pastor and continuing the vision with the same zeal they had under our leadership. The people did accept the sovereignty of God and bore witness that the Holy Spirit had given us a word to move to Portland. I gave the congregation the following three scriptures:

A man's heart plans his way, but the Lord directs his steps (Prov. 16:9).

The steps of a good man are ordered by the Lord, and He delights in his way (Ps. 37:23).

A man's steps are of the Lord; how then can a man understand his own way? (Prov. 20:24).

In Portland, Pastor Iverson (who, with his parents, had founded Bible Temple forty years earlier) announced to his congregation about his appointment of Sharon and me to be his successors. He comforted the church with the fact that the transition itself would take three years and then he would still be ministering out from Bible Temple as his home church.

• *God's sovereign choice.* It was not something I had desired or sought. I had done nothing to bring it about by any of my actions. I did not ask to be his successor.

The account of the prophet Samuel anointing David as king leaped off the pages of the Bible and sprang to life with new meaning for me. Jesse's seven sons had to appear before the prophet, but the Lord divinely chose David to replace Saul (1 Sam. 16:7-11). About one thousand years later, Christ's eleven apostles also had to replace a leader.

> And they prayed and said, "You, O Lord, who know the hearts of all, show which of these two You have chosen to take part in this ministry and apostleship from which Judas by transgression fell, that he might go to his own place." And they cast their lots, and the lot fell on Matthias. And he was numbered with the eleven apostles (Acts 1:24-26).

A leader with a heart for the church thinks very seriously about the future of the congregation he pastors. I was not concerned just for my own ministry. When leaving this congregation, I was concerned that the church would outlive me and accomplish the work God had given it to do. It was imperative that the local elders support the transition. Their support would protect the church from losing ground because of the change.

Every church going through a change in leadership may find these insights of some value.

Wisdom and warning for transitions

Transitions and changes always create vulnerable times. Anxiety and restlessness stir the people. Motives come into question, and the enemy attacks with great vigor. The apostle Paul warned the Ephesian elders to expect pressures on the church after his departure (Acts 20:28). The Scripture "Strike the shepherd and the sheep will be scattered" becomes very practical (Zech. 13:7).

Stable leadership ushers the church through change. Leaders in every department—from deacons to elders to lay people—must stand strong like pillars. In a relay race, the baton passing is the most critical time. Change always creates tension, but believers know who holds the future.

Transitions and changes always create an atmosphere of adjustments. The absence of a familiar leader and the introduction of a new pastor forces adjustments for everyone. The new pastor adjusts to his new responsibilities and new congregation. Every family in the church has to adjust. If they become angry, fearful, anxious or critical, they need to understand their emotions. Everyone needs to be careful to have faith and a positive attitude in the church, but transition requires adjustments and people do express their emotions as they adapt their thinking. People will embrace change as an exciting adventure if they see the sovereignty of God with spiritual eyes.

In our time of adjustment, I assured the church the succeeding pastor loved the same biblical principles and vision, but that his own leadership style would become evident as he takes the helm. Every leader must make his own waves. God gives each leader certain gifts and talents as well as a unique blend of personality, education, training and emotions. Churches in transition need to adjust to new leadership styles in the grace of God. People have to allow for differences without becoming nervous or critical.

Transitions and changes always cause the domino effect. Transitions force leaders to shift responsibilities between themselves. Effects from a transition ripple through leaders and staff like dominoes falling in a row. The man who succeeded me left vacant his previous area of responsibility. Someone had to shift to pick up his old duties. Change rippled through the staff. We had not planned to shift people around during the transition, but it was forced on us. The domino effect should be anticipated.

On the bright side, new leaders emerge during times like this. People who never appeared to be leaders and those hiding in the stuff step forward. I watched as my mantle shifted to my successor and his mantle shifted to others. Leaders took on new fervor, new passion, and new anointing. New responsibilities called for a new spirit and new frame of mind. God has the right leaders in the right places if you trust Him.

Transitions and changes help us to focus on the unchangeable factors. Even though change affects pastors, leaders, church locations, congregations, and church buildings, God never changes.

> For I am the LORD, I do not change;
> therefore you are not consumed, O sons
> of Jacob (Mal. 3:6).

God is faithful. He has been faithful in the past and will be faithful in the future. He has done marvelous miracles in the past and will continue to move on behalf of His people because he doesn't change. Even though the pastor might change, the Holy Spirit is the same. God's Word also is immovable and unchangeable. The same congregational faith that brought them to the point of transition will continue to take them forward. Things of greatest value will never change, such as prayer, worship, the Word of God, and the presence of the Lord.

Transitions and changes usually are affirmed by a new power of the Holy Spirit. Transition brings new, supernatural moves of God. To encourage the hearts of the people, God moves in fresh, powerful ways. God did new miracles for Joshua that He had not done for Moses. The people experienced God moving in novel, distinct ways under Joshua's leadership. God said to Joshua, "I will not fail you or forsake you. Be strong. Be courageous. Be careful to walk in the ways of the Lord and I will give you great success" (Josh. 1:1-9).

Leaders can encourage the church to believe God for supernatural moves of the Holy Spirit during changes in leadership. The church does not need to lose ground or wither. New leadership can mean new ground is taken for the Lord.

Transitions and changes must be shouldered by experienced warriors. Church leaders need to be valiant warriors during transitions. In Josh. 1:14 the Lord exhorted the leaders to cross before the people in full battle dress, so all the mighty men of valor led the way. Leaders need to be united together with a valiant warrior mentality.

The senior pastor never should make a transition until the leaders—whether they are on a deacon board, eldership board or lay ministry team—are in unity and bear witness that the change is of God. Then the church can draw strength from its leaders. Most transitions fail when a pastor tries to move without agreement from the rest of his leaders.

It is extremely important that the pastor make time to talk with the leaders, individually and collectively, to make sure they understand the total vision. They need to know why he is making the change. The leaders need to bear witness that God sovereignly orchestrated the change.

Transitions and changes are successful when the new leader is highly respected. Respect for God's house and its new leader is critical. A transition is not the time for families to look elsewhere for a new church. The new leader needs every family to dig in and believe God for a fresh anointing. The new leader needs the anointing for greater authority and power to expand his abilities.

> And they answered Joshua, saying, "All that you command us we will do, and wherever you send us we will go. Just as we heeded Moses in all things, so we will heed you. Only the LORD your God be with you, as He was with Moses. Whoever rebels against your command and does not heed your words, in all that you command him, shall be put to death. Only be strong and of good courage" (Josh. 1:16-18).

The congregation should show respect for its new leader. Even if people disagree with his style or have reservations about his age or ability to teach, preach or guide the church, these concerns should be put on hold. Give the man a chance to let God confirm his ministry. After the mantle of a senior leader comes to rest upon a man, he is different than he was before. A person can function as a department head, youth pastor, young adult pastor, Sunday school superintendent or hold a variety of responsibilities in the church. Each time he takes a new responsibility, he receives a new anointing and mantle for that duty. When a man emerges through the ranks and takes the lead role in a church, God gives him the senior man's mantle. He becomes the first among equals in the eldership. He receives the anointing to lead the church, make decisions, preach the word, rebuke the gainsayer and seek the mind of God for decisions. But the church needs to pray for him and stand with him. The church cannot afford to have a spirit of criticism or critique everything he does. Families must stand like pillars to support the new leader and believe God has truly placed His hand upon him.

Transitions and changes are the time to keep the focus on Christ who owns the church. The church belongs to God. It is His property. Jesus said, "I will build *My* church" (Matt. 16:16-18). It is not the pastor's church. The pastor is only an undershepherd. It is not the elders' vineyard. Elders are only farmers with responsibility to till it. The church belongs to Christ, and He knows who He wants to lead it, and when He wants to replace leaders. So leaders must keep their eyes on the Lord of the church.

Joshua told the Israelites not to cross the Jordan River until they could see the ark of the covenant. Then the priests took up the ark and went ahead of the people (Josh. 3:1-3). The ark of the covenant represented the presence of God. Moving through transitions, church leaders and congregations must keep their eyes on God. If they fast, pray and keep their focus on Christ, then God will give them wisdom, and leaders will pass the baton successfully.

Appointment of new leaders

Appointment comes from God through man. Moses appointed Joshua. Elijah appointed Elisha. David appointed Solomon. Paul appointed Timothy. Congregations confirm the new leaders just as the early church confirmed the replacement among the apostles (Acts 1:23-26). Leaders cannot force the mind of God upon the congregation but can lead the congregation into decisions.

• First, the pastor should seek the Lord to find out who the successor should be.

• Next, the pastor should take the man's name to the eldership.

• After the eldership confirms it, the congregation should be given the opportunity to confirm it. Then they will have a three-fold witness: the pastor's heart, the eldership's heart and the heart of the congregation.

Passing the baton to my successor was exciting. The Lord led us through every step. The elders, my wife, and I laid hands on the new man and his wife and prayed for them. Ahead of time, I had a baton made to give to him. On it, I had a message engraved: *Keep the vision. Run with integrity.* I blessed him and handed the baton to him. I exhorted him and the elders to run faster and harder in the race. I exhorted the congregation to continue with the vision.

As I handed the baton to my successor, I felt a virtue leave me and enter him supernaturally. In my spirit I saw the mantle lift off my wife and me and rest on him and his wife. I could see the congregation's love transfer to them. In a moment, they were exalted in the eyes of the congregation. The people stood clapping and crying. The people now would follow him as they had followed me. The change was complete. We were free to go and accomplish the will of God for us.

Biblical patterns of leadership replacement

Leaders who follow biblical patterns invest their time and energy in others. Jesus invested and reproduced his life in his chosen disciples. In similar ways, church leaders give their strength to others to see Christ's self-sharing life and spirit reproduced. Reproduction of the life of Christ in His followers brings Him glory on earth. Christ's leadership is more than a historical curiosity. It is an ongoing reality. The same choosing, investing and reproducing goes on now and should continue into the twenty-first century.

The biblical pattern for replacement of leaders can be seen in examples from the Old and New Testaments. Five models demonstrate how God appoints successors.

First, Elisha succeeded Elijah.

> And Elisha the son of Shaphat of Abel Meholah you shall anoint as prophet in your place (1 Kings 19:16).

Elisha was not seeking Elijah's prophetic mantle. Elisha was fulfilling his God-given responsibilities as a farmer with his family. God knew where Elisha was and God knew that Elisha had the character capacity and spiritual capacity to succeed Elijah. It was clearly a

God-initiated act for Elijah to anoint Elisha in his place.

Second, Solomon succeeded David. David had many sons, some of whom already had prepared to take the throne. In the people's minds, Solomon was the least likely of all his brothers to take the throne. Nevertheless, the Lord chose him and he succeeded his father.

> And of all my sons (for the Lord has given me many sons) He has chosen my son Solomon to sit on the throne of the kingdom of the Lord over Israel... Consider now, for the Lord has chosen you to build a house for the sanctuary; be strong, and do it (1 Chron. 28:5, 10).

Third, Eleazar succeeded Aaron.

> "Aaron shall be gathered to his people, for he shall not enter the land which I have given to the children of Israel, because you rebelled against My word at the water of Meribah. Take Aaron and Eleazar his son, and bring them up to Mount Hor; and strip Aaron of his garments and put them on Eleazar his son; for Aaron shall be gathered to his people and die there." So Moses did just as the LORD commanded, and they went up to Mount Hor in the sight of all the congregation. Moses stripped Aaron of his garments and put them on Eleazar his son; and Aaron died there on the top of the mountain. Then Moses and Eleazar came down from the mountain.

Now when all the congregation saw that Aaron was dead, all the house of Israel mourned for Aaron thirty days (Num. 20:24-29).

Fourth, Timothy succeeded Paul. Paul had many disciples, but Timothy received special attention. In Paul's last years, he poured more of his time into training Timothy than anyone else. The choice was clear. Timothy became Paul's successor and carried on as an apostolic pastor in the city of Ephesus (Phil. 2:19; Acts 16:1-3; 17:14-15; 18:5; 20:4; 1 Cor. 4:17; 1 Tim. 1:2; 4:14; 2 Tim. 1:2; 3:15).

Fifth, Joshua succeeded Moses. Moses was a visionary and builder. According to the pattern he saw in his vision, he built the tabernacle of God. Joshua was a warrior. He possessed the land where the vision could be extended and lived out. Moses laid the foundation for Joshua's ministry. When the time came for Moses to pass his leadership mantle to someone else, the Lord selected Joshua and Moses discerned it (Exod. 17:9-11; 24:13-14; 32:17; Num. 11:28; 27:16-23).

In each of these five examples, the successor and the leader had shared a godly relationship. Succession seems to follow a father-son relationship, proven and tested over a period of time. God chooses the successor, and the predecessor trains and places him in leadership. God clearly guides the process.

Moses: The profile of a predecessor

The predecessor has to discern several things: who his successor will be, what God's timing for the change is, and how to protect the congregation through the transition. Here is how Moses did it.

1. *God's timing.* The timing for Moses to be replaced must have seemed odd to many people. He got close enough to see—but not possess—the land he had heard about all his life (Deut. 3:23-27; Num. 27:12-14). He did not grieve at his own loss because he knew he had sinned. He had struck the rock twice. In anger he had lost control, and God removed his last leadership duty, which was to possess the Promised Land. Nevertheless God spoke to Moses and told him when to promote his successor. Moses still was a man of God hearing from the Lord. Moses knew he was replaced at God's bidding so he prayed for his successor. Imagine how solemnly Joshua pondered the reason behind Moses' departure. Imagine how Joshua must have seen lessons and warnings for himself and the congregation.

2. *The congregation's welfare.* A godly leader always has the welfare of the congregation as his number-one priority. The congregation cannot be left leaderless at vulnerable times.

> Then Moses spoke to the Lord, saying:
> "Let the Lord, the God of the spirits of all
> flesh, set a man over the congregation"
> (Num. 27:15-16).

The Berkeley translation reads, "Let the Lord, the God who knows the disposition of all mankind, put a man in charge of the congregation." The Tay translation reads, "O Jehovah, the God of the spirits of all mankind, before I am taken away, please appoint a new leader for the people."

The congregation had approached the Promised Land. The promise was within reach. Being a wise leader, Moses understood that all the nation's past experiences had been orchestrated to prepare God's people for this hour. He prayed earnestly, "O God, at this point do not leave the congregation without a leader."

3. *The successor's name.* In Moses' day, succeeding leaders usually came from within the ranks of a man's own family. It would have been natural for Moses to appoint one of his own sons. The priesthood was held by the family of Moses' brother, Aaron, so one of Aaron's sons might have been considered. However, Moses left the selection entirely in the Lord's hands. He received and obeyed the word of God by ordaining Joshua, who had served as a leader under Moses for many years.

> And the Lord said to Moses: "Take Joshua the son of Nun with you, a man in whom is the Spirit, and lay your hand on him" (Num. 27:18).

A predecessor should receive the name of his successor from the Lord, not from the board, a wife or a family member. In many transitions, churches choose wrong men. Wrong leaders produce spiritual and numerical decline. Given wrong leaders, some congregations have split.

Congregations can suffer when a father presses his son or when a son presses his father to keep succession within the family. It is dangerous for a senior pastor to determine to make one of his own family members his successor. It may be natural for a son to succeed a father if the son is called and anointed by God. However, a son or daughter may be called into the ministry and not be called to succeed his or her own father at that particular church.

4. *The divine order.* God gave Moses specific steps to follow in the transition (Num. 27:18-23).

Now Joshua the son of Nun was full of
the spirit of wisdom, for Moses had laid
his hands on him; so the children of
Israel heeded him, and did as the LORD
had commanded Moses (Deut. 34:9).

Moses needed to decrease and Joshua needed
to increase. Many pastors have a hard time
backing out of leadership.

First, he was to "take Joshua" (Num. 27:18). Moses
was to personally appoint Joshua before doing
anything else. Second, he was to set him before the
other leaders so they could bear witness with the
appointment and support it (v. 19). Third, he was to
set him before the congregation (v. 19). Then Moses
was to commission Joshua or give him a charge. The
godly charge was spoken before the congregation so
the people could hear it. Moses imparted not only an
anointing but also honor. The people had bonded
with him, and for many years they had honored the
one who spoke with God face-to-face, but now they
needed to honor another man.

Moses needed to decrease and Joshua needed to
increase. Many pastors have a hard time backing out
of leadership. Pride comes in. The flesh rises up and
causes contention, strife and arguments. A leader
must have humility to decrease so another man can
increase. Out-of-control pride or carnality running
rampant in either man will devastate the
congregation. Governed by God, Moses obeyed and
gave some of his honor to Joshua. He decreased
while Joshua increased in the people's eyes.

God told Moses to lay hands publicly upon Joshua
to impart his spirit and mantle of ministry onto

Joshua. When transitions do not take place publicly, leaders leave a lot of room for doubt and murmuring among the congregation. Awkward, unscriptural transitions cause grief to the people of God. Sometimes predecessors do not leave on good terms. The one leaving must be able to lay his hands publicly on the one coming in to bless him. The event assures the people of unity and consistency between the two leaders. The departing pastor must impart all he can so the new leader can go further in the vision and extend what God has given to the church.

He had not lost vision for the people of God to take the land. He was not an old, depleted leader.

Finally, Moses was told to release leadership authority to Joshua. A leader can believe he wants someone to take his place, but when it comes right down to releasing his grip on leadership and giving another man responsibility and authority, it is another story. Release means you have to stop making decisions. You give up the pulpit. You cease ruling the eldership or the board. You give up the right to act independently. You turn over leadership to the person you have trained for the job.

5. *Release while strong.* Moses was still strong when he appointed Joshua.

> Moses was one hundred and twenty years old when he died. His eyes were not dim nor his natural vigor abated (Deut. 34:7).

He was vigorous. He still had strength to achieve. The Jerusalem Bible reads, "His eye undimmed, his vigor unimpaired." Moses was still young in spirit and heart. He had not lost vision for the people of God to take the land. He was not an old, depleted leader. It was just God's will and time for Moses to give up that particular position. If God says release, then it is time to release.

Do not wait too long to release your leadership. Release it while you are strong. Release it while you have a good, healthy mind and still have a hold on your position. Many men do not release their hold on leadership until they are too old. Many wait until the church has declined and their own authority is in jeopardy. That is too late. When decline occurs, the saints become discouraged and some may try to take control. More murmuring makes things difficult for the new man.

Joshua, the divinely appointed successor

Young men need older men as Joshua needed Moses. Many young men want to do great things for God but do not have the necessary wisdom. Moses was able to instill in Joshua the wisdom and insight needed to lead the people of God. Aristotle said, "Young men have strong passions. They would rather do noble deeds than useful ones. They think they know everything and are always quite sure about it. This, in fact, is why they overdo everything."

Successors must qualify for leadership by building track records of service, loyalty, and leadership ability. Here is how Joshua did it.

1. *Faithful servant.* Joshua had proven himself as a servant to Moses and to the congregation. He had served Moses faithfully for forty years (Exod. 11:28; 17:9; 24:13; 32:14-17). He had stood with Moses against

opposition, through pressure and trials. Joshua went to war when others refused. Faithfulness in small things qualifies a man to rule over larger things. Loyalty in service leads to the royalty of the throne. Joshua's single goal had been to enhance Moses' glory and relieve his cares. He submerged his personality in his master"s. Joshua was the perfect successor. He had been molded by God as well as Moses.

2. *Divine appointment.* Christ selects ministers for His church. Ministers should seek their appointments and commissions directly from God. Like Moses, Joshua was divinely appointed by God. Joshua may have thought Caleb the lion-hearted, Phineas the godly priest, or one of Moses' sons might take Moses" place, but the Lord had something else in mind. The Lord put His hand on Joshua and appointed him.

> Let the Lord, the God of the spirits of all
> flesh, set a man over the congregation
> (Num. 27:16).

The word *appoint* in Hebrew means to choose, select, prefer, or place a person over something. Joshua probably never dreamed of such a high honor or such a vast responsibility. He had been content to serve Moses. He was satisfied waiting on the mountain while Moses climbed higher to meet with God in the cloud. He stayed in the tent to serve Moses and to guard its contents. He was jealous for his master's honor when Eldad and Medad prophesied. He was loyal to Moses.

3. *Trusted example.* Both Moses and the congregation trusted Joshua. He had gone out and come in before the congregation and had set an example for others to follow.

who may go out before them and go in
before them (Num. 27:17).

Joshua's name had become prominent forty years
earlier when he was one of twelve men sent to spy
out the Promised Land. He and Caleb had returned
with a good report to inspire the people forward. In
hard times, Joshua showed enthusiasm and
optimism by embracing the vision. He was willing to
live and die for it. He showed leadership ability,
decisiveness, and courage by standing with Moses
when others would not. Many times Joshua had laid
down his life for the people and the vision. The
people had seen his leadership character and had
confidence in him.

The character of a godly leader is shaped through
long years of self-discipline, courage and ministry to
others. It is not formed in a sudden outburst of
energy. Commitment keeps successful leaders going
even though they have enough excuses to satisfy a
thousand failures.

4. *Proven leader.* Joshua had proven leadership
ability and gifts. Joshua proved himself in the battle
against Amalek, recorded in Exodus, chapter 17. He
did not shrink back looking at the enemy or obstacles.
He kept his eyes only on the accomplishment. He did
not fret over hard tasks or boring routine. Through
them, God prepared him for bigger things even
though he had no idea what God was training him
for.

Leadership is an art. Management is a science.
Leadership sees the destination. Management
oversees the journey. Leadership starts projects, but
management finishes them. Joshua was a leader first
and then a manager. He saw the destination and
could oversee the journey.

5. *Shepherd's heart.* A senior pastor must provide pastoral care to nurture people and bring them to Christian maturity. Some leaders have an anointing to see, visualize, and make decisions, but not to care, love and nurture. Some leaders push their congregations toward the vision so strongly they kill off the lambs of the flock. Joshua had vision and a shepherd's heart. This combination is rare in leaders today.

> that the congregation of the Lord may not be like sheep which have no shepherd (Num. 27:17).

In contrast, some leaders go overboard shepherding, loving, and nurturing people while losing sight of the vision and failing to lead.

6. *Spiritually gifted.* Leadership is a spiritual gift given to some people, according to Rom. 12:6-8. Joshua possessed this particular gift.

> And the Lord said to Moses, "Take Joshua the son of Nun with you, a man in whom is the spirit" (Num. 27:18).

The word *spirit* in Hebrew may refer to Joshua's own capacity to lead. It could read, "a man in whom is the spirit of leadership." When choosing a successor, be careful to make sure he has leadership as well as pastoral gifts. People who have only a pastoral gift tend to manage instead of lead. Merge the two together to fulfill the vision as well as to shepherd the flock.

7. *Laying on of hands.* Moses laid his hands on Joshua. The act symbolically expressed continuity

between the two men and their terms of leadership. It was important for Joshua and for the people to see.

> and lay your hands on him (Num. 27:18).

Through the ceremony, Joshua identified with Moses and was made Moses' representative for the future. Laying his hands on Joshua, Moses imparted spiritual gifts, authority and anointing. As the recipient, Joshua accepted the promotion and added responsibility that came with the transfer of leadership (1 Tim. 4:14, 5:22; 2 Tim. 1:6; Deut. 34:9). Joshua was filled with the spirit of wisdom because Moses had laid his hands upon him.

8. *Public inspection.* Joshua's life was observed by other leaders and by the congregation for a period of time.

> set him before Eleazar the priest and before all the congregation (Num. 27:19).

His observers were the immortal souls for whom he was to live and labor. By seeing him, the congregation would be moved to honor and pray for him. The people would be encouraged to commit themselves to support him and help in any way to accomplish the vision.

9. *A godly charge.* Joshua received a godly charge from his predecessor to keep the faith, fight the good fight, and finish the race.

> and inaugurate him in their sight (Num. 27:19).

F.B. Meyer once said, "Words pass on to man the heroic thoughts which thrill the souls of those who speak them first. Words, when uttered, encourage man to dare and do, to attempt and achieve." Receiving a charge from godly leadership is one of the most encouraging and important aspects of leadership transitions. For more insight on this principle, read 1 Tim. 1:18-19; 4:14; 4:15-16; 5:21; 6:20; 2 Tim. 4:1-15.

10. *Honor given.* Joshua received honor from his predecessor. Experienced, honored leaders who know the person they ordain bestow honor on him by uniting to lay hands on him. It is very important that a number of godly men respected by the church and by the successor participate in the ceremony.

> And you shall give some of your authority to him (Num. 27:20).

The spiritual transfer and impartation does not meet the natural eye, but something godly takes place in the heavenlies and in the spirit of the man.

The leadership styles of any two men will not be identical, but biblical principles remain the same.

---

11. *Keep proven principles.* Joshua walked in the proven principles of his predecessor. He held fast to what was good.

> Only be strong and very courageous, that you may observe to do according to all the law *which Moses My servant* commanded you; *do not turn from it to*

> the right hand or to the left, that you
> may prosper wherever you go...
> Remember the word which Moses the
> servant of the Lord commanded you,
> saying, "The Lord your God is giving
> you rest and is giving you this land"
> (Josh. 1:7, 13; emphasis added).

> I thank God, whom I serve with a pure
> conscience, *as my forefathers did*, as
> without ceasing I remember you in my
> prayers night and day (2 Tim. 1:3;
> emphasis added).

> Test all things; hold fast what is good (1
> Thess. 5:21).

The word *hold* in Greek means to grasp, clutch, grip, take ownership, seize, defend, protect and guard. It means to watch, to hold intensely, to keep even if it takes force to keep it.

A successor is wise to continue the same vision and principles his predecessor gave the church. Moses had received vision and principles from God and Joshua followed the same principles. The leadership styles of any two men will not be identical, but biblical principles remain the same. When a man changes the *vision* and the *principles* just because his leadership style is different, he causes confusion in the congregation, although I understand that every leader will begin to add to or change parts of the vision to fit his own unique calling for that local church. But even in this it should be done *slowly* and *carefully*, and principles should remain the same. Altering the vision has caused more than one local church to split.

> Then David gave his son Solomon the
> plans for the vestibule, its houses, its
> treasuries, its upper chambers, its inner
> chambers, and the place of the mercy
> seat; and the plans for all that he had by
> the Spirit, of the courts of the house of
> the Lord, of all the chambers all around,
> of the treasuries of the house of God,
> and of the treasuries for the dedicated
> things (1 Chron. 28:11-12).

Following the pattern laid down by the predecessor
extends the success of the vision. If a predecessor laid
down principles that are not biblical, they should be
adjusted very carefully, wisely, and slowly.

Great leaders prepare the next generation to do
things for God. Vanguard leaders seriously accept the
charge to pass the baton so future generations are not
left without leaders. Train every generation from the
ground up. Pass your knowledge and wisdom to
other leaders so the baton does not fall to the ground.
During the 1984 Olympics, the torch relay across
America involved four thousand runners from New
York to Los Angeles. Four thousand times the baton
changed hands. During those four thousand
handoffs, the baton was not dropped. Careful
handling by each runner allowed the baton a safe
arrival in Los Angeles to light the torch signaling the
opening of the Olympic games.

I believe it will be helpful for the reader to hear
from two pastors who went through a baton passing
event. One pastor received the baton, the other is
passing it. One was successful; one had many
difficulties.

Receiving the baton

The first is Gary Clark, who has been through a leadership transition as a successor. He became senior pastor of the church my wife and I pioneered and has presided over a smooth transition. As a member of the church-planting team that pioneered the church, he labored for twelve years helping to establish the church. At the time this book was written, he has led the church for two years. Following are his comments and observations:

"I never had an interest in being the senior leader of a congregation. I cut my ecclesiastical teeth on the team ministry concept and enjoyed seeing it work without being responsible for any of it. Adjusting to the reality of ultimate responsibility for a congregation of 1,000 people and the livelihood of 10 staff members caused me more than a few sleepless nights. I lost the luxuries of:

•Not being required to have an opinion.

•Having only marginal impact on the church with a bad decision.

•Being involved only in areas of personal interest.

"The congregation was accustomed to strong leadership. For me to exercise confident leadership without being arrogant, presumptuous or disrespectful of my predecessor's life and ministry was awkward at first. During the six months of transition, it was tricky knowing when and how to act. The congregation appreciated my gratitude to Frank but needed to sense that I possessed a degree of godly confidence in myself, in the office I was assuming and in God's calling on our congregation. It would have been deadly for the congregation to sense that the most exciting chapters of the book had already been written.

"For a leadership change like this to work, the egos of the predecessor and successor must diminish or at least be well-hinged. The predecessor cannot afford to take anything personally. The successor has to deal with a deluge of new emotions and responsibilities, while making every effort to accommodate the trauma surrounding the predecessor.

"For several months, emotions of fear, insecurity, and incompetence came over me. I felt abandoned. I felt inferior because I would have to be content with less than what I thought Frank could lead us to accomplish. I had to remind my human nature that God was orchestrating all this.

"Others who had "bought the field" and moved here to pioneer this church with the founding pastor also had to work through these emotions. So did the saints who had joined us and the new Christians who had put their trust and faith in their leaders. These emotions could have destroyed wonderful things that had been built here. It's scary to think how dangerously close we come to disaster during these crossroad experiences.

Learning to fly

"In my first year as senior pastor, I felt more like a novice pilot learning to read an airplane's instrument panel, discover the strength and durability of the aircraft and respond correctly to various "weather patterns." The staff and eldership remained strong and positive from the beginning. The value of their stabilizing influence cannot be overestimated.

"Nearly the entire congregation survived. We had always emphasized the value of every team member and tried to nurture the congregation away from dependence on any one figure, yet the change did reveal some who were attached to the personality, ministry style and charisma of the departing pastor. I try to convince myself that it would have happened regardless of who succeeded Frank, but it remains difficult not to take it personally. I'm grateful to Frank for his diligent and wise crafting of this church that was most evident when he handed it to someone else with relatively little disruption.

Moving on with vision

"In my second year, it was time to clarify and restate the vision to move the congregation ahead. I did not change the vision this church possessed from the beginning. However, the congregation needed to hear it from me. New and exciting chapters are being written now. New signs of life include new people, new converts, new members, new ministries, and new mission projects. These new signs of life prove that the vision belonged to the congregation and not only to a particular leader.

"Twelve years ago I "saw" the vision God gave my predecessor for the church. Many committed their lives to fulfill that vision, and it has been the joy of my life to see it. However, now I must originate, own, cast, communicate, and inspire others in this vision. This has been the greatest challenge because it requires the gifts and skills to lead a congregation. I am grateful for the opportunity because it has given me a greater awareness of Christ's faithful presence and headship of this church."

Handing off the baton

This is the story of a minister who pastored a church for 30 years and what happened when he tried to pass the baton. Under this pastors care, the church grew from only 25 members into one of the most significant Charismatic churches in the area. He

recounted that when the time came for him to pass
the baton to a successor, "all the fireworks started
with unbelievable demonic activity." Here is his story
and four lessons he learned:

"God gave me specific direction to transfer
leadership to one of my spiritual sons. Prophetic and
apostolic brethren had confirmed him to be God's
choice, but he was rejected. It was a power struggle for
the steering wheel of the church. My wife and I
never experienced such a devastating time in
ministry. Looking back, I can't believe how naive I
was about such an awesome, crucial event.

Pastor needs elders' support

"Lesson#1: The senior pastor must accept the
responsibility to raise a successor, and the eldership
must understand and support the process. A senior
pastor knows he will turn his work over to a
successor one day, but he never really wants to step
back. The change is inevitable, but it never comes
easily. He needs to be like Moses who wanted only
what was best for the future of God's people (Num.
27:15-17).

"Like Moses, a successful senior pastor governs
the church with a team of elders. Disagreement over
a biblical, orderly succession of senior leaders stirs up
dissention that leads to regrettable mistakes with
painful consequences.

"A successor should have served in the local
church with the pastor and elders long enough to
know the direction of the church. Like Joshua who
trained under Moses for many years, a successor
maintains stability in the church by carrying the same
heart as the previous pastor. He accepts the legacy and
vision God has given the church and commits
himself to perpetuate it. The selection of Joshua came
as no surprise to the elders because Moses had been

preparing him for many years. The transition went smoothly, as it should.

"The Bible does not record any efforts by Joshua to raise a successor. He did not pass his mantle of authority to anyone or publicly recognize a new leader to replace him before he died. The consequence of this derelict action was the tragic period of the judges with its apostasy, rebellion, and anarchy.

Bylaws should define roles

"Lesson #2: The bylaws of the local church must clearly identify the senior pastor's responsibility to initiate the procedure. Bylaws should define the process step by step and spell out the eldership's role so the whole church can be aware of it.

"I assumed we never would have a problem in this area because we all loved one another, but ambitious men with hidden agendas and vested interests seize times like this to come forward and assert themselves.

"When elders have times of misunderstanding or disagreement, they usually turn to their bylaws to justify a course of action. Bylaws need to be in harmony with the Scriptures because they serve as a legal expression of biblical principles. An old church adage says that bylaws are written for times of war, not for times of peace.

"During a change of senior pastors, demonic attacks aim to confuse, divide, and thwart the ministry of the church. The reason is that during this period, the government of the church, to some degree, is no longer fixed or in place. Elders need to be deeply involved in the succession process in prayer, fasting, honest discussion of the candidate, and ultimately in endorsing of him.

Relationships must be harmonious

"Lesson #3: Pass the baton during a season of relational unity. Never start the process until the chemistry on the eldership is right. Conflict is inevitable as brothers walk together over the years, but covenant relationships survive on honesty, openness and vulnerability.

"Pastors of large churches can easily neglect relationships with their elders while distracted traveling in mobile ministry, serving various Christian organizations, and administering church operations and building programs.

"An overt emphasis on wanting unanimity in all decisions of the church board also can create a fantasy land of purported togetherness. Senior pastors help create it. To protect a false notion of unity, brothers hide their concerns. Disagreements never surface, and contrary opinions are not stated until it is time to select a new senior leader. Then buried issues and offenses come out.

"Chemistry on the eldership needs to be apologetic and forgiving so that a change of senior pastors will not be traumatic or disastrous for the church. Love and togetherness lays level ground for the brothers to deal with this momentous issue.

Wait for God's timing

"Lesson #4: Timing is important. Patience is essential for success. This lengthy, deliberate procedure cannot be hurried. One day the senior leader's mantle will rest on another man. The big question is: When? God the Father had patience over thousands of years to develop His great plan. We need the same patience so we don't miss God's timing. Resist premature action motivated by lack of energy, vision, or boredom.

"After the elders and the church has given its "Amen" to the newly appointed leader, the two men need to co-pastor for a few months or a few years for the stability and security of the people. During this time:

• The elders are encouraged to relate to the successor.

• The senior pastor honors and supports him publicly.

• The senior pastor treats him as an equal.

• The senior pastor gradually turns over more and more responsibility to him.

• The senior pastor helps set his salary and benefits so that he is not faced with this matter.

• The senior pastor plans a grand and glorious installation to pass the baton.

• The senior pastor steps out of the way but remains available for counsel."

Let us pass the baton carefully. Let us light the torch for the next generation, and let us accomplish all that God has given us to do in our day.

Appendix: Things I Have Learned

•Always overestimate people, even when you think you already have. People are mighty miracles of potential under the hand of God.

•A positive approach to life pays off in the long run. Positive attitudes are a thousand times better than negative attitudes.

•Life's best and most wonderful moments are usually unplanned surprises.

•Adversity, pressure, setbacks and disappointments are where the "gold" is to be found. Out of crisis comes something much more beautiful than could ever be expected.

•Serving God is best accomplished when you are willing to serve people. Bury your own needs and desires to reach out to others.

•Friendships are the most precious commodity in life. To love is to risk being hurt. It is worth the risk. Out of hurts come a more special love. Building bridges is much better than building walls.

•Discipline of time is the greatest discipline of all. You live out only a small portion of what you are capable of doing. Everyone settles for so much less.

•A group of people with vision and willingness to stretch for it can accomplish awesome things for God and His kingdom.

•If you do not pray earnestly before you make decisions, you have a great possibility of making wrong decisions that are very painful to turn around.

•Expressing love takes time and thought. It is better than just thinking love; actions are important. Little things, little expressions of love, make up the spice of life.

•Enjoy the journey and not just the destination. Live life daily. Take time to smell the flowers.

•Leadership is much more than a set of principles to be imparted to followers. It is life itself. It is impartation of your total being. You may be accepted, rejected or abused, but that is the essence of true leadership impartation.

•Leadership is the willingness to be hurt by those you lead. True leadership does not isolate or insulate itself when hurt. It does not lose trust in people, but accepts this as a cross to bear and will continue to risk being hurt.

•Leadership fruitfulness happens slowly, almost imperceptibly, over a period of many years. Consistency and perseverance are the hands on the plow that produces fruitfulness.

•Leadership finds its hope and anchor in the vision God imparts. This vision will lead you through many nightmares of disillusionment, hopelessness and defeat. Those who remember the dream live through the nightmare.

•Leadership is working in partnership with Christ to bring the church to its ultimate goals: maturity and expressing Christ's presence without imbalance or spiritual negligence.

•The anointing of God is more precious and valuable than all the books ever written, all the sermons ever preached, and all the knowledge ever attained. How the anointing comes is sometimes mysterious but when it lifts, it is immediately noticeable. You need to hunger for the anointing, for more understanding of it and for more respect for the powerful potential of the oil of God.

•The church declining in spiritual excellence may be characterized by many commendable qualities which, in themselves, become issues which only true spiritual discernment may see through.

•The church in spiritual decline is not aware of its serious state until a divine rebuke is received and believed.

•The health of the church is greatly determined by the spiritual health of the leadership.

•There are key prophetic turning points in the history of every church when dramatic change must take place in order to rise to the next level. If these prophetic moments are missed, spiritual decline is probable as status quo and stagnation sets in.

•Succeeding leaders fail when they have a caretaker mentality dedicated to maintaining past institutions. They must have fresh faith and vision for the future.

•Failure is imminent when a church becomes encased in time, never keeping up with change in people and culture around them.

•Leadership must maintain a constant forward-moving faith-spirit. Never lead for safety reasons; it is the most dangerous leadership style!

Bibliography

Colson, Charles W. *The Body*. Dallas, Texas: Word Publishing, 1992.

Colson, Charles W. *The God of Stones and Spiders*. Wheaton, Illinois: Crossway Books, 1990.

Earle, Ralph. *Word Meanings in the New Testament*. Grand Rapids: Baker Book House, 1974.

Fettke, Tom and Ken Barker. *The Hymnal for Worship and Celebration*. Waco, Texas: Word Music, 1986.

Ford, Leighton. *Transforming Leadership*. Downer's Grove, Illinois: Intervarsity Press, 1991.

Harris, Laird R., Gleason L. Archer, and Bruce K. Waltke. *Theological Wordbook of the Old Testament*. Chicago: Moody Press, 1980.

Lewis, C.S. *Inspirational Writings of C.S. Lewis*. Inspirational Press, n.d.

MacArthur, John Jr.. *Expository Preaching.* Dallas, Texas: Word Publishing, 1992.

Peters, Thomas J. *In Search of Excellence.* New York: Harper and Row, 1982.

Renner, Rick. *Merchandising the Anointing.* Rick Renner Ministries, n.d.

Richards, Lawrence O. *Expository Dictionary of Bible Words.* Grand Rapids, Michigan: Zondervan, 1985.

Schaeffer, Francis A. *How Should We then Live?* Old Tappan, NJ: F.H. Revell Co., 1976.

Spurgeon, C.H. *The Treasury of David.* Nashville: Thomas Nelson, 1984.

Tan, Paul Lee. *Encyclopedia of 7700 Illustrations.* Rockville, Maryland: Assurance Pub., 1979.

Toffler, Alvin. *Future Shock.* New York: Bantam Books, 1970.

Toynbee, Arnold J. *Cities of Destiny.* New York: McGraw-Hill, 1967.

Vos, Howard Frederic. *Archaeology in Bible Lands.* Chicago: Moody Press, 1977.